THE
SUPERFOOD
SWAP

Lentil Meatballs and Pasta (page 195)

THE SUPERFOOD SWAP

THE 4-WEEK PLAN TO EAT WHAT YOU CRAVE WITHOUT THE C.R.A.P.

Dawn Jackson Blatner, R.D.N.

WITH CINDY KUZMA

FOOD PHOTOGRAPHS BY TINA RUPP

A RUX MARTIN BOOK
HOUGHTON MIFFLIN HARCOURT
BOSTON · NEW YORK · 2017

Copyright © 2017 by Dawn Jackson Blatner

Food photographs copyright © Tina Rupp

For information about permission to reproduce selections from this book, write to trade.permissions@hmhco.com or to Permissions, Houghton Mifflin Harcourt Publishing Company, 3 Park Avenue, 19th Floor, New York, New York 10016.

www.hmhco.com

Library of Congress Cataloging-in-Publication Data is available.

ISBN 978-0-544-53555-8 (hardcover); 978-0-544-53556-5 (ebook)

Book design by Laura Palese
Food styling by Carrie Purcell
Prop styling by Stephanie Hanes

Printed in China
SCP 10 9 8 7 6 5 4 3 2 1

» A LITTLE « STORY

I have no idea how old I was, but I remember sitting cross-legged on the floor watching a health video in school about brushing your teeth. In the video, each tooth was an animated little guy complete with hands, eyes, and a smile.

AS THE TOOTHBRUSH with sudsy toothpaste scrubbed, each tooth would giggle, clap, and cheer. They felt so good when they were clean! "Whoa," I remember thinking, "I want *my* teeth to feel that good." This was a silly but powerful moment in my life—the first time I began to think my body parts and cells had feelings and that I was in charge of taking care of them.

Decades later, this same lesson motivates me to take good care of myself. I believe all my cells depend on me to feel good. Decisions I make about what to eat, how much to exercise, when to rest, and more all impact these little cells. I think about them giggling, clapping, and cheering when I eat a kale salad, do an hour-long yoga class, or take a break when I'm starting to feel run down.

Learning how to take care of my body has not always been an easy task. Conflicting opinions and schools of thought about what to eat and how to live abound. I drew wisdom from my parents, who made healthy changes to our diet when I was young; then I went to college and became a dietitian to learn all I could about food. I have traveled all over the world to experience different food and lifestyle philosophies. In the end, I've learned three important lessons:

1

YOU GOTTA PRACTICE
BODY LOVE

Another way to say it: Be nice to *you*. Eat well and exercise because you love your body and want to take care of it, not because you hate it and wish it were different. The only way to be successful and stay motivated is to stop judging yourself and be kind. That doesn't mean you have to accept the weight and health you have, but it does mean saying nice things to yourself and being your own biggest cheerleader as you work to create change and improvements. Good news—the more you practice this on yourself, the less judgmental and more compassionate you will be toward others.

2

YOU'RE ≫ THE ≪
BOSS

No *one* magic way to eat or live works for everyone. Celebrities, the health-nut chicks in your office, and even reputable gurus contradict one another. Research studies are often at odds with one another as well. You can draw inspiration from all these sources— but you have to test their ideas and then tune in to see what works for *your* body. And when I talk about what works, I'm talking not only about the foods and lifestyle that make you healthy, but also those that please your inner wild child (I've got just the trick for this balance—the vice/virtue bundle— and you'll read all about it later).

3

FUN
≫ IS THE ≪
SECRET INGREDIENT

Focusing on change that is complicated or boring is a recipe for failure. Keep change simple. Start with a few basic habits and add more complicated stuff after each win. And above all, start with things you want to change, instead of those things you think you "should" or "have to." Something magical happens to people when they are excited about what they are doing.

I encourage clients to choose to work only on things they want to and to learn to listen to their bodies. This book is packed with real food, good fun, and no B.S.

Tomato Soup with Grilled Cheese
Croutons (page 189)

A LOT OF
» ACKNOWLEDGMENTS «

From the beginning, I set out to have fun and find joy
with this project. I did it by surrounding myself with amazing people.
I want to give my most sincere thanks to them.

Stacey Glick, my literary agent. Our NYC margarita celebration on Cinco de Mayo launched this project with the perfect fiesta vibe.

Rux Martin and Houghton Mifflin Harcourt, for believing in me and being pumped about this project from the very beginning.

Cindy Kuzma. It was the universe that brought us together. I knew from the moment I met her that she would be the perfect writer to work on *The Superfood Swap.* Cindy is a smart, creative, organized power woman. She's become a great friend in the process and I'm excited to have her in my life.

Laura Georgy, for recipe edits, testing, and nutrition analysis. She reached the finish line with me and along the way was willing to jump in and help anywhere.

The kitchen and blogging crew: Jessica Dogert, Karen Formanski, Kristina Kubik, Katie Perkowska, and Taylor Wessel, for grocery shopping, random recipe testing, brainstorming, and positive vibes.

Melissa Ford, a kickass business coach and so much more, for helping me guess and test, create joyful success, and learn to get high on the "ladder."

Gina Marotta, for her moon circle inspirations and reminders to add more me, fairy dust, and love to everything I do.

Christian Blatner, my stepson. I am inspired by his outgoing personality, can-do attitude, and willingness to persist even when things get hard. I am one lucky lady that my husband came with such an amazing kid, who has become such an incredible adult.

Herb, Shannon, Sofia, and Herbie. No surprise that my amazing brother has an amazing wife and kids. Their flexible, warm entertaining style and delicious kitchen creations are an inspiration to me. I want to hang out and eat at their cozy house every day.

My parents, Nance and Herb Jackson. Every single day of my life I have felt encouragement, support, and love from them. They are, and always have been, my most influential role models for living a life with energy, honesty, follow-through, strength, and a positive outlook.

My husband, Chris Blatner. I hit the jackpot with this guy. He's my best friend, an awesome cook, and super hot. I appreciate all the extra grocery shopping trips, help cleaning up the kitchen after I make a huge mess, and taste tests. Every day I'm blown away by how thoughtful, resourceful, and supportive he is. I am so lucky to have him and our part-time dog, Mr. Nuts.

Jasmin Queen, my partner on the show *My Diet Is Better Than Yours*. She showed up ready and excited to make big changes in her life—and along the way, she transformed mine. She gave me more confidence in myself and proved that this plan is a winner. And to her husband, Kevin, and daughter, Callie, for their support and love during our journey.

And a special thanks to everyone who reads this book. You aren't picking this up by accident. You are drawn to the same ideas that I am: Health is everything, superfoods are magic, living well shouldn't be boring, and healthy people have more fun.

—DAWN JACKSON BLATNER

AND A COUPLE MORE WORDS OF THANKS

When I first agreed to help write a nutrition book, I figured I'd learn a thing or two about healthy eating. And I did pick up quite a few new details about how diet affects our bodies and minds—plus a love of Super Lattes (page 213), a raw-cashew habit, and a brand-new appreciation for the versatility of cauliflower.

But the most powerful lessons have less to do with food and more to do with exactly how to change your life for the better. After all, having healthy goals doesn't mean much if you can't execute them. The powerful insights Dawn shares have made me a better eater, athlete, writer, and person. So the first thanks go to her for giving me the opportunity to work on this project and absorb a bit of her brilliance and joy along the way.

I'd also like to thank Julia Turan, for her super-sharp editorial assistance; my parents, Bill and Mary Szelag, for always supporting my writing career and never failing to ask for an update; and most of all, my husband, Matt, for all the good things. You remain the best decision I've made, and I'm not sure where I'd be without you on my team.

—CINDY KUZMA

Brussels Sprout Pad
Thai (page 182)

CONTENTS

» INTRODUCTION «

I SWAPPED **C.R.A.P.** FOR SUPERFOODS—
AND *YOU* CAN, TOO

You picked up this book because you want to eat better.
With all the mixed messages about nutrition
out there, it's hard to know what that means—and even harder to
actually make changes to your eating habits.

———————————————————

I'**M HERE TO HELP YOU** solve both problems. In my life and as a registered
dietitian-nutritionist, I've experienced firsthand that eating better means
eating more superfoods—they give you wholesome nutrition for a slimmer,
healthier, more energized body. I've also learned that the most successful long-
term changes occur when you enjoy what you're doing. The Superfood Swap
brings these 2 components together, combining superfood magic with the fun,
simple strategy of swapping. You'll eat what you crave, but swap superfoods for
C.R.A.P. ingredients.

Throughout the entire Superfood Swap plan, I'll teach you to master a tech-
nique called the **SuperSwap** and then use it to eat, look, feel, and perform your
best—and have fun along the way. In fact, enjoying yourself isn't just a perk—it's
an essential component of making the plan work. So get ready to SuperSwap,
and you'll see and feel supercharged results!

Sprouted Pizza (page 157)

SUPERFOOD SWAP VOCAB

BEFORE WE BEGIN, it helps if we speak the same language. A few words you'll need to know:

- **C.R.A.P.:** An acronym that can help you remember how to spot processed foods. It stands for **C**hemicals you don't use in your kitchen; **R**efined flour and sugar; **A**rtificial sweeteners, colors, and flavors; and **P**reservatives.

- **Superfoods:** Foods (mostly plants) that deliver the maximum dose of antioxidants, vitamins, healthy fats, and other good stuff your body needs to thrive.

- **SuperSwap:** Add something better and drop something of lower quality. And by quality, I'm not just talking about price or brand names—I mean things that provide benefits to your body and mind. You might want to write this on a sticky note—it's the key strategy of the Superfood Swap.

WHO SHOULD SUPERSWAP?

YOU, IF YOU FEEL:

>> pretty good about your eating habits but have a hunch you could feel even better if you kicked it up a notch.

>> you're working harder than you'd like to stick with a healthy routine—and getting minimal results. You know there must be an easier way.

>> caught in a good/bad eating cycle. You're sometimes very disciplined, sometimes off the wagon.

>> rushed, confused, and overwhelmed by nutrition information and choices in the grocery store. You just grab what's available, familiar, and easy.

>> confident in your eating and exercise plans—but too busy or tired to actually follow through with them.

>> stuck in a rut with the food you eat, as well as with life in general. You're ready to bust out of the plateau and on to the next level.

CHANGE = HARD, SUPERSWAP = EASY

You try to eat pretty well. You don't feel terrible, but you have big goals—and your current routine hasn't allowed you to reach them. Your scale's stuck on a number just a little higher than you'd like. You don't have as much energy, creativity, or focus as you need to truly reach your potential.

You know that making a shift in how you feed your body could change all that for the better. But it's hard to do for 3 reasons:

1 **Sneaky foods.** You know certain foods aren't good for your body, but they make your brain feel so good you indulge anyway. The more you eat them, the more you crave them, and the harder they become to resist. Food manufacturers create processed food full of C.R.A.P. specifically designed to keep you trapped in this harmful cycle.

2 **Set routines.** Your brain develops mental shortcuts—habits—to help make sense of your busy life. It's all too easy to go through your day on autopilot, complacent about your eating patterns. You might not even realize you've developed bad habits or that they can be broken.

3 **Mistaken identities.** You may have preconceived notions of who you are and what you can and can't do, even if you don't realize it. Conscious or not, these self-descriptions have enormous power. If you've ever said or even thought something like "I'm not a runner," "I don't cook," or "I have an out-of-control sweet tooth," you've boxed yourself into a corner before you even begin.

THE SUPERFOOD SWAP PLAN HELPS YOU MAKE THESE CHANGES:

≫ You'll learn how to remove the C.R.A.P. and naturally change your cravings. A study from Tufts University showed that if you start eating more wholesome food, you can indeed retrain your brain over time to automatically crave nutritious stuff.

≫ You'll practice shaking up your routine and trying new things—even on your busiest days. Whether you do the complete 4-week program or just start randomly sampling recipes, you'll bust right out of autopilot mode.

≫ You'll shed stale definitions of yourself and try new foods, activities, and mind-sets. Keep an open mind through the process and you will most definitely surprise yourself about who you are and what is possible for you.

DIETS STINK—SUPERSWAP IS DIFFERENT

In order to lose weight or "clean up" their diet, people typically feel they have 2 options:

1 **Deprivation:** Deny cravings and feel deprived. They cut out foods they enjoy and blame themselves when the unrealistic routine they've established can't be maintained.

2 **Fake food:** Swap their favorite unhealthy food for low-calorie imitations with artificial ingredients. All they pay attention to are calories, leaving their body deprived of nutrients.

Sound familiar? We all know complete denial doesn't work in the long run. No one can simply white-knuckle their way through each day, using willpower alone to turn down every temptation. Eventually, you'll slip up and maybe even binge, entering a downward spiral of guilt, shame, and failure. That's no way to live.

As for low-cal swapping—well, I have a *serious* problem with it. Sure, you may lose a few pounds, but the scale isn't the only—or even the best—measure of success. Focusing only on cutting calories doesn't take into account the quality of food you put into your body. Replacing food with processed, synthetic imitations robs your cells of nutrients.

Listen, you don't need deprivation or fake food. You really *can* SuperSwap and satisfy cravings with foods that are good for your body.

WHY IT WORKS

Say the word "diet," and most people immediately think about giving up their favorite foods. That's what most plans do—they take out the things you love the most and make it impossible to follow the diet long-term.

LEARNING TO SUPERSWAP DOES require some effort at first. Fortunately, our energy tends to be highest at the start of a new adventure—and baby, we're going to make the most of it! I'll guide you through a month-long process of setting yourself up for success before letting you loose in the kitchen. Here's the scoop:

- **Week 1:** Supercharge with Superfoods. You'll meet these dietary wonders and start adding them to your day.
- **Week 2:** Cut the C.R.A.P. We'll call B.S. on fake food and potentially harmful ingredients and begin breaking your ties to them.
- **Week 3:** Take Superfoods to the Streets. You'll learn to dine out, entertain, and vacation, SuperSwap style.
- **Week 4:** Maintain Your Mojo. You'll never fear failure again with this ultimate guide to keeping your motivation high—now, and for months and years to come.
- **Cookbook:** You'll find about 100 recipes to keep the party going. What you crave . . . made with the healthiest stuff on earth.

EACH WEEK FEATURES:

- **A Superfood Swap Truth:** Simple wisdom that can change your life.
- **Science-Based Lessons:** Don't worry; I'm not taking you back to high school biology—these are brief but enlightening!
- **SuperSwap Challenges:** Fun to-dos that help you put food, fitness, and happiness ideas into practice.

RESULTS YOU CAN EXPECT:

At the end of the 4-week program:

- You will be a full-fledged superfood junkie.
- You'll feel the high of superfoods pumping through your veins.
- You will reboot your taste buds so that you crave more superfoods.
- Your house will smell of craveable foods packed with superfood nutrition.
- You'll have a kitchen stocked with superfoods.
- You'll be armed with smart cooking skills.
- You will glow with superfood health and energy.
- Plus, if you SuperSwap most meals and snacks, you will lose 2 to 4 pounds per week.

The secret to the SuperSwap is this: You're following, instead of denying, your cravings. You ask yourself what you really want to eat. Then you make it with superfoods in the right ratios—heavy on the veggies, with a little grain, protein, and fat. Remember, when you eat what you want, you'll feel excited about your plan— and magical things happen when people are excited about what they're doing.

This book is chock-full of the tools you need to transform your life—scientifically sound strategies and superfood recipes that have worked for me and my clients. For example, I'll teach you to:

- **Bake** chocolate chip cookies that feed your brain (see page 199).

- **Stay active** with short, sweatless workouts.

- **Whip up** ranch dressing with metabolism-boosting cashews (page 178).

- **Rock your day** with an uplifting playlist (see page 33).

- **Recharge** with a quick, chemical-free energy drink (page 221).

When you SuperSwap your eating—and your life—you can make a profound difference in how you look and feel. And you'll protect your health for years to come. Let me help you learn to master the SuperSwap—and have fun along the way.

LET'S TALK CALORIES

We live in a state of utter calorie confusion. Most popular diets and nutrition gurus fall into one of two equally flawed calorie camps:

> ### THE ORIGINAL SUPERSWAP: TRADE SHAME FOR
> # BODY LOVE
>
> MOST PEOPLE START DIETS with a negative body image—a feeling that their thighs are too big, their gut too bulging, their butt too squishy. Well, I call that crap thinking. The very first SuperSwap to make is one of mind-set: Instead of trying the Superfood Swap plan because you hate your body, do it because you love your body and want to treat it right. I bought myself a heart-shaped necklace and wear it every day to symbolize my commitment to body love. Think kind and loving thoughts about your body, prioritizing both relaxation and exercise, and nourish it with superfoods.

>> The **calorie counters** focus solely on numbers without regard for nutrition or the quality of the food. Follow this strategy and you may lose weight, but you'll also deprive your body of real-food nutrients. Plus, obsessive counting leads to joyless eating.

>> The **calorie clueless** focus only on quality without regard to calories. Many diets lead you to think that if you just avoid "junk" and choose "healthy" food (based on their particular definitions), that's all there is to it. Problem is, you absolutely can overdo it, even with the highest-quality foods. You'll gain weight, which leads to low energy, increased risk of disease, and frustration.

I don't advocate strictly counting calories. But I don't advocate ignoring them completely, especially if you aim to lose weight. My solution is called **calorie consciousness**.

The calorie conscious believe that calories *and* quality matter. Calorie for calorie, high-quality foods give you more supercharged nutrients for overall health and long-term wellness. Plus, quality foods may stimulate your body to burn more calories, making it easier to lose weight.

How does calorie consciousness fit in with the Superfood Swap plan? I've made all the recipes in this book calorie conscious. Each contains quality ingredients *and* clocks in at around 400 calories. If you eat 3 Superfood Swap meals a day and then add 2 snacks of 100 to 200 calories each, you'll have a total of 1,400 to 1,600 calories a day. Depending on your starting weight and how much you exercise, you can lose 2 to 4 pounds per week—while getting all the nutrients you need to live an energized life. You'll feel physically full from eating real food and mentally satisfied from eating recipes inspired by your favorite foods.

FRESH START: Almond Butter and Chia Jam Sandwich (page 137)

MORE WAYS TO STAY CALORIE CONSCIOUS

>> **Dine in.** Make your own food as often as you can. Put in a little kitchen effort, and research shows you'll automatically eat less while enjoying each bite more. And don't worry, you'll learn how to SuperSwap at restaurants in week 3 of my plan.

>> **Visualize.** Looking at your plate can quickly reveal whether you have the right ratios. Vegetables have the most nutrients for the fewest calories—you want them filling half your plate. Aim for smaller portions of whole grains, proteins, fats, and fruits. They have more calories and sometimes more sugars than veggies, so you can't eat them with abandon and expect to lose weight.

>> **Eat mindfully.** Put your food on a plate. Sit down at the table. Pay attention to what you're eating. Listen to your "inner wisdom," really tasting each bite and honoring hunger and fullness cues. Studies have found that doing so results in eating less.

>> **Weigh in.** Step on the scale weekly. Most people who successfully maintain weight loss do. If the number creeps up, you'll know you're eating too many calories. (Don't beat yourself up about it, though. Use it as just one nonjudgmental measure—and keep track of other non-scale victories, too.)

Bottom line? Educate yourself about the basics of calories and stay aware of them, but don't obsess or play games (for instance, "saving up" calories for a later binge). And always aim for the highest-quality food you have available.

MORE THAN A NUMBER

You better believe that cutting C.R.A.P. and eating more superfoods leads to more than just weight loss. Notice—and enjoy—these benefits beyond the scale:

- Feeling and looking younger

- Higher confidence levels

- More energy—and less need for crutches like sugar and caffeine

- Better attitude—and ability to find joy in everyday situations

- Clearer thinking

- Better digestive health, which includes less bloating and more regularity

- Improved health markers like cholesterol, blood sugar, and blood pressure

- Fewer cravings for junk

- Improved focus and productivity

- Healthier hair, skin, and nails

- Fewer colds and flu

- Less apt to feel guilt, shame, and stress

Join my online community so we can share swaptastic superfood tips with each other. Visit my website, dawnjacksonblatner.com, and sign up for my weekly Nutrition WOW email. Congratulations on taking this step to supercharge your health and life. Your body loves you for it.

PEACE, LOVE, AND SUPERSWAP,

Dawn

SEVEN EASY SUPERSWAPS: *clockwise from top:* extra-virgin olive oil, unsweetened coconut flakes, hemp seeds, coconut oil, raw cashews, pistachios, chia seeds

PART 1

THE 4-WEEK PLAN

WEEK 1

1

SUPERCHARGE
WITH
SUPERFOODS

MANY EATING PLANS start by telling you what not to eat. Not this one. To get started, I actually want you to *add* something to your diet: superfoods.

Superfoods stand out as the rock stars of the nutrition world: foods that deliver the maximum dose of antioxidants, vitamins, healthy fats, and other primo ingredients your body needs to thrive. Sure, you might be able to *survive* on a diet of processed foods (more on that C.R.A.P. next week), but if you fill your plate with superfoods, mostly plants, you'll *thrive*.

You won't have to scour the top shelves of health food stores or search exotic websites to find my favorite superfoods. The ingredients you'll meet in this first week (see the complete list on page 74) are easy to find, versatile enough to work in multiple recipes, and loaded with health benefits. Plus, they're delicious.

THE POWER OF THE POSITIVE

If the idea of kicking off a new way of eating by adding foods—not taking them away—sounds strange to you, you're not alone. It completely contradicts how we've been conditioned to think about healthy eating.

And here's something else that's different from most diets: We're also going to focus on what foods do for your *whole body*, not just your waistline.

With Americans' near-obsessive focus on how food affects weight, it's easy to forget what actually happens when you eat. After each swallow, food travels through your esophagus, breaks down in your stomach, and then hits your intestines. Special cells in your intestinal walls send the digested food molecules directly into your bloodstream.

SUPERFOOD SWAP »> TRUTH

Superfoods are the secret sauce that brings out your slimmer, healthier, more energized self.

Whole, high-quality foods (superfoods) infuse your blood with powerful nutrients to energize and strengthen every single cell in your body. They fight disease, fire up your metabolism, and transform your appearance, among other benefits. This is the magic of superfoods—they have the power to change how you look and feel on a cellular level.

Of course, the biology of digestion is only part of the story. Food also appeals to our more sensual, emotional nature. Thanks to our evolutionary history of feast or famine, we crave foods that are sweet, salty, fatty, and full of flavor. In fact, in every area of our lives—food, sex, art, work, music—we are hardwired to seek pleasure. Part of the brain called the reward circuit lights up when we get what we want. Think about how you feel when you hear the first few notes of your favorite summer song, when your boss gives you a glowing review, or when a hottie looks your way. There's an instant burst of electricity and excitement—the same thing that happens when we sit down to a delicious meal.

In effect, we each have a little bit of dietary split personality disorder—an inner health nut who wants to do right by our bodies, and a pleasure-seeking wild child who wants the next food-induced high.

Good news, my friends: You can feed both at the same time! Starting this week, we'll prepare the foods your wild child craves (like pizza, cookies, and soda) with ultranourishing superfoods. You'll eat what you love *and* what you need at the same time. Fulfill your cravings—and your nutritional requirements.

Food fuels us, but we're not cars that can rev up on the same old regular unleaded every day. We're humans, with culture, relationships, and senses. Enjoying ourselves while eating well isn't merely a gimmick or a luxury—it's actually a critical part of creating healthy habits we can live with for the rest of our lives.

THE SUPERPOWERS OF SUPERFOOD

What makes superfoods so super? Their weight-loss, beauty, energy, and health-promoting powers come from compounds that nourish your cells and help fight wear, tear, and disease (see pages 26 and 27). Many are phytochemicals—which just means substances produced by plants—while others are living organisms themselves. Check out the highlights of the head-to-toe benefits of eating superfoods. This isn't an exhaustive list, but a superfood sampling—so many more fruits, vegetables, whole grains, proteins, and fats have similar health-promoting powers.

SUPERFOODS SLIM YOUR WAIST BY:

» **Changing your calorie math.** High-quality superfoods take more energy—about 10% more—to digest. It's called the thermic effect of food, and it means digesting a 400-calorie bean burger on a sprouted whole-grain bun with avocado burns 40 more calories than digesting a 400-calorie turkey sandwich on white bread with fake American cheese.

SUPERSWAP CHALLENGES

☐ **Make these meals.** Or you can swap in any other breakfast/lunch/dinner from the book.

    Breakfast: Avocado Toast (page 91)
    Lunch: Sunflower Caesar (page 100); Hummus Bowl (page 99)
    Dinner: Quick Kale Pizza (page 106); Guac and Greens Tacos (page 107);
    BBQ Salmon and Cauliflower Mash (page 108)

☐ **Snack only when you're hungry**—0 to 2 times per day—preferably from the list on page 126, or from any of the treats sections if you're craving something special.

☐ **Take inventory.** Read over the superfood list on page 74. Highlight the foods you already eat regularly—and give yourself a high-five! Then use a different color marker to highlight foods you've never tried—and get excited! Working your way through the Superfood Swap recipes will help you explore these new foods.

☐ **Make a list of your most frequent cravings.** Think of the comfort food meals and snacks you turn to when you need a lift. Consult the SuperSwap Cravings chart (page 28)—or flip through the rest of the book to find superfood-containing dishes that have similar flavors and textures. Try one of them the next time you're confronted with a craving.

☐ **Create an exercise calendar.** Right now, plug in the days, times, and places you're going to work out for the next 4 weeks. That's right—schedule your workouts like you would any other important appointment. What should you do? It doesn't matter—anything is better than nothing.

☐ **Connect and share.** You're not in this alone—I'm rooting for you every step of the way. As you go through the plan, snap pics of yourself, your SuperSwap meals, and swaptastic tips and post them on social media; tag me (I'm @djblatner on Instagram, Facebook, and Twitter) and use the #SuperSwap hashtag.

>> **Keeping you satisfied. Fiber** and **unsaturated fats** have cravings-busting staying power. Eat them for breakfast or lunch and you'll subconsciously cut calories at your next meal, say researchers at Purdue University and the University of Toronto. **Superfood All-Stars:** almonds, avocados, chickpeas, and lentils.

>> **Stabilizing your hunger hormones.** Mice on high-fat diets gained less weight if their meals were also rich in the compounds inulin and beta-glucan, according to a study in the journal *PLOS ONE*. As your body breaks down these compounds, which are called fermentable carbohydrates, your blood levels of fullness hormones rise, sending the signal to your brain that it's time to put down the fork. **Superfood All-Stars:** asparagus, oats, and mushrooms.

>> **Speeding your metabolism.** Compounds called catechins turn up your total daily calorie burn by about 4%. According to a study in the *Journal of Research in Medical Sciences*, people who drink 4 cups a day of catechin-rich green tea shed 3 pounds in 2 months without making any other changes to their diet and exercise program. And Danish researchers found that combining catechins with foods rich in tyrosine (like spinach and eggs), capsaicin (which gives chile peppers their heat), and caffeine could help you burn an extra 21 calories per day. **Superfood All-Stars:** green tea, spinach, eggs, and cayenne.

HEY, HOTTIE! SUPERFOODS HELP YOU:

>> **Get your glow on.** In a recent British study, men and women were rated more attractive when their skin glimmered from carotenoids (orange pigments that subtly tint the skin) rather than from the sun. Carotenoids are found in red, orange, and dark green produce. **Superfood All-Stars:** red bell peppers, carrots, oranges, pumpkin, and kale.

>> **Shave years off your face.** The more vitamin C you eat, the less dry and wrinkled your skin appears, according to research published in the *American Journal of Clinical Nutrition*. And omega-3 fatty acids, essential fats your body can't produce on its own, keep your skin hydrated and dewy fresh. **Superfood All-Stars:** grapefruit, strawberries, fatty fish, and walnuts.

>> **Star in your own shampoo commercial.** Protein strengthens hair strands and prevents them from falling out. The mineral silica gives you a thick, lush mane. And minerals like iron, copper, and zinc (abundant in seeds) speed hair growth. **Superfood All-Stars:** bananas, sunflower seeds, and eggs.

>> **Make the most of your manicure.** Vitamin D and calcium strengthen nails, while folate, protein, and iron keep them smooth and shiny. Biotin-rich eggs prevent frustrating peeling and breakage. **Superfood All-Stars:** spinach, eggs, yogurt, and kefir.

POWER UP! WITH SUPERFOODS YOU'LL:

» **See the bright side.** Keep your plate full of red, orange, and green produce. The more carotenoids in your bloodstream, the more optimistic your outlook, Harvard research shows. **Superfood All-Stars:** carrots, mangoes, butternut squash, and spinach.

» **Crush your workouts.** Cyclists who ate ½ cup of almonds per day could pedal an extra mile during a 20-minute timed test—and bananas, raisins, and chia seeds work as natural energy boosters during long workouts (with less C.R.A.P. than a sports drink). It's the complex carbohydrates, antioxidants, and potassium in these foods that fuel all-star performances. **Superfood All-Stars:** chia seeds, almonds, raisins, and bananas.

» **Beat the blues.** In one large study, foods rich in folate were linked to a lower risk of depression. In another, polyphenols and other anti-inflammatory compounds in leafy green and yellow vegetables reduced women's chances of feeling down. **Superfood All-Stars:** black beans, collards, chard, and arugula.

» **Sharpen your thinking.** Fish has earned its rep as a brain food. The more omega-3 fatty acids in your diet, Tufts University researchers found, the lower your risk of cognitive decline—the brain fog that often occurs with aging. **Superfood All-Stars:** flaxseeds, pumpkin seeds, and fish. Seaweed, walnuts, and even broccoli and cauliflower also boast these brain-boosting fats.

EAT SUPERFOODS AND YOU'LL:

» **Stay above the weather.** Aim for a healthy dose of immune-boosting compounds like allyl sulfides, vitamins C and E, and probiotics to ward off colds, flu, and other common illnesses. In a meta-analysis of research, the "good" bacteria in yogurt and kefir slashed the risk of colds by 62%. And regular garlic consumption can cut your risk of catching a respiratory infection by 58% (and shorten the length of the colds or flu you do develop by 60%). **Superfood All-Stars:** yogurt and kefir, honey, onion, and garlic.

» **Fight inflammation.** When you catch a bug, slice your finger, or twist your ankle, your bloodstream floods with compounds like C-reactive protein and cytokines to help repair the damage. That's good—but our crazy-stressful lives cause inflammation to linger and damage healthy cells. This chronic inflammation increases the risk of joint pain, type 2 diabetes, obesity, and heart disease. Magnesium, quercetin, and oxylipins calm down our body's reaction to injury. **Superfood All-Stars:** kale, citrus, apples, onions, brown rice, soybeans, and cocoa powder.

» **Cancer-proof your cells.** Just ½ teaspoon of flaxseeds per day contains enough estrogenlike compounds called lignans to reduce breast cancer risk by 18%, according to a recent study in the journal *Cancer Causes & Control*. And isothiocyanates in cruciferous vegetables help ward off breast, prostate, and liver cancer. **Superfood All-Stars:** flaxseeds, cauliflower, broccoli, and Brussels sprouts.

SUPERSWAP CRAVINGS

YOU CRAVE	TRY THESE QUICKIES (and see page 76 for many more)	OR THESE RECIPES
SWEET STARCHY CARBS	• Pureed fruit instead of pancake syrup • Handful of nuts and raisins instead of a granola bar	• Cereal Puff Bowl (page 92) • Blender Pancakes (page 176) • Cinnamon Oatmeal Muffins (page 172) • Zucchini Bread French Toast (page 175)
SUGARY DRINKS	• Sparkling water with a shot of 100% juice instead of soda • Brewed chai tea instead of a chai latte	• Super Latte (page 213) • Super Soda (page 213) • Real Ginger Ale (page 214) • Coconut Lemonade (page 214)
FRIED FOODS	• Nuts instead of bread crumb coating • Grill for flavor instead of frying	• Fast Falafel Bowl (page 144) • Cauliflower Fried Rice Bowl (page 149) • Carrot and Green Bean Fries (page 227) • Buffalo Cauliflower Poppers (page 226)
SALTY	• Nuts instead of pretzels • Guacamole instead of processed cheese dip	• Superseed Crackers (page 207) • Wasabi Chickpeas (page 206) • Spinach Chips (page 121) • Superfood Party Mix (page 125)
SAVORY STARCHY CARBS	• Cauliflower rice instead of rice • Zoodles or spaghetti squash instead of noodles	• Sprouted Pizza (page 157) • Kale Burgers and Veggie Dippers (page 154) • Mexican Burrito Bowl (page 99) • Tomato Soup with Grilled Cheese Croutons (page 189)
CHEESY OR CREAMY	• Plain 2% Greek yogurt instead of sour cream or mayo • Coconut milk instead of flavored coffee creamers	• Cashew Ranch Dressing (page 178) • Cauliflower Mac and Cheese (page 150) • Butternut Squash Lasagna (page 198) • Cheddar Grits with Beans and Greens (page 116)
MEAT	• Seasoned lentils instead of ground beef • Sliced chicken or turkey breast instead of processed lunch meat	• Lentil Meatballs and Pasta (page 195) • Beet Burgers (page 153) • BBQ Sandwich and Collard Chips (page 142) • Superfood Chili (page 192)
ICE CREAM	• Frozen grapes instead of push-pops • Frozen banana slices instead of a banana split	• Nice Cream (page 163) • Green Smoothie Ice Pops (page 160) • Dark Chocolate Cherry Milk Shake (page 160) • Cashew Whip and Berries (page 159)
CHOCOLATY	• Dark chocolate instead of packaged cakes and cookies • Unsweetened cocoa powder instead of sugary chocolate syrup (see page 237)	• 5-Minute Chocolate (page 117) • Chocolate Yogurt Mousse (page 120) • Brownie Bites (page 159) • Chia Chocolate Chunk Cookies (page 199)
SWEET	• Plain yogurt with berries instead of berry-flavored light yogurt • Dried mango (no sugar added) instead of gummy bears	• No-Bake Peanut Butter Cookies (page 121) • Brown Rice Crispy Treats (page 206) • Mini Yogurt Cheesecake (page 162) • Gingersnap Cookies (page 203)

>> **Protect your heart.** Sweet news: Thanks to the flavonoids it contains, cocoa improves blood pressure, cholesterol, and a measure of blood vessel health known as arterial stiffness. And nuts contain phytosterols and unsaturated fats that also cut your cardio-vascular risk—in one Pennsylvania State University study, a serving of pistachios per day reduced blood pressure by about 5 points. **Superfood All-Stars:** cocoa powder and pistachios.

GO FISH

Most of the healthiest foods on earth grow in the ground—but a few swim in the sea. In fact, health experts recommend eating fish (especially fatty varieties like salmon and sardines) at least twice a week for omega-3 fatty acids that boost heart, brain, and skin health.

When you buy fish, look for these things: high in omega-3 fatty acids, low mercury levels, and sustainability (caught or farmed in ways that cause little harm to habitats or other wildlife). Your very best bets are wild salmon, sardines, mussels, rainbow trout, and Atlantic mackerel. Other good choices include oysters, anchovies, herring, shrimp, catfish, tilapia, clams, and scallops.

For more reading on the best choices for your body and the oceans, head to the Monterey Bay Aquarium's comprehensive site (complete with downloadable chart and app) at seafoodwatch.org. And for personalized fish recommendations based on your age, weight, and gender, check out Environmental Working Group Seafood Calculator at ewg.org/research/ewgs-good-seafood-guide.

LIKE IT RAW?

Raw fruits and vegetables are incredibly good for us, but I don't promote a totally raw-food diet—adding heat has benefits. Cooking adds variety to our diets and may actually increase key nutrients (for instance, cooked tomato products like paste and sauces contain more lycopene than fresh tomatoes).

The flip side: Other health-promoting compounds, such as vitamin C, can break down with heat. The solution? Strive for a balance of cooked *and* raw produce throughout each day. Try the raw versions of these traditionally cooked foods—you just might see them in a whole new light.

>> **Asparagus.** Toss fresh, well-washed spears in your salad.

>> **Beets.** Peel and chop these root beauties and blend them into smoothies (try the Chocolate Beetberry Smoothie, page 134).

>> **Cashews.** Typically salted and roasted, the uncooked version of these nuts offers less sodium and has a cleaner, sweeter flavor. Use them in Cashew Ranch Dressing (page 178), Cashew Alfredo (page 158), and Cashew Whip and Berries (page 159).

>> **Kale.** Massaging it gently breaks down some of the tougher fibers, making kale salads easier to digest and more delicious.

>> **Zucchini.** Use it to create grain-free noodles (aka zoodles!). See the recipe for Pesto Zoodles with Garlic Bread (page 111).

GREEN BASE

THE ONE THING THAT should always be in a healthy fridge is, without a doubt, washed-and-ready leafy greens. Arugula, baby spinach, kale mix, mixed salad greens, shredded cabbage, romaine . . . stock up! Leafy greens are real miracle workers for health and weight. You can use them for salads of course, but my favorite way to use them is as a Green Base.

THE INGREDIENTS

3 cups of your favorite salad greens (or, really, any veggie you have on hand)

Anything you like to eat: pizza, fried chicken, Chinese takeout, pasta, etc.

THE STEPS

1 **Assemble:** Put undressed leafy greens in a bowl and put whatever you want to eat on top, but not too much.

2 **Chop or toss:** Chop or toss everything together. This is the ultimate vice/virtue combo . . . a base of greens for a healthy body and topping them with what you crave.

ENJOY IT AS A MEAL . . .

Put almost anything you eat on a Green Base. My faves:

- **Pizza:** Cut pizza into squares and use as croutons.
- **Pasta dishes:** Put hot noodles on greens to wilt them perfectly.
- **Tacos:** Pour taco filling onto greens and make it taco salad night.
- **Steak and potatoes:** Top greens with these dinner classics.

- **BBQ meats or fish:** Combine sweet BBQ and bitter greens, yes!
- **Fried chicken:** Chop chicken into bite-size pieces and toss with greens.
- **Chinese takeout:** Dump half your usual entrée onto the greens.

BY THE WAY, SUPERSWAPPERS, THIS COUNTS AS THE MOST

SIMPLE AND LOW-DRAMA WAY

TO SUPERSWAP YOUR MEAL.

Sure, this book is all about making your favorites with superfoods—but using a Green Base offers a super quick, no-recipe-needed strategy to improve your nutrition. Just eat a smaller portion of your original dish and round it out with a heaping pile of veggies.

Fast Falafel Bowl (page 144)

YOUR F.I.T.T. RX

Get ready for a surprise: Exercise is actually *not* the best weight-loss tool. Your diet reigns supreme when it comes to shedding pounds, but physical activity does help you prevent weight *gain*. And it does pretty much everything else for you, too—soothes your sleep, boosts your mood, zaps stress, and fights disease.

Any workout is better than none, of course. Government experts advise adults to get 150 minutes of moderate activity per week (if you like to exercise intensely, you can aim for 75 minutes). Further supercharge your workouts by changing any of the 4 factors of F.I.T.T.:

>> **Frequency:** How often are you working out? My rule of thumb: Never let 2 days go by without a workout, even if it's short and sweatless.

PUT YOUR
BEST FACE FORWARD

SUPERFOODS DON'T JUST GO *in* your body. You can also score beauty benefits by applying them to your skin and hair. Check it out:

- **Coconut oil** works just as well as any chemical-laden makeup remover. Soak round or square cotton pads in melted coconut oil and then let it cool. Store the pads in your bathroom or gym bag for easy wipes on the go.
- **Honey** exfoliates and clears skin naturally, thanks to its antibiotic properties. You'll avoid artificial microbeads that harm your skin and the environment—and you can easily store some honey in a contact case for travel.
- **Cinnamon** plumps lips. Channel your inner Angelina by dipping your finger in coconut oil and then into ground cinnamon. Massage the mixture on your lips for a minute, wipe or lick it off, then reapply a little oil for shine on top.

» **Intensity:** How hard are you working? If you're just starting out, keep it easy to moderate (you should be able to talk but not sing while walking, jogging, or cycling). After a few weeks of consistent exercise, add short bouts of high-intensity efforts—say, a 30-second sprint every few minutes during your easy run. Research shows this nets you the same health and fitness benefits as a longer workout in less time.

» **Time:** Start where you are and then gradually increase your amount of activity. The rule of thumb is to add about 10% per week to give your body time to gain strength and fitness. For instance, if you walk for 30 minutes 4 times this week, add about 12 minutes total to your walking time next week.

» **Type:** You need both cardiovascular exercise—which moves large muscles and gets your heart beating harder—and strength training. But the options within those rules are nearly endless (dancing, swimming, running, or rowing for cardio; weight lifting, gardening, yoga, or Pilates for strength).

MAKE TIME FOR PLAY

Whether you went for the tiara and crown or picked out a pair of superhero underwear, remember how much fun you had playing dress-up as a kid? Somewhere along the way to adulthood, we lose the ability to make play a key part of every day (not just something to enjoy every now and then on vacation). R&R doesn't take $1,000 or a week on a beach; reclaim that childhood sense of delight by including a small, simple pleasure each day. Some of my faves:

» **Drinking cinnamon-apple or spiced tea.** In the summer, make it iced and serve it in a pretty glass goblet.

» **Listening to music.** Each time you find yourself grooving to a tune or hear a song that takes you back to a happy time, add it to whatever music service you use. Presto: your own custom, mood-boosting playlist.

» **Wearing one bright accessory.** Even if you've stocked your closet with neutral basics, a splash of color on a scarf, tie, or necklace does the trick.

» **Coloring.** Use crayons, markers, or colored pencils. Now there's no one to tell you to stay inside the lines, or that trees can't be blue or purple. Let your imagination run wild!

DRINK UP!

WHEN IT COMES to weight loss, water might be the original metabolism-boosting superfood. In a Virginia Tech study, researchers found that drinking 2 cups of cold H_2O before a meal led people to consume up to 90 fewer calories. Over 12 weeks, participants who gulped water before every meal lost 5 pounds more than those who didn't. Women should aim for at least 9 glasses per day; men, 12. Beat boredom by adding superfoods—think cucumber, berries, or lemon—or herbs and spices like mint, ginger, or cayenne to your water.

SMART SEASONINGS

Put zest into your meals with these value-added SuperSwap seasonings.
Store dried herbs and spices away from light, heat, and moisture
(not near the stove or the dishwasher). This extends their shelf life,
but they'll still eventually lose flavor and potency—so taste-test jars
you've had around for a while before you use them.
If they're flavorless, replace them.

SEASONING	WHAT IT DOES	HOW TO USE IT
CAYENNE	• Boosts metabolism	• In soups or on pizza or egg dishes • To spice up the Wellness Shot (page 220)
CINNAMON	• Lowers blood glucose, promotes weight loss	• In breakfast oats, smoothies, or coffee • To sweeten up the Banana Bread Cookies (page 171)
COCOA	• Lowers blood pressure and cholesterol	• With yogurt or fruit for a sweet treat • Blended into the Chocolate Beetberry Smoothie (page 134)
GARLIC (FRESH)	• Lowers heart disease risk, fights bacteria	• Cooked in soups and stews or chopped raw with tomatoes for a quick homemade salsa • To make natural Garlic Bread (page 111)
GINGER (FRESH)	• Eases bloating, helps digestion, reduces post-workout soreness	• Grated in salad dressings or blended in smoothies • To bake fresh Gingersnap Cookies (page 203)

SEASONING	WHAT IT DOES	HOW TO USE IT
OREGANO (DRIED)	• Controls blood glucose • Kills bacteria that cause food poisoning	• Atop pizza, pasta, and other Italian-inspired dishes • To season Eggplant Parmesan (page 190)
LEMON/LIME	• Boosts your immune system	• Squeezed over other fruits, veggies, tofu, or fish • To add oomph to Matcha Jolt (page 212)
PARSLEY (FRESH)	• Keeps blood healthy • Inhibits tumor growth • Decreases water retention and bloating	• Stirred into sauces and dressings, tossed into salads, or blended into smoothies • To freshen up Chickpea Noodle Soup (page 179)
SEAWEED	• Contains essential minerals like iodine, can reduce sodium intake	• As a stand-in anywhere you'd use salt • To add savory flavor to Sesame Seaweed Popcorn (page 122)
TURMERIC	• Fights inflammation and relieves joint and muscle pain	• Heated as tea or to season curries and stir-fries • To add a beautiful hue to Golden Milk (page 216)
VINEGAR	• Boosts metabolism and mood	• Blended with nuts, cheese, or avocado as a salad dressing • To make 15-Minute Pickles (page 153)

Lentil Tacos (page 185)

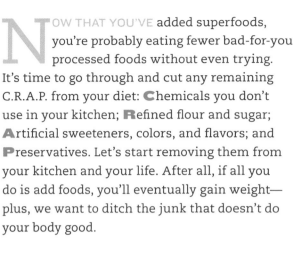

WEEK 2

CUT THE C.R.A.P.

NOW THAT YOU'VE added superfoods, you're probably eating fewer bad-for-you processed foods without even trying. It's time to go through and cut any remaining C.R.A.P. from your diet: **C**hemicals you don't use in your kitchen; **R**efined flour and sugar; **A**rtificial sweeteners, colors, and flavors; and **P**reservatives. Let's start removing them from your kitchen and your life. After all, if all you do is add foods, you'll eventually gain weight—plus, we want to ditch the junk that doesn't do your body good.

SHOW C.R.A.P. THE DOOR

Not all processing is bad. Throughout human history, we've processed foods to make them safer, easier to digest, and more nutritious. Harvesting plants, cracking hard shells, simmering on a stove, or roasting over an open flame are "processes," after all—and they fit right in with healthy eating.

But somewhere along the way, things changed. Manufacturers began pumping our meals full of lab-created ingredients not to enhance nutrition but to make food cheaper and hyperappetizing, almost addictive. As a result, our grocery stores are now full of things our ancestors would barely recognize as edible.

Understand: I'm not vilifying everything that comes in a carton or package. I personally employ a lot of healthy convenience in my daily routine—and if you're a busy working parent, these kinds of things are practically necessities. Check out the Healthy Convenience Cheat Sheet on page 42 for my list of top time-saving picks.

That said, it's critically important to distinguish between healthy convenience and processed C.R.A.P. Remember how superfoods nourish every cell? Well, C.R.A.P. gives your

SUPERFOOD SWAP TRUTH »

Processed foods containing C.R.A.P. are full of empty calories that don't nourish your cells.

organs and tissues absolutely nothing to thrive on. C.R.A.P. clogs your taste buds and keeps you locked into craving yet more C.R.A.P. And in some cases C.R.A.P. can actually harm you—studies have shown associations between some of these ingredients and health problems, from allergic reactions to cancer.

Please note: I don't want you to live in fear of every bite. You won't keel over if C.R.A.P. passes your lips. But start paying attention, and you'll notice that C.R.A.P. makes you feel like crap. Once you swap in superfoods instead, you will become addicted to how they make you feel, both mentally and physically. You'll avoid C.R.A.P. not because you feel like you should but because you want to—and because you feel the difference inside and out.

SPOT THE C.R.A.P.

Here are the ingredients you need to ditch—and how to spot them.

» **Chemicals you don't use in your kitchen.** Currently, the U.S. Food and Drug Administration (FDA) allows more than 10,000 additives in our food supply. About a third of them haven't undergone complete testing to ensure they're safe for human consumption. Many have been linked to health risks in humans and animals—from cancer to obesity to developmental problems. **Look for words like:** azodicarbonamide, carrageenan, potassium bromate, soy isolate, brominated vegetable oil, and partially hydrogenated vegetable oil.

» **Refined grains and sugars.** Whole grains contain 3 parts: the bran, the germ, and the endosperm. Refining removes the outer bran and inner germ, as well as key nutrients such as filling fiber, blood-boosting iron, and stress-reducing B vitamins. Plus, refined grains and white sugars get you stuck on a blood-sugar roller coaster that over time contributes to the development of obesity, type 2 diabetes, and other metabolic problems. Since these foods aren't filling, you get hungry in no time and start craving the rush again—up and down and up and down. This yo-yo feeling affects focus, mood, and energy. **Look for words like:** refined flour, enriched wheat, high-fructose corn syrup, sugar, and anything ending in -ose.

» **Artificial sweeteners, colors, and flavors.** The ultimate in food fakery, these compounds alter foods' taste or appearance. Many low-calorie or calorie-free sweeteners have caused cancer in animal studies, and some research suggests that they trick your brain into craving more sugar and sweet foods. Food dyes may trigger allergic reactions, contribute to hyperactivity in children, cause cancer in animals, and damage nerve reactions. **Look for words like:** caramel coloring, saccharin, aspartame, acesulfame-potassium, dyes, diacetyl, or just plain "artificial flavoring."

WEEK 2 SUPERSWAP CHALLENGES

❏ **Make these meals.** Or you can swap in any other breakfast/lunch/dinner from the book.
 Breakfast: Peanut Butter Oatmeal (page 92)
 Lunch: Mexican Burrito Bowl (page 99); Ramen Jar (page 181)
 Dinner: Kale Burgers and Veggie Dippers (page 154); Olive Oil Pasta (page 115)

❏ **Snack only when you're hungry**—0 to 2 times per day—preferably from the list on page 126, or from any of the treats sections if you're craving something special.

❏ **Practice bottom-up label reading.** Before you buy something, turn it over and look at the label—starting with the ingredients. Don't get distracted by the health claims on the front or the numbers and percentages at the top. If you find something containing C.R.A.P., don't buy it—and if you don't recognize an ingredient, eliminate or investigate it. Make no assumptions. Question everything, especially the 10 things that regularly top your grocery list. These foods are the most important to check because they form the core of your diet. (For more on decoding nutrition facts, read the SuperSwap Label-Reading Guide on page 41.)

❏ **Go on a C.R.A.P.-cutting mission.** Scour your refrigerator, freezer, and cabinets—and don't forget your office. Dispose of items with obvious C.R.A.P. by starting with the 7 foods in the C.R.A.P.-tastic Hall of Fame on page 43, then by reading ingredient lists. Hate waste? Make a note not to buy these items again when you run out.

❏ **Save food receipts for the week.** If you eat out (or order takeout) more than a couple of times, you run the risk of weight gain—and of eating C.R.A.P. you don't even know about. Consider how to cut back. Some ideas: make Brussels Sprout Pad Thai (page 182) instead of having dinner delivered; make a Belly Love Smoothie (page 96) to drink on the way to work instead of hitting the drive-through; host a Superfood Swap dinner party (see page 59) instead of girls' night out.

❏ **Track your workouts.** Every day, pull out your exercise calendar and give yourself a smiley face or checkmark when you successfully complete your workout. On days you don't, figure out what stood in your way and fix it.

>> **Preservatives.** True, you don't want your chips or dried apricots to go bad on the shelf, which happens without preservatives. However, compounds used to preserve these foods also can trigger severe, asthmalike reactions in some people and even contribute to cancer in lab animals. **Look for words like:** sodium nitrate/nitrite, BHA, TBHQ, BHT, heptyl paraben, and propyl gallate.

DON'T GET FOOLED

Food manufacturers put C.R.A.P. in our foods to trick us by:

- using color and flavor to transform cheap chemicals into faux fruit juice, fruit, and meat

- adding vitamins and minerals to processed junk so it seems healthy

- producing cakes, cookies, and snack foods that can last for months or even years on store shelves

- sticking small bits of protein together into a bigger sausage, patty, or steak

- coloring farmed fish to make it look like wild caught

Cut the C.R.A.P.!

TAKE A STAND AGAINST S.A.D.

If you find your cabinets, cart, and desk drawer stuffed with C.R.A.P., you're far from alone. When researchers study the so-called Western or Standard American Diet (S.A.D.—another fitting acronym), they literally define it as high in cake, pizza, salty snacks, and ice cream, and low in fruits, vegetables, whole grains, and lean protein like seafood. Yikes, that's embarrassing. This is the way we've been taught to eat, the way the people around us eat, and the way our environment encourages us to eat. As a result:

>> **We're gaining weight.** Research shows high-quality foods burn 10% more calories as you consume them—so a 400-calorie meal of white pasta with fake cheese sauce burns 40 calories fewer than the same 400 calories made with whole-grain pasta, shredded Parmesan, and veggies.

>> **We're unhappy.** A recent Norwegian study found high-quality diets full of fruits, veggies, and unprocessed meats reduce the risk of depression, while Western diets provoke anxiety. A separate study from Spain linked trans fats to a blue mood.

>> **We look old.** High-fat, high-sugar, and fried foods contain more compounds called advanced glycation end products (A.G.E.). These accumulate in your skin, decreasing its vibrant elasticity and increasing sun sensitivity, discoloration, and wrinkles.

>> **Our minds and bodies are run down.** Those who eat more processed foods are 58% *less* likely to reach their golden years in good mental and physical shape, British researchers found. They tend to die earlier—and if they do survive, they struggle with illness and disability.

I don't know about you, but I'm ready to change the status quo!

THE SUPERSWAP LABEL-READING GUIDE

In theory, food labels give us all the details we need to choose our foods wisely. In practice, companies use a variety of sneaky techniques to sell us more C.R.A.P. Outsmart them with these 5 steps:

1 **Ignore the claims on the front of the package.** Most have no meaning at all, and even those with a definition don't have much to do with basic nutrition. Words like "anti-oxidants," "heart healthy," "whole-grain," and "all natural" prime you to think a food is good for you regardless of the truth. Instead, flip over the bag or box and evaluate the contents yourself. Don't let fancy advertising make your decisions for you.

2 **Immediately read the ingredients.** Start from the bottom up. Numbers can quickly steer you wrong (in one study, numbers led 1 in 5 label-readers to rate Spam as more healthful than salmon!). Scope out the ingredients first. In general, the shorter and easier to pronounce this list is, the better. Ingredients are listed in order of weight, so choose items with the real whole foods you'd use in your own kitchen high on the list. Skip those containing C.R.A.P., especially if it appears in the first 3 or 4 spots.

3 **Check the serving size.** It often differs from the amount you actually eat. For instance, if a cereal box has a serving size of ¾ cup but you pour 1½ cups, you're getting a double dose of everything inside.

4 **Assess—but don't obsess over—the calorie count.** Staying calorie conscious is important, especially if you're trying to lose weight. This number should *never* be the main reason you choose a food, but you should be aware of it.

5 **Note the percentages.** These numbers are super helpful—they make it easy to put nutrients into perspective. Here's the rule: **5% or less is low** for that nutrient and **20% or more is high** for that nutrient (and anything

C.R.A.P.-SPOTTING EXAMPLE

LET'S SAY YOU PICK up a bag of frozen french fries. You see that they contain potatoes, vegetable oil, salt, and spices. Okay—those are all things you probably have in your pantry.

But keep reading and you'll notice there's also "natural flavor," dextrose, and disodium dihydrogen pyrophosphate. You might recognize that dextrose is a type of sugar—but you certainly don't have a canister of it in your cabinet. Nor would you add in a heaping spoonful of disodium dihydrogen pyrophosphate to homemade oven fries. You don't need to know what it is to recognize that it probably is not doing your cells any favors (if you're wondering, it's a white powder that prevents potatoes from turning brown).

I'm not calling this stuff toxic poison. What I *am* saying is if your body doesn't need it, why eat it? Just cut up a fresh potato instead and bake your own simple fries. And for that matter, add other veggies, too, like parsnips, green beans, and carrots.

I HAVE A GOOD FRIEND—let's called her Heather—who is an old soul. Even in college, her hobbies included gardening, canning, and baking bread from scratch.

If that describes you—awesome! A passion for preparing your own foods gives you a huge advantage in the nutrition arena (not to mention endless potluck invitations). But for the rest of us who wouldn't live long on *Little House on the Prairie*, here are my favorite nutritious shortcuts that can save you time while helping you cut C.R.A.P. Sometimes they cost a little more, but other times they're less expensive—and either way, you might find they're worth it.

- **Bagged greens.** Lettuce, spinach, kale, arugula, preshredded coleslaw mix—take your pick! Precut, prewashed ingredients can go directly into a salad, soup, omelet, or stir-fry.

- **Cooked whole grains.** Check the freezer or refrigerator sections of the supermarket for precooked brown rice, quinoa, hulled barley, or whole-grain farro. Choose simple versions without sauces or seasonings. Simply heat and enjoy.

- **Frozen fruits and vegetables.** Picked and preserved at the height of freshness, these come in handy between trips to the grocery store or if what you want isn't in season. Choose versions that have no added sauces or syrups.

- **Sprouted whole-grain bread, pizza crust, and tortillas.** Sprouting makes whole grains even more nutritious by increasing the amount of vitamins and minerals your body can absorb. I can tell you from experience it's a major pain to sprout the grains on your own, and that's even before you get around to making dough and baking a loaf. My favorite brand of sprouted whole-grain bread contains sprouted wheat, barley, millet, and spelt.

- **Canned beans.** Dried beans cooked in the slow cooker (see page 241) taste better than canned and are better for digestion—and if you plan ahead, they don't add much extra time to your routine. But canned beans are far better than no beans at all. Just rinse them first to get rid of extra salt.

- **Sauces and seasoning mixes.** You have to read labels closely—some are nothing more than packets or jars full of C.R.A.P. like monosodium glutamate, artificial flavorings, and high-fructose corn syrup. But the right mix can make dips, stir-fries, and curries a snap. I have a favorite French onion dip mix for veggies, plus a few go-to simmer and pasta sauces that I love—and when I find new ones that pass the C.R.A.P. test, I stock up.

in between is average). So if you see that a product has 20% vitamin C, 10% fiber, and 5% sodium, you can quickly determine that it's high/excellent in vitamin C, average in fiber, and low in sodium.

THE SUPERFOOD SWAP DIFFERENCE

Every day, I scan blogs, email newsletters, and social media posts from influential "nutrition gurus" and find it astounding how much bad advice out there promotes C.R.A.P. Keep an eye out for these 2 types of offenders:

>> **The low-cal empty promises.** I saw a popular 87-calorie "5-ingredient" dessert recipe posted online. But each "ingredient" had its own lengthy list of ingredients. I added them all up and got a shocking total of 56, including 5 types of sugar, 7 oils (2 partially hydrogenated), 4 artificial sweeteners, and 20 stabilizing or preservative chemicals. The moral: Even if it looks like a simple 5-ingredient recipe, check those 5 foods closely. They may harbor hidden C.R.A.P.

>> **The health-food fakers.** Another day, I clicked on an article about how to throw a vegan, gluten-free barbecue. The recommended grocery list would load your picnic table with refined-grain buns, processed veggie dogs and burgers, and dairy-free frozen desserts that pack in almost 5 teaspoons of white sugar per ½ cup. The moral? A food may have *no* sugar, gluten, animal products, or dairy, but ask yourself: What *does* this food actually contain? Let me say this again: A food may have no sugar, no gluten, no animal products, no dairy, but what *does* it actually contain should be the

> ## TRASH THE C.R.A.P.-TASTIC
> # HALL of FAME
>
> **WANT TO CUT THE MOST C.R.A.P.** in the least amount of time? Trash these 7 foods, which have multiple types of harmful ingredients.
>
> - "diet" foods, usually labeled "sugar-free, fat-free"
> - packaged cookies and other baked sweets
> - packaged crackers, chips, and other snack foods
> - sausage and bacon
> - fake veggie "meats" like soy burgers and hot dogs
> - soda—diet or sugar-sweetened
> - white bread and rolls

question. Don't lose sight of the fact that eating is supposed to provide nutrients to our body cells. It's not just about keeping calories low and cutting out food villains. Instead of avoiding specific ingredients, ask yourself this big-picture question: Does it have nutrients that will supercharge my body or is this just a health-food faker full of C.R.A.P.?

Here are the facts: You absolutely must eat high-quality foods to maintain your health and to lose weight. "Low-calorie," "low-fat," "natural," "vegan," "gluten-free," or "sugar-free" labels tell you nothing about the nutrition a food provides.

I WANT A PEANUT BUTTER TREAT!

Let's look at a side-by-side comparison of options.

SIDE-BY-SIDE COMPARISON:	Low-cal empty promise dessert recipe: low-calorie peanut butter shake	Health-food faker dessert product: chocolate peanut butter–flavored soy ice cream	Superfood Swap whole food dessert: No-Bake Peanut Butter Cookies (page 121)
INGREDIENTS IN RECIPE:	powdered peanut butter, light vanilla soymilk, light vanilla ice cream, low-fat peanut butter–flavored cereal (like Jif Peanut Butter Cereal), vanilla extract, no-calorie sweetener (like Splenda or Truvia), fat-free Reddi-Wip, maraschino cherry	N/A	oats, peanut butter, flaxseeds
INGREDIENTS ON LABELS:	In alphabetical order: baking soda, BHT for freshness, brown sugar syrup, calcium carbonate, cane sugar, canola oil, carrageenan, cellulose gel, cellulose gum, cherries, citric acid, corn bran, corn syrup, cream, degerminated yellow cornmeal, dextrose, FD&C red #40, guar gum, high-fructose corn syrup, inulin (chicory extract), maltodextrin, milk, mono and diglycerides, natural and artificial flavors, nonfat milk, peanut butter (peanuts, sugar, salt, hydrogenated vegetable oil [rapeseed, cottonseed, soybean], dextrose, molasses, monoglycerides, peanut oil), peanut powder, polydextrose, polysorbate 80, potassium sorbate and sodium benzoate, propylene glycol monoesters, reb A (stevia leaf sweetener), salt, sea salt, soymilk (filtered water, soy flour), sucralose or stevia, sugar, sulfur dioxide, vanilla bean, vanilla bean extractives in water and alcohol, vitamin A, vitamin D_3, water, whey, wheat flour, whole-grain yellow corn flour	Organic soymilk (water, organic soybeans), organic tapioca syrup, organic dried cane syrup, organic peanut butter (organic peanuts, salt), organic soybean oil, organic cocoa powder processed with alkali, chicory root extract, locust bean gum, tapioca dextrose, natural flavors, guar gum, carrageenan, sea salt	Same as above: oats, peanut butter, flaxseeds

Practicing the techniques in this chapter can help you develop your natural food–sleuthing abilities so you can more quickly judge for yourself whether you're making a healthy choice rather than relying on guidance from a flawed guru.

BREWS AND BOOZE

What about coffee and alcohol? While most people can incorporate both into a healthy diet, they're worth discussing because they're not just food—they're drugs, even if you don't typically think of them that way.

Coffee contains caffeine, which boosts your heart rate and metabolism. Small doses can sharpen your thinking, help you crush a hard workout, and even contribute to weight loss. And java has other health perks. In one recent study, adding a cup a day decreased participants' risk of developing type 2 diabetes by 11%, and a recent meta-analysis linked 2 to 4 small 8-ounce cups per day to longer life.

Of course, too much of a good thing can keep you awake at night, make you jittery and anxious, and upset your stomach. Most healthy people should stop at about 400 milligrams of caffeine—about the amount in 4 cups of coffee. If you feel symptoms sooner, set lower limits. And cut yourself off 8 hours before bedtime to avoid disrupting sleep.

As for alcohol—well, I don't have to tell you that some people should steer clear of it altogether, including pregnant women, people with a personal or family history of alcohol abuse, and patients with liver disease. For healthy adults, risky drinking—that's more than 7 drinks a week for women or 14 for men—increases the risk of heart disease, cancer, and other health problems. But light to moderate drinking may actually protect your heart, especially if red wine is your beverage of choice. Oh, and 1 drink is 5 ounces of wine, 12 ounces of beer, or a 1½-ounce shot of hard alcohol. (Watch out for heavy-handed bartenders.)

Like any drug, these two can help when taken in the right dose by the right person. Overdose, though, and you'll put your health at risk.

KNOW YOUR SUGAR SYNONYMS

SOMETIMES A FOOD CONTAINS several types of sugars. **Learn to spot all the synonyms for sugar:** agave nectar, anhydrous dextrose, barley malt syrup*, beet sugar, brown rice syrup*, brown sugar, cane juice, cane sugar, confectioners' sugar, corn syrup, corn syrup solids, crystal dextrose, date sugar*, dextrose, evaporated cane sweetener, evaporated corn sweetener, fructose, fruit juice concentrate, fruit nectar, glucose, high-fructose corn syrup (HFCS), honey*, invert sugar, lactose, liquid fructose, maltose, maple syrup*, molasses (blackstrap or dark)*, nectars (e.g., peach nectar, pear nectar), pancake syrup, raw sugar, rice syrup, sucrose, sugar cane juice, and white granulated sugar.

*These have more antioxidants than other sweeteners—choose them when possible, though in limited amounts

REAL-WORLD LABEL COMPARISONS

Here are actual examples of what to drop and how to SuperSwap.

DROP	⤳ SUPERSWAP
Quaker Chewy Chocolate Chip Granola Bars Ingredients: granola (whole-grain rolled oats, brown sugar, crisp rice [rice flour, sugar, salt, malted barley extract], whole-grain rolled wheat, soybean oil, dried coconut, whole wheat flour, sodium bicarbonate, soy lecithin, caramel color, nonfat dry milk), semisweet chocolate chips (sugar, chocolate liquor, cocoa butter, soy lecithin, vanilla extract), corn syrup, brown rice crisp (whole-grain brown rice, sugar, malted barley flour, salt), invert sugar, sugar, corn syrup solids, glycerin, soybean oil. Contains 2% or less of: sorbitol, calcium carbonate, salt, water, soy lecithin, molasses, natural and artificial flavor, BHT (preservative), citric acid	**Almond Joy Snack Mix** (page 118) Ingredients: raw almonds, unsweetened coconut flakes, cacao nibs
Dannon Fruit-on-the-Bottom Yogurt Ingredients: cultured grade A low-fat milk, blueberries, sugar, fructose syrup, high-fructose corn syrup, fructose. Contains less than 1% of: modified cornstarch, cornstarch, pectin, kosher gelatin, malic acid, natural flavor, disodium phosphate, tricalcium phosphate, carmine (for color)	**Fage Total 2% Yogurt** Ingredients: grade A pasteurized skimmed milk and cream, live active yogurt cultures (*L. bulgaricus*, *S. thermophilus*, *L. acidophilus*, *Bifidus*, *L. casei*). Add your own fresh fruit (ingredients: blueberries, strawberries, etc.).
Strawberry Pop-Tarts Ingredients: enriched flour (wheat flour, niacin, reduced iron, thiamine mononitrate, riboflavin, folic acid), corn syrup, high-fructose corn syrup, dextrose, soybean oil, palm oil, TBHQ, sugar. Contains 2% or less of: cracker meal, wheat starch, salt, dried strawberries, dried pears, dried apples, cornstarch, leavening (baking soda, sodium acid pyrophosphate, monocalcium phosphate), citric acid, corn cereal, gelatin, partially hydrogenated soybean oil, caramel color, modified cornstarch, soy lecithin, xanthan gum, modified wheat starch, tricalcium phosphate, color added, turmeric color, vitamin A palmitate, red #40, niacinamide, reduced iron, pyridoxine hydrochloride, yellow #6, riboflavin, thiamin hydrochloride, folic acid, blue #1	**Almond Butter and Chia Jam Sandwich** (page 137) Ingredients: Almond butter, sprouted whole grain bread, chia jam (ingredients: fresh fruit, chia seeds)
Jif Creamy Peanut Butter Ingredients: roasted peanuts, sugar. Contains 2% or less of: molasses, fully hydrogenated vegetable oils (rapeseed and soybean), mono and diglycerides, salt	**365 Organic Creamy Peanut Butter** Ingredients: peanuts, salt
Keebler Cheese & Peanut Butter Sandwich Crackers Ingredients: enriched flour (wheat flour, niacin, reduced iron, thiamin mononitrate [vitamin B₁], riboflavin [vitamin B₂], folic acid), peanut butter (roasted peanuts), soybean oil with TBHQ for freshness, sugar, dextrose, salt. Contains 2% or less of: leavening (baking soda, sodium acid pyrophosphate, monocalcium phosphate), cheddar cheese (milk, cheese cultures, salt, enzymes), yellow #6, cornstarch, whey, red pepper, buttermilk, disodium phosphate, soy lecithin	**Nabisco Triscuit Original** Ingredients: whole-grain soft white wheat, soybean oil, sea salt. Add natural peanut butter (ingredients: peanuts, salt).

DROP	🔖 SUPERSWAP
Slim-Jim Beef Jerky Original Ingredients: beef, mechanically separated chicken, water, corn syrup, soy protein concentrate. Contains less than 2% of: salt, spices, dextrose, paprika and paprika extractives, flavoring, hydrolyzed soy, corn, and wheat proteins, lactic acid starter culture, sodium nitrate	**Seaweed Snack Strips** (page 165) Ingredients: Nori seaweed, honey, sesame oil, cayenne, sesame seeds, sea salt
Butternut Honey Wheat Bread Ingredients: enriched wheat flour (wheat flour, malted barley, niacin, iron, thiamin mononitrate, riboflavin, folic acid), water, whole wheat flour, honey, high-fructose corn syrup, yeast, soybean oil (nonhydrogenated), salt, wheat gluten, sesame seeds. Contains 2% or less of: dough conditioners (monoglycerides, ethoxylated mono and diglycerides, sodium stearoyl lactylate, ascorbic acid, enzymes), caramel color, calcium propionate (to retain freshness), calcium sulfate	**Food for Life 7 Sprouted Grains Bread** Ingredients: organic sprouted wheat, filtered water, organic malted barley, organic sprouted rye, organic sprouted barley, organic sprouted oats, organic sprouted millet, organic sprouted corn, organic sprouted brown rice, fresh yeast, organic wheat gluten, sea salt
Hillshire Farms Thin Sliced Oven Roasted Turkey Breast Ingredients: turkey breast, turkey broth, modified cornstarch. Contains 2% or less of: salt, natural flavor, carrageenan, sodium phosphate, yeast extract, sodium nitrite, sodium propionate, caramel color **Fast Fixin' Chicken Breast Nuggets** Ingredients: chicken breast with rib meat, water, soy protein concentrate. Contains 2% or less of: salt, sodium phosphate, tricalcium phosphate, potassium lactate, soy lecithin. Battered and breaded with: wheat flour, water, 2% or less of wheat starch, buttermilk, whey, potassium chloride, sodium acid pyrophosphate, sodium bicarbonate, corn starch, monocalcium phosphate, spice, salt, dextrose, maltodextrin, flavor, caramel color, extractives of paprika	**Perdue Harvestland Organic Chicken Breast** Ingredients: Chicken
Rice-A-Roni Long Grain & Wild Rice Ingredients: parboiled long-grain rice, wild rice, onions, hydrolyzed soy protein, monosodium glutamate, maltodextrin, salt, autolyzed yeast extract, sugar, parsley, garlic, hydrolyzed corn gluten, caramel color, spices, hydrolyzed torula and brewers yeasts, hydrolyzed wheat gluten, niacin, ferric orthophosphate, thiamin mononitrate, folic acid	**Rice Expressions Organic Brown Rice** Ingredients: cooked organic whole-grain brown rice. And add your own seasonings (see Smart Seasonings Chart on page 34 for ideas).
Kraft Original Barbecue Sauce Ingredients: water, vinegar, sugar, tomato paste, modified food starch, salt. Contains less than 2% of: citric acid, molasses, caramel color, mustard flour, dried garlic, spice, guar gum, dried onions, potassium sorbate as a preservative, natural hickory smoke flavor, paprika, sucralose (sweetener)	**DIY BBQ Rub** Ingredients: sea salt, chili powder, garlic powder, cumin, cayenne
Snickers Ingredients: milk chocolate (sugar, cocoa butter, chocolate, skim milk, lactose, milkfat, soy lecithin, artificial flavor), peanuts, corn syrup, sugar, palm oil, skim milk, lactose, partially hydrogenated soybean oil, salt, egg whites, artificial flavor	**Chocolate Pecan Candy Clusters** (page 200) Ingredients: pecans, Medjool dates, coconut oil, unsweetened cocoa powder, maple syrup, sea salt

SHOULD YOU GO ORGANIC?

We talked about what's *in* your food—but what about how it's grown? Many people worry about the health risks of pesticides and related chemicals. And then there is the complicated issue of genetically modified organisms (commonly called GMOs). This process changes the DNA of seeds to create plants with specific traits, such as hardiness to resist viruses.

Well, let me get right to the bottom line:

>> Start eating more fruits and vegetables— organic or not. Nine out of 10 Americans don't eat enough produce as it is. You should worry about eating the recommended dose before you worry about chemicals or genetic engineering.

>> Once you've formed a solid fruit and veggie habit, buy organic when you can. A recent research review suggests organic fruits and veggies may contain more disease-fighting antioxidants. Start buying organic versions of the produce "Dirty Dozen," a list of fruits and vegetables the nonprofit Environmental Working Group (EWG) found to contain the most pesticides: apples, bell peppers, celery, cherry tomatoes, cherries, cucumbers, grapes, nectarines, peaches, spinach, strawberries, and tomatoes (and also kale and collard greens). Check the website ewg .org for regular updates. As a general rule of thumb, if the produce is something you'd peel, like a banana, don't worry as much about whether it's organic. Most pesticide residue is found on the skin you will be throwing away.

>> Cutting C.R.A.P. will automatically reduce your exposure to GMOs. The most common genetically modified plants—corn, canola, soybean, and cotton—are used to make ingredients like high-fructose corn syrup and cottonseed or canola oil found in packaged foods.

>> Aim to buy organic, grass-fed beef and organic, pasture-raised pork, poultry, and eggs. Cows, pigs, chickens, and turkeys whose meat or eggs are labeled "USDA certified organic" eat an organic, non-GMO diet, usually have access to the outdoors, aren't treated with antibiotics, and are raised under more stringent health and welfare standards than conventionally managed animals. Plus, organic cows aren't given added growth hormones (these are always banned in pigs and poultry).

Now, I know organic, grass-fed or pasture-raised meat costs more. However, the animals are healthier (and happier). Plus, paying more will help you remember to limit portion sizes and fill the rest of your plate with superfood plants—veggies, fruits, beans, nuts, seeds, and whole grains.

DITCH PUNISHMENT WORKOUTS

How many times do you endure a workout because you feel like you have to atone for that extra slice of cake or because you are unhappy with how your arms/belly/thighs look? Well, it's time to stop. **Exercise because you love your body, not because you hate it.** Instead of thinking of exercise as punishment, view it as a gift you give your body (and approach it with gratitude—it's also a gift to be healthy enough to exercise!). View exercise as an opportunity to move your muscles, clear your mind, and produce brain-boosting, happy chemicals. Pick a workout that you like, not one you dread. You'll find it easier to develop a fitness habit—and you just might have a good time.

HARNESS THE POWER OF WORDS

Constant exposure to negative words and phrases can sabotage your positive efforts. Surround yourself with positive statements instead.

>> Start the minute you get out of bed. Instead of a harsh beep, set your phone alarm to an upbeat song—or better yet, a positive phrase like "Good morning. Today is going to be a beautiful day."

>> Change your passwords to motivating health mantras. Include numbers and symbols for greater security. For instance: Eat>Greens (eat more greens); Lungesb4BED (lunges before bed); 2dayisGR8! (today is great!).

>> Reframe your goals as desires. Tell yourself you *want* to eat more superfoods, start a new fitness routine, or dump C.R.A.P. from your cupboard rather than that you *should*. This simple word shift has had dramatic effects for my clients—and in my own life.

>> Practice the catch and flip. When you *catch* yourself saying something hateful, *flip* to the exact opposite statement. The words you use create your reality, so cut your crap thinking. If you catch yourself saying "I have flabby thighs," flip it to "I have tight, toned thighs."

GET RID OF C.R.A.P. KITCHEN GEAR

DITCH THE THINGS THAT drive you crazy or prevent you from having fun while preparing or eating healthy meals. Scrap scratched or chipped cookware, dull knives, old takeout or other plastic containers, and stained plastic cutting boards. Not only are these things ugly, but chipped nonstick pans and old plastic containers can also leach dangerous compounds into our food. Also get rid of—or store out of reach—extra-large wineglasses and oversized bowls and plates that tempt you to serve too-large portions.

Pesto Zoodles with Garlic Bread
(page 111)

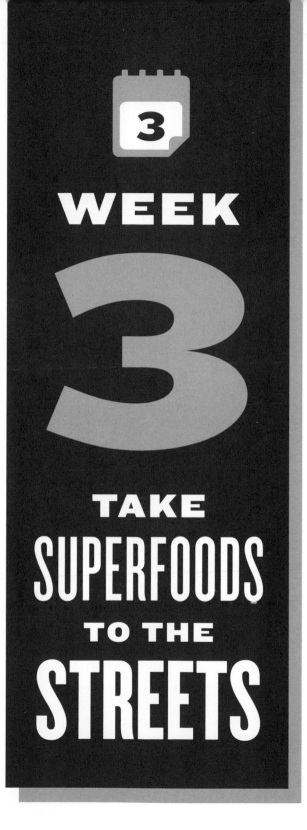

WEEK 3

TAKE SUPERFOODS TO THE STREETS

Y OU'VE TOSSED THE C.R.A.P. from your cabinets and drawers and transformed your kitchen into a haven for superfoods. What happens when you step outside this zone of complete control and into a restaurant, party, or family gathering—or for that matter, when you're forced to wing a meal instead of following a recipe?

Believe it or not, it is possible to stay true to the Superfood Swap anywhere you are in life, whether you're networking at a business dinner, attending a generously catered reunion, sitting down to a decadent anniversary meal with your sweetie, or feeling exhausted from a long day and can't fathom cooking but still need to eat. What's more, I'll show you how to do so in a way that doesn't leave you feeling deprived—and makes people around you jealous rather than judgmental.

CHANGE YOUR MIND, CHANGE YOUR DIET

You might think the biggest challenge when eating out boils down to finding nutritious options among dishes laden with extra calories and C.R.A.P. While it's true that many menus are minefields—and I'll offer you tips on safely navigating them—I'm going to suggest something that may sound a little strange at first. The biggest obstacle to healthful eating in restaurants and social situations lies not in the list of entrées or at the bottom of the deep fryer, but in our brains.

Even if we successfully change our habits in our carefully controlled everyday environment, eating becomes a whole different sport when we're with others. Whether it's at a restaurant, at a party, or on vacation, we face two distinct challenges:

>>> **Our definitions of ourselves.** This is the main barrier to smart decision-making in a crowd. Perhaps you view yourself as the life of the party, always ordering the extra bottle of wine for the table and making sure everyone has a good time. The person you believe yourself to be would never order a salad with dressing on the side or sip a club soda. On the flip side, you may think of yourself as a virtuous eater who can't loosen the strings even a tiny bit. When you try to adhere to this extreme, you run the risk that even a bite of a bacon-wrapped appetizer will send you into a tailspin and leave you feeling like a failure. Remember, we all have dietary split personality disorder—a little bit wild child, a little bit health nut. Try to find the balance of both sides, even in your own mind.

>>> **The expectations of others.** Peer pressure is a real thing (and later on, I'll show you how to harness it for good instead of evil). But chances are, you're putting a lot of that weight on yourself. Other people are thinking far less about your choices and more about their own—and what they react most strongly to is your attitude, not what's on your plate. Think about it—why do you like your friends? Is it because they shovel down burritos and candy? No, it's because they're happy, fun, and kind to you, regardless of what they're feeding themselves.

On one hand, this news kind of stinks. After all, it seems a lot easier to just order a spinach salad than it is to make big changes in your thought and behavior patterns. But on the other hand, this means that a little hard work

on adjusting your attitude can have powerful effects in every area of your life.

So how, exactly, do you go about this mind-set shift when dining out? Go back to the idea of seeking not perfection, but balance. With each meal away from home, you strive to fulfill both your body's physical nutrition requirements *and* your emotional desire for satisfaction. Eat mostly superfoods that protect and strengthen your cells, but leave room for treats that feed your deepest cravings. Strike this balance and you'll leave the table 100% happy and well nourished.

GREEN BASE 101

Here's the truth: We all need to wing it from time to time. The simple, foolproof way? Cover your plate with a Green Base—like I mentioned on page 30, this can be arugula, spinach, romaine, kale, or whichever leafy green you like. Or chop any vegetable you have around the house and put it in a bowl. Then pile about 400 calories of other foods on top: pizza, Chinese leftovers, hard-boiled egg, extra brown rice from last night's dinner, or drained canned beans. This method serves as a catchall for anything in your fridge, freezer, or pantry. Choose 3 options from the list on page 54, and you're pretty much there. (The same strategy works at salad bars, too.)

SUPERSWAP CHALLENGES

☐ **Make these meals.** Or you can swap in any other breakfast/lunch/dinner from the book.

    Breakfast: Superfood Scramble Bowl (page 93)
    Lunch: Avocado Tuna Sandwich (page 101); Asian Peanut Bowl (page 102)
    Dinner: Pesto Zoodles with Garlic Bread (page 111); Superfood Chili (page 192); Cauliflower Mac and Cheese (page 150)

☐ **Snack only when you're hungry**—0 to 2 times per day—preferably from the list on page 126, or from any of the treats sections if you're craving something special.

☐ **Make a rule: table-plate-chair.** This is the most powerful tip while socializing, and beyond. For the next 7 days, eat everything from a plate while seated at a table. If you graze, you will overeat. When we put food on a plate, our mind takes a mental snapshot to gauge hunger and fullness.

☐ **Make a food backup plan.** Create a list of 4 veggie-rich dishes you can buy in a pinch from stores or restaurants near your home or office. That way, you'll have healthy go-tos when a home-cooked SuperSwap meal just isn't in the cards.

☐ **Make a fitness backup plan.** Find some workouts you can do quickly when you don't have an hour or access to gym equipment. Search for 5- to 20-minute routines on phone apps, online, or in articles in your favorite health and fitness magazines—for example, a 12.5-minute sprint routine or a 7-minute full-body workout.

Fried chicken: ⅓ cup or 2 ounces

Steak: ⅓ cup or 2 ounces

Pulled pork: ⅓ cup or 2 ounces

Grilled salmon: ⅔ cup or 4 ounces

Tuna salad (with mayo): ⅓ cup or 2 ounces

Hard-boiled egg (chopped): ½ cup

Beans (chickpeas, kidney, edamame, etc.): ½ cup

Fried tofu/falafel: ⅓ cup

Nuts: 2½ tablespoons

Dried fruit: 5 tablespoons

Dressing: 2 tablespoons

Cheese: 5 tablespoons

Avocado: ⅓ whole avocado or ½ cup cubed avocado

Guacamole: ¼ cup

Brown rice (cooked): ½ cup

Quinoa (cooked): ½ cup

Pasta (cooked): ¾ cup

Croutons: 12 pieces or ½ cup

Tortillas chips/strips: 12 chips or ½ cup

Pizza: ½ slice pizza, chopped

Roasted or baked potato: ¾ cup cubed potato

Egg roll: ⅔ egg roll, chopped

DINING OUT HOW-TO

It's a special occasion and the verdict's in—you're going out! Take this opportunity to nourish your inner health nut with superfoods while simultaneously indulging your wild child.

》》 **Plan ahead.** Do a few minutes of research *before* you're swept up in a whirlwind of socializing and drinking. This could be as simple as perusing the online menu on your phone on the ride to the restaurant.

》》 **Order a vice/virtue bundle.** Pair a healthy superfood with a less-healthy craving. It's the only way to honor both your inner health nut and wild child. At a barbecue joint and really want the pulled pork? Get it—but instead of plopping it on a refined-grain bun, ask to put it on or alongside a salad. In fact, you can immediately cut the calorie count and increase the superfood content of any sandwich or wrap by turning it into a satisfying salad instead. Other bundle ideas:

- pizza with a basic green salad

- burger with a garden salad instead of fries

- side of pasta marinara with Parmesan paired with an order of roasted broccoli

- a half sandwich with veggie soup instead of a full sandwich or side of chips

- hash browns with a poached egg and sliced tomatoes instead of hash browns with a large cheesy omelet and toast

- a single pancake with an egg and fresh berries instead of a stack of pancakes. Ask for a side of honey for the pancake, unless you know it's pure maple syrup. (Many restaurants use imitation syrup, which is full of refined sugar, caramel coloring, and other C.R.A.P.)

For other great bundles, see There's an App for That on page 55.

>> **Don't worry about being high maintenance.** Don't feel bad or make apologies for asking for things done your way—99 out of 100 times, the restaurant staff just wants you to leave happy. Ask nicely and tip well. Far better to order what you want than to pile on C.R.A.P. trying to people-please the waitstaff.

>> **Prioritize your favorites.** If you find yourself at a buffet or facing a tableful of small plates, commit to your absolute favorites rather than sampling every option. Research shows variety stimulates appetite—so little bits of everything never satisfy you, keeping you going back for more. (You can use this at parties with full appetizer tables, too— works like a charm.)

>> **Activate your portion ninja.** Sometimes you really have no options—for instance, when you are served something at someone's house or you are at a wedding with preplated food. When this is the case, remember there are only two variables with food: choice and portion size. Drink 2 glasses of water before the meal and chew each bite 10 times to really slow down and savor.

>> **Limit accessories.** It's often not just the meal that racks up C.R.A.P. calories, it's also the add-on apps, drinks, and desserts. Focus on your main and skip these extras, or at least just pick your favorite *one*.

THERE'S AN APP FOR THAT

To keep portions in check, skip the main and make a meal out of appetizers and side dishes. Here are a few good ideas:

ENJOY YOUR TREATS

IF YOU REALLY WANT something:

- **Pay for it**. This transforms treating yourself from a passive, shame-filled process to an active, enjoyable experience. Don't secretly shovel down leftover brownies from a meeting you didn't even attend—instead, walk down the street and buy your favorite decadent dessert and eat it there with a cup of tea. Or even better, wait until later and make it at home.

- **Socialize.** Go out for ice cream with your spouse or get on your favorite dating site to invite a hottie out for a piece of chocolate cake. When you eat (and drink!) with others there's more enjoyment and less guilt. Think about it: Chocolate cake on a date feels much more satisfying than chocolate cake alone on the couch. Healthy eating isn't always about just the food. It's about the feeling and location, too.

>> **Crab cakes.** Sure, they're often fried, but they're small. They're awesome on top of a house salad without dressing—you can use a little of the tartar sauce that comes with the cakes.

>> **Satay.** Chicken, steak, shrimp, or tofu on a skewer—usually simply prepared by grilling or broiling. Great with a green salad

HACK HAPPY HOUR

Try these SuperSwaps at your next post-work get-together and you won't stick out for being a goody-goody or for how tipsy you get in front of your coworkers.

DROP	⌄ SUPERSWAP
Margaritas: Salt-rimmed calorie bombs at best, and at worst, made from mixes full of C.R.A.P. like high-fructose corn syrup.	**Light Mexican beer with lime:** Or order a no-sugar margarita: a large club soda with a shot of tequila and lots of fresh lime wedges. You can also ask for a few slices of fresh jalapeño since the extra spice naturally slows drinking pace.
Gin and tonic: Don't be fooled by the clean taste—tonic water has just as much sugar as regular soda.	**Gin and club soda:** Just as light, refreshing, and fizzy, but C.R.A.P.-free.
Cheap cocktails at the dive bar: Extra calories plus crappy booze equals one bad idea.	**Club soda with flavored rum or vodka:** Try citrus for a fruity flavor or cucumber for a fresh, clean finish.
Craft cocktails at the latest hot spot: Delicious and artisan, but often contain as much alcohol as 4 or more standard drinks—not good for your waistline or your judgment.	**Custom made:** Ask the mixologist for a club soda with house-made bitters. You'll enjoy signature craftsmanship for a fraction of the calories—and without a hangover.
Sangria: Sure, there's fruit—but also plenty of pure white sugar.	**Red or white wine** with a few slices of lemon, lime, or orange. Lose the sweetener, keep the festive feel.
10 Bud Lights: Beer specials (buckets, anyone?) can tempt you to overdo it on even low-cal, low-flavor options.	**One craft beer:** Sure, the calorie count is higher, but you'll be able to sip it slowly and feel satisfied. Or go for a pint of Guinness—surprisingly, this thick, dark brew clocks in at a mere 125 calories per 12-ounce bottle.
Wings: Fried bits of chicken and skin, sometimes covered in fluorescent hot sauce? Totally C.R.A.P.-tastic.	**Veggies and hummus:** If it's spice you crave, ask for crushed red pepper flakes or Tabasco sauce to stir in, and replace refined-grain pita with extra veggies.
Fried calamari: Healthful seafood coated in refined flour and deep-fried in oils that probably contain trans fats.	**Grilled calamari:** Same flavor profile, less C.R.A.P. Ask for it even if it's not on the menu; the kitchen has squid back there, after all, and they can probably prepare it differently.
Nachos or quesadillas: Pick your poison—either deep-fried corn crisps or refined-flour tortillas paired with too much cheese, lard-flavored beans, and ground beef.	**Chips and dips:** You can have your tortilla chips and eat them too; just pair them with good-for-you guac or salsa. Plus—and this is key—put them on a plate instead of taking them straight from basket to mouth for a better picture of how many you're eating.
Flatbread: Refined-carb crusts that usually come with toppings skimpy on the veggies.	**Italian soup:** Satisfy your cravings for tomatoes, herbs, and cheese with a hearty minestrone or pasta e fagioli sprinkled with Parmesan. Bonus: Eat a broth-based soup before your meal and you'll naturally cut back on the main course.

or veggie of the day. Use the satay dipping sauce as dressing.

>> **Grilled fish tacos.** Not fried, these often come with healthy fats from guacamole. Ask for extra shredded lettuce or cabbage.

>> **Mussels.** This can be a low-calorie, healthy choice as long as you aren't drinking the buttery broth. Get them with a slice of sourdough to dip into the broth.

If all you see on the menu are small plates of cheesy fried C.R.A.P., you're absolutely better off ordering an entrée and asking for double vegetables on the side.

POSITIVE PEER PRESSURE

Research shows that what the people around us eat has a powerful influence on what we choose. In fact, a recent study in the journal *Appetite* found that we tend to eat more if our friends do, even when we're not actually *with* them.

That influence poses a challenge, but also an awesome opportunity. Seek power in numbers, and take these steps to set a positive and healthful tone:

>> **Join the planning committee.** When you dine out, help pick the restaurant. That way, you can nominate a spot where you know there are superfoods.

>> **Buddy up.** Sit next to someone whose eating habits match yours—*not* the person who either judges others for their choices or who tends to order the diet disaster.

>> **Order first.** Don't be the one to say, "I'll have what she's having." Put in your superfood-

rich order first. You'll subtly encourage everyone to order smarter instead of calling up 5 supersized bacon burgers in a row.

>> **Be happy.** No one wants to hear you apologize for "only" ordering small plates. Make it a point to quickly mention one part of the meal you're excited about before ordering—say, the fennel in your salad, the seasoning on your tofu skewers, or the anti-inflammatory powers of the turmeric in your curry. Other people pick up on your cues. Plus, mustering a little excitement will make your food taste better, too!

SUPERSWAP YOUR SANDWICH

The average American eats about 200 sandwiches a year—that's 200 chances to take it up a notch from run-of-the-mill baloney on white bread. Here's how to SuperSwap your tried-and-true lunch.

1 **Salad-ify it.** Ditch the bread altogether and pile your hoagie filling onto a bed of greens.

2 **Go open-faced.** Pile toppings—heavy on the veggies—on just 1 slice of bread.

3 **Choose bread wisely.** Go sprouted whole-grain whenever possible (and don't be fooled by "wheat" or "multigrain" options—they're usually not truly whole grain). Other good options: rye or pumpernickel, which are rich in fiber and resistant starch, or sourdough with a fermented base. These options keep your blood sugar steadier.

4 **Think beyond iceberg.** Boost your sub with a heaping helping of superfood veggies—besides the traditional lettuce and tomato,

THE SUPERSWAP **GETS SOCIAL**

YOU ARE...	YOU NEED SOMETHING THAT...	SUPERSWAP SOLUTION
WITH YOUR GIRLFRIENDS	Goes well with gossip—and will leave your girls in awe	Enjoy Spinach Enchilada Casserole (page 193) and Hibiscus Sangria (page 219)
AT A FAMILY REUNION OR HOLIDAY GATHERING	Will please your superfood palate—without freaking out meat-and-potato-loving Uncle Joe	Carry over some Butternut Squash Lasagna (page 198)
AT A NEIGHBORHOOD BARBECUE	Stands up to Ann's famous super-creamy potato salad	Toss some Crunchy Cabbage Slaw (page 151)
GOING TO A BABY OR WEDDING SHOWER	Will look beautiful next to the boozy punch and sugary cupcakes	Bring some Vanilla "Sugar" Cookies (page 204)—use natural food coloring to dye them pink, blue, or your bride's fave shade
HAVING A DATE NIGHT	Pairs well with wine and romance	Serve up Olive Oil Pasta (page 115)
HAVING A PLAYDATE	Kids will love and moms will approve	Whip up Brown Rice Crispy Treats (page 206)
HOSTING BRUNCH	Satisfies sweet and savory brunchers without much fuss	Offer both Zucchini Bread French Toast (page 175) and Burrito Omelet Cups (page 173)
COOKING FOR THE OFFICE POTLUCK	Travels well and will stand out	Clock in with Cauliflower Mac and Cheese (page 150)
PLANNING A BOARD GAME NIGHT	Offers snacky fun	Play along with Spinach Dip (page 167) or French Onion Dip (page 205)
HEADING TO BOOK CLUB	Fills your hands and mouth between insightful observations	Tote Superfood Party Mix (page 125)
GOING TO A FOOTBALL PARTY	Feels hearty and manly	Cheer with Superfood Chili (page 192)

YOU DON'T HAVE TO spend a fortune on serving dishes—scope out clearance sales, discount stores, and even thrift shops. Or consider it an investment and splurge.

- **Cocktail glasses.** Use these for Super Soda (page 213), Mojito Water (page 215), and Sparkling Bitters (page 220). You can also use glasses to hold stand-up veggies like green beans and carrot or zucchini sticks.

- **Large wood or stone cutting board.** Use this for piles of olives, nuts, fruits, veggies (fresh, pickled, or marinated), and flavorful cheeses, plus a dollop of Chia Jam (page 137).

- **An assortment of sassy small plates.** Use these for unsweetened dried mango, broken pieces of a dark chocolate bar, and Superseed Crackers (page 207).

- **An assortment of classy, clear bowls.** Clear bowls are key so guests can actually see what they are eating. Never serve salad in ugly plastic containers—you'll just end up with boatloads of leftovers. Use small bowls for dips and party mixes like Spinach Dip (page 167), Superfood Party Mix (page 125), and Almond Joy Snack Mix (page 118).

- **Tiered dessert or cake stand.** Use this for petite desserts like Mini Yogurt Cheesecake (page 162), Brownie Bites (page 159), and Gingersnap Cookies (page 203).

add superfoods like cucumber, mushrooms, red bell pepper, zucchini, and watercress.

5 **Switch up your proteins.** Packaged, processed lunch meat? Textbook C.R.A.P. You can do a lot better. Try grilled tofu, tuna, or hummus instead. And remember, a grilled chicken breast is better than chicken lunch meat any day.

SUPERSWAP YOUR PARTY

It's a scenario I see again and again with my clients. Slim, healthy people who love superfoods flat-out freeze up when it's time to entertain. Suddenly they're in the junk-food aisle, loading up on bulk snacks they'd never eat themselves but have somehow been convinced are what their guests desire. It's time to SuperSwap more than your own life. Here's how to plan the perfect SuperSwap party:

≫ **Don't flaunt it.** Avoid branding your fare as health food. After all, you aren't sacrificing good taste! If people ask about the ingredients, it's okay to share your superfood excitement. But don't give them a chance to prejudge the food as bland and boring.

≫ **Go for finger foods.** Light hors d'oeuvres placed strategically offer more opportunities for mingling and fitting in superfoods than a formal sit-down dinner party. Provide plates and plenty of places to perch to discourage mindless grazing.

≫ **Think variety.** Sure, not everyone will love kale chips or lentil meatballs. But if you set out an impressive spread of superfood dishes, everyone will find something to groove on.

Kombucha Margarita (page 216)

>>> **Serve a signature cocktail.** Encourage fun and moderation. Offer something that can be made spiked or virgin, like the Kombucha Margarita (page 216).

>>> **Make it beautiful.** Everything tastes better when it's presented well—even the simplest foods get rave reviews when they're elegantly prepared and plated.

CHOOSE YOUR FIT MIX

People who completed at least 2 different types of workouts burned an extra 1,500 calories per week, says a recent University of Tennessee study. Shake it up with these tips:

>>> **Go back to a workout you loved as a kid.** Jump rope, play hopscotch, or jump on a trampoline (now called rebounding)—the bouncing motion boosts bone health and keeps lymph, the body's cleansing fluid, flowing.

>> **Try a fun, innovative piece of gear or a new class.** Working out with something like sand ropes, which are rubberlike tubes packed with heavy sand, can sizzle calories and build strength. Or try old-school dance aerobics classes, aerial yoga, or adventure parkour (obstacle course) classes.

>> **Download an app.** Look for one based on the amount of time you have—say, a 20-minute high-intensity interval routine if you're time-crunched, an hour-long yoga class if you're not. Or try targeting a different body part each time (better-butt boot camp, anyone?). While you can't really spot-tone one specific area, you're still likely to uncover some new strength or cardio moves.

TASTE TRANSITION

EVER WONDER WHY DESSERT seems like the natural next step after a big meal? We crave a signal of doneness, a move away from the flavors of the meal. But you don't need to consume C.R.A.P. to clear your palate. Instead, recycle a mini mint tin, fill it with fennel seeds, chew on 5 to 10 after a meal. They freshen your breath and have the added bonus of helping digestion. Or have some decaf or herbal coffee with a splash of coconut milk or a cup of herbal tea like mint or cinnamon.

EVERYDAY AMBIANCE

Why wait for a party to have a veggie tray? Make your superfoods stylish for the most important guest of honor: you! A touch of festivity makes every meal taste better—and makes you feel happier.

>> **Pretty plating.** Don't keep all those fun platters and bowls hidden until guests arrive.

>> **Candles.** Light them at the dinner table— even for a solo meal.

>> **Music.** Pump up the party tunes while you're cooking, just like you would when getting ready for a gathering. Fire up a sophisticated playlist for dining—my favorite are pop songs gone classical.

>> **Bright color and fun shapes.** Neon measuring cups, animal-shaped sponges, and tropical-print napkins make every step—from prep work to cleanup—more pleasant.

Belly Love Smoothie (page 96)

WEEK 4

MAINTAIN YOUR MOJO

SO WE'RE NEARING the finish line of this month-long journey. Let's talk about how to maintain your motivation for this last week—and beyond.

In this chapter, you'll find a list of simple, easy, and joyful tips and tricks. You can use them when you're already cruising. Motivation isn't something you're born with—you have to keep putting wood on the fire to keep the flame burning. And when you're stuck in a full-on funk, don't stress—you haven't unlearned everything you've been doing, you just need a little refresher.

FILL YOUR MOJO TANK

I hear things like this all the time from clients and friends:

"I wish I had more motivation to eat well."

"I was doing great but something happened to my motivation and now I'm stuck."

Motivation can seem like something magical with a mysterious on/off switch you don't know how to control. But staying motivated or kicking your mojo into high gear is simple, once you know the secret. And here it is: *You have to want the behavior to get the results. You can't just want the results.* Success means enjoying the process, not rushing to get to the finish line.

Most attempts at change start out great, but a couple of mojo killers often get in the way: feeling overwhelmed or feeling underwhelmed (aka not excited). Kick-starting motivation is as easy as asking yourself, **"How can I make this change less daunting and more fun?"**

To keep motivation steady and buzzing along, invest a little bit of time and energy regularly (say, every week or month) into filling up your "motivation tank." How do you do that?

SUPERFOOD SWAP TRUTH »

Add joy, fun, and excitement, and ultimately success will follow.

With simple, fun actions that shake up your routine. It doesn't matter if you start with food, fitness, or happiness—they're all intertwined. Motivation in one area splatters over into all the others and beyond.

Don't wait until you have reached rock bottom before you start making changes. Preemptively try new things that make you happy and challenge you in a good way.

MENU OF MOJO ENHANCERS

Try these simple, fun shakeups to add energy to your Superfood Swap lifestyle. How to choose? Read them all and see if one jumps out at you, either because it sounds particularly enjoyable or because it speaks to a problem you have had trouble solving. Or just put your finger down and pick one at random.

FOOD

» **Shake it up.** Identify your trigger routines—maybe you tend to overeat after dinner or hit the doughnut drive-through on your morning commute. Now do something different. For example, watch TV from a different chair (or even better, play a board game instead of turning on the tube). Exit the expressway at a different spot on your way to the office. After dinner, sit outside with a little sip of wine spritzer. When you shake up even just a small piece of your routine, it's easier to snap out of those bad habits that are on autopilot.

» **Seek out stealth C.R.A.P.** On page 39, you learned how to sweep your home and office for C.R.A.P. Sometimes it doesn't take much for unhealthy convenience foods to sneak back in. Repeat this process, replacing C.R.A.P. with healthy SuperSwaps. Use the SuperSwap Quickies on page 76 for inspiration.

» **Flip bad influences.** Have a friend or partner who eats poorly? Recognize it and do your best to neutralize the impact. Try to enjoy some of their food on top of a salad or Green Base. Don't push your healthier choices on them, but *do* eat healthful foods with enthusiasm. If you are excited about superfoods, it will rub off on them.

» **Snap a pic.** You might be eating more C.R.A.P. than you'd think or admit. Use an app to create a photo food log. Upload and track how your meals and snacks align with your results.

» **Go back to basics.** Return to the fundamentals of healthful eating: 3 meals and 2 snacks per day. A regular schedule keeps cravings at bay.

» **Banish "last chance" eating.** You think: "I'll get back on track on Monday. Just one last binge." The problem is that Monday never comes, and all those last-ditch calories add up. Instead, take the view that *now* matters. You don't have to be perfect, but *what one small thing* can you do right now to make a little progress?

SUPERSWAP CHALLENGES

❏ **Make these meals.** Or you can swap in any other breakfast/lunch/dinner from the book.
> **Breakfast:** No-Sugar Granola Parfait (page 138)
> **Lunch:** Collard Green Burrito (page 105); Lox Lunch Plate (page 102)
> **Dinner:** Lentil Meatballs and Pasta (page 195); Coconut Curry and Super Rice (page 112); Cheddar Grits with Beans and Greens (page 116)

❏ **Snack only when you're hungry**—0 to 2 times per day—preferably from the list on page 126, or from any of the treats sections if you're craving something special.

❏ **Congratulate yourself!** You deserve props for even giving a damn about your diet and your health. So many people mindlessly consume C.R.A.P. without a second thought. Just the fact that you know you can do better deserves recognition and respect.

❏ **Show off your success.** Now's the time to show off your "before" and "after" pics. Post them on social media, tag me @djblatner, use #SuperSwap, and watch the likes roll in!

❏ **Then try a new strategy.** This can either maintain your awesome mojo or rev you up a bit if you're feeling stuck. Every week or month, try a new simple strategy from this list or anything beyond that keeps your mojo tank filled.

≫ **Break the cycle.** Prone to binging, even on healthy foods? Chances are you feel restricted, either denying what you truly want to eat or eating what you want but judging yourself for doing it. The only way to fix the binging is to correct the restriction. Here's how: Ask yourself, "What do I really *want* to eat?" and then, "Can I SuperSwap any part of it?" Whatever you end up eating, own it, enjoy it, and then move on. Portion control and peace with food is easy with this method.

≫ **Play games with your cravings.** Try something I call urge surfing. Cravings are like waves that ebb and flow; they don't just keep getting worse if you don't give in. When you feel a craving on its high, ride it out until it goes away—distract yourself, and it will be gone within 15 minutes. The more you practice this, the stronger your craving willpower muscle will be.

≫ **Google your visions.** Open the search engine, type in the name of a superfood you like, and then hit "image." You'll be bombarded with delicious-looking, motivating photos of dishes made with that item. Make your own version of what you see.

≫ **Explore your temper tantrums.** Any time you overeat mindlessly or binge, recognize it for what it is. Instead of pounding our feet and crying like disappointed kids, adults often use food (and even drugs and alcohol) to throw a tantrum. Next time you overdo it, don't beat yourself up or feel guilty. Instead, ask yourself, "What's not going my way, and how can I do something about it?"

≫ **Delay, don't deprive.** If there's something you crave, don't tell yourself you can't have it. Instead, promise yourself you'll wait it out awhile, and if you truly want it later, it will be yours. So, say you have a late-night craving for leftover pizza—tell yourself that you can have it for breakfast with eggs or for lunch with greens. Check in with yourself at the appointed time, and if the craving hasn't subsided, eat it and own it.

FITNESS

≫ **Habit first, effort later.** Can't seem to get into an exercise groove? Blame overly aggressive expectations. Instead of starting with full 30- to 60-minute gym sessions, aim for 7 days of putting on your workout gear, going to the place you'd exercise, and moving for no more than 5 minutes. Nailing the logistics helps you form the habit— and that's the toughest part. After that, extending your exercise time is easy.

≫ **Make it "opposite" day.** Your body craves new and different types of challenges. Think of an exercise that seems the exact opposite of your go-to workout and give it a shot. Fast runner? Do a slow, restorative yoga class. Swim by yourself? Try a team sport that's nowhere near the water, like basketball. Even try things you did once before and hated. You'll broaden your physical capabilities—and your mental ones, too.

≫ **Be antsy.** You can torch 350 calories per day without working out at all. Just fidget, take the stairs instead of the elevator, or schedule walking meetings. Researchers call it NEAT—non-exercise activity thermogenesis—and say it can melt 10 to 30 pounds a year.

>> **Join the team.** Grab a pal and make your workout social. A little healthy competition encourages you to push harder—plus, a recent study in the *American Journal of Physiology* shows the camaraderie of group sweat sessions may stabilize hormone levels in women.

>> **Remove exercise excuses.** Pack your gym bag the night before. Sleep in your running clothes. Book an expensive class with a no-cancellation policy. Take whatever steps you need so that *not* working out involves more effort and grief than just doing it already.

>> **Studio hop.** Check to see if tools like ClassPass have hit your city yet—they allow you to sample a wide range of fitness options for one monthly fee. Or try new exercises by taking advantage of intro specials at yoga, Pilates, and other fitness studios. Because they're designed for newbies, the staff usually take extra steps to make you feel at home, and you can keep trying new things until you find something that you truly love (or keep it up if what you love is always trying the newest thing).

>> **Take a fit trip.** Don't think of a vacation as time to take a break from your fitness routine—instead, see it as an opportunity to break out of the mold and try a new way to move. Check out a big-city bike-sharing program, take a walking or running tour, kayak in a lake or lagoon, do laps in a pool, frolic in the ocean, or join the locals moving to the music on the dance floor.

>> **Start a streak.** Many activity trackers, like those from Fitbit and Shine, give you badges for days of continuously meeting your goals. Try one of those programs, or just give yourself a star on your calendar for every day you intentionally move, even if it's just for 10 minutes. See how long you can keep the trend going, and plan a reward for each milestone (a new playlist at 10 days, a new pair of workout pants at 30).

>> **Relive your greatest hits.** Recalling a positive exercise-related memory made study participants more likely to work out the following week, researchers at the University of New Hampshire found. Keep a log of your workouts and any particularly compelling moments—that time you pushed through fatigue to excel in spin class or the view when you summited the hill on a tough hike.

HAPPINESS

>> **Schedule you time.** Make sure your appointment calendar includes the most important person in your life—you! Block out 15 minutes or more every day for something that's 100% pure happiness and relaxation, whether that's meditating, listening to music, painting, gardening, or shopping. Just a couple of rules: The activity has to be something that feels a little lazy, and you cannot feel guilty about doing it.

>> **Toss your fat clothes.** Two meanings here: First, if weight loss is your goal, throw out the things that don't fit the minute they become too big. That eliminates any permission you might feel to slip back into

them. Second, toss anything that makes you feel frumpy, dumpy, or bored right now. Even if you can't immediately splurge on a new wardrobe, it's far better to have fewer clothes and feel good in them than to have more options that make you feel crappy.

>>> **Treat, don't eat, your emotions.** The extremes of emotion—tension and fatigue—can bring on cravings. Instead of turning to C.R.A.P. or comfort food to soothe them, try one of these tactics instead:

TENSE EMOTIONS
- Nervous—Sip hot tea.
- Stressed—Stand up and touch your toes.
- Anxious—Make a to-do list.
- Angry—Look at pictures.
- Frustrated—Call a friend.

TIRED EMOTIONS
- Exhausted—Take a nap.
- Bored—Listen to music.
- Unfocused—Exercise.
- Lonely—Change locations.

>>> **Use daily affirmations.** Keep your focus and vision alive daily with a steady diet of healthy, motivating thoughts. Select from the list below, or choose your own:

- I love the energy I feel when I exercise.
- I am in charge of what I put in my body.
- I am in charge of my schedule and make self-care a priority.
- I crave foods that give me energy and health.
- I take time and care to prepare meals for myself.

>>> **Set alarms.** Use your phone or computer calendar to schedule things like lunch, packing up leftovers, and even drinking water. That tiny *ding*, vibration, or pop-up screen will jolt you out of autopilot and remind you to care for yourself.

>>> **Come up with a healthy add-on.** Tack on a new healthy habit to something you already do. For instance, aim to make more green drinks with your new juicer. You automatically make coffee every morning, so make a green juice alongside your brewing routine. Next morning, repeat! Repetition helps the new habit stick. Think of your current habits as a wave to carry your new healthy behavior.

>>> **Chill out.** Creating a relaxed environment automatically cuts calorie consumption by 18%, according to a study in *Psychological Science*. Soften the lighting, turn on soothing tunes, and take a few deep breaths before picking up your fork.

>>> **Prioritize your ZZZs.** Research shows that lack of sleep stimulates your hunger hormones and makes fattening foods more appealing. In fact, people who don't get enough sleep consume about 130 extra calories a day—and are 30% more likely to be obese. Aim for 7 to 8 hours, and get there by maintaining a steady sleep schedule (even on the weekends). Keep your bedroom dark, quiet, and cool and turn your screens off 2 hours before bedtime (they emit blue light that suppresses the sleep hormone melatonin).

>> **Write it down.** Buy a cool-looking journal. Fill it with the things you see or hear healthy people doing that seem like something you'd like to try. Stuff like going on a yoga retreat, drinking hot lemon water in the morning, or doing 10 minutes of meditation. Gradually start checking things off your healthy bucket list.

>> **Reinvent yourself.** What would people see if they looked you up in the dictionary? Try on a new definition to motivate change. If you've always said you're a dessert person—well, now say you're not. Think you're a person who can't pull off wearing hot pink pants? Tell yourself you can. Do you hate running? Revise that: You love how it makes you feel. Choose how you define yourself very carefully, because at the end of the day, you are who you say you are.

>> **Fun it up.** During any mundane task, ask yourself this question: Is there any way to infuse more joy into the moment? Buy a funky-colored pen to write your shopping list, choose a fancy keychain to make errands more lighthearted, jazz up your phone case with rhinestones. Even little things that make you smile add up to big-picture happiness.

>> **Cut out comparisons.** The moment you stop comparing yourself to others, your happiness will increase. If you do find yourself feeling envious of someone, use that as a guide to plan your future goals and dreams. Because your friend took a dream vacation, got a great work assignment, or won an award doesn't mean you can't aim for the same things. Instead of letting jealousy create a rift between you and others, follow its compass to find your own bliss.

>> **Reflect on the real reason.** When special occasions arise, take time to remember what they're really about. Yes, food comforts us and helps us celebrate, but it's never the main focus. Even at Thanksgiving, the most food-centric holiday, the emphasis is on homecoming and family togetherness. Even if you're not one to say grace, pause before a meal to acknowledge and express feelings of gratitude, and you'll dine more mindfully.

>> **Get sexy—right now.** Do things to make you feel hot at any weight or point in time. Don't wait for a number on a scale or a slimmer pant size to feel attractive. Get a slick new hairstyle, a funky accessory, designer shoes . . . you get the idea. You deserve to feel happy and enjoy your body all the time, not just when you reach some arbitrary number.

>> **Redecorate.** Don't suffer with the things that bug you about your home, car, or office. Take the leap and paint that boring wall, invest in a support pad for your desk chair, or fix the dent in the bumper or the annoying squeaky garage door. You'll feel an instant lift—and all the energy you spent fussing about the issue can be used to make positive change instead.

>> **Believe in abundance.** The world is full of opportunities for success, joy, and love. It can take work to find them, but you can—and you don't have to settle for things that don't make you truly happy. Learn to say no or let go of the jobs, relationships, and activities that don't truly help you achieve your goals.

MEET S.L.I.P.—YOUR MOTIVATION SABOTAGE

Despite your best efforts, outside forces can suck the wind out of your sails. Keep a lookout for the 4 sabotaging forces of S.L.I.P.: **S**urroundings, **L**ack of results, **I**ndifference, and **P**ressure/stress.

THE S.L.I.P. LIST

>> **Surroundings.** Your environment triggers you to fail. If you think this is your problem, try breaking it up. Notice when you've paired food with a specific place or activity. For example, do you always eat lunch at the computer, snack while watching TV, or drink alcohol in front of a fire? Just like Pavlov's dogs salivating at the dinner bell, our bodies come to expect treats in situations where we habitually eat them, creating a craving. Acknowledge these bonds and then find a healthy way to replace them—say, by turning on a special playlist when it's time to get to work and walking away from your desk to eat lunch in the break room.

>> **Lack of results.** Despite your best efforts, you're not seeing changes in your body, health, or energy level. If this is your problem, try gut-checking your goals and efforts. Honestly assess your situation. If it's just that you're not making progress quickly, your expectations may be a little too lofty. However, if you're truly getting no results, make a list of the concrete actions you've taken to achieve your goals. You may find it's shorter than you think. Our minds sometimes trick us into believing that worrying about something is the same as *doing* something—but it's not.

>> **Indifference.** You feel bored with your healthy choices and can't muster the excitement to stick with your plan. If you think this is your problem, try surrounding yourself with inspiration. When you lack energy within, you can find it outside. Look around a health-food store to find new stuff, sign up for a 5K race, read wellness magazines. Immerse yourself in a world of positive, health-affirming people and places.

>> **Pressure/stress.** Healthy habits take time to establish—and time is one thing you don't have to spare. If you think this is your problem, try picking one. Don't obsess about everything you're not doing. Instead, choose one simple SuperSwap you can commit to. This may mean adding a glass of veggie juice to your breakfast, snacking on nuts instead of pretzels, or turning your lunch wrap into a bowl of greens. Create a physical way to check that item off as completed each day, whether it's on your calendar or a sticky note on the fridge. When that behavior feels like a habit, move on and pick another behavior to build on the success.

SHHH: LISTEN TO THE SYMPTOMS

If you lose your way, forces even bigger than S.L.I.P. may be at play. Falling offtrack can often serve as a symptom of a larger problem. You may be avoiding a bigger life question about your career, relationships, or place in the world. Instead of beating yourself up or feeling like a failure, view getting offtrack as a sign that something bigger is wrong.

When you get an itch in your throat or your eyes feel a little achy, you can tell a cold is coming on. These symptoms are our body's way of waving a little flag to get our attention, telling us something isn't right—often when we still have time to nip it in the bud. I feel the same about slipups. In fact, I had one as I started writing this book. In retrospect, I'm glad I did, because it changed the book for the better.

During a particular day of recipe testing, I was trying out a recipe for scones. The first batch didn't taste great, yet before I knew it, I had wolfed down four of them. It was at that point that I realized those four scones were a symptom of a much bigger problem. I was struggling to create overly complicated recipes that weren't true to my passions and expertise. I listened to my inner voice, changed gears, and had a blast writing from that point forward. The moral? Don't beat yourself up over four scones. Listen to them—they are probably telling you something very important.

I GIVE YOU PERMISSION:
GO FOR THE QUICK FIX

SO OFTEN, CLIENTS WHO fall into a funk come to me looking for a whole new plan—a complete reboot. I say, why start from scratch? Getting back on track doesn't have to be as dramatic or intimidating as many people make it out to be. After all, you're not at ground zero. You haven't magically unlearned all the stuff you've already picked up on your quest. You just need to refine and adjust your strategies to spark your momentum and get that mojo back. In fact, I'd argue that setbacks are an essential part of the process of creating the Superfood Swap lifestyle that works for you. The journey is never a straight line—and it's in the twists and turns and offshoots that you'll find the fabulous, healthy self that is completely, uniquely *you*.

FUNDAMENTALS
OF THE
SUPERFOOD
SWAP

SUPERFOOD GROUPS

WHOLE GRAINS

- Amaranth
- Barley, not pearled
- Bread*
- Brown rice
- Buckwheat
- Bulgur wheat
- Corn on the cob**
- Cornmeal/polenta*
- Couscous, brown rice
- Crackers, whole-grain and seed
- English muffin*
- Flatbread*
- Kamut
- Millet
- Oats
- Pasta, quinoa or brown rice
- Pita*
- Popcorn
- Potatoes, with skin**
- Quinoa
- Rye
- Sorghum
- Spelt
- Sweet potatoes, with skin**
- Teff
- Tortillas, corn*
- Triticale
- Wheat berries
- Wild rice

PROTEINS

- Beans:
    Black
    Chickpeas
    Kidney
    Pinto
    White/cannellini
- Lentils and peas
- Nuts and seeds, raw:
    Almonds
    Brazil nuts
    Cashews
    Hazelnuts
    Peanuts
    Pecans
    Pine nuts
    Pistachios
    Pumpkin/pepitas
    Sesame
    Sunflower
    Walnuts
- Edamame
- Nut and seed butters:
    Almond
    Peanut
    Sesame
    Sunflower
- Tempeh
- Tofu
- Cheese, natural
- Eggs
- Kefir, plain 2%
- Yogurt, plain 2%
- Beef
- Chicken/turkey
- Fish
- Pork
- Shellfish

VEGETABLES

- Artichokes
- Asparagus
- Beets
- Bok choy
- Broccoli
- Broccoli rabe
- Brussels sprouts
- Butternut squash
- Cabbage
- Carrots
- Cauliflower
- Celery
- Collard greens
- Cucumbers
- Daikon
- Dandelion greens
- Eggplant
- Fennel
- Green beans
- Green onions
- Hearts of palm
- Jicama
- Kale
- Kohlrabi
- Leeks
- Mushrooms
- Mustard greens
- Okra
- Onions
- Parsnips
- Pea pods
- Peppers, all colors
- Pumpkin
- Radishes
- Rhubarb
- Rutabaga
- Salad greens:
    Arugula
    Endive
    Romaine
    Spring mix
    Watercress
- Spaghetti squash
- Spinach
- Sunchokes
- Swiss chard
- Tomatoes
- Tomatillos
- Grape tomatoes
- Turnips
- Zucchini and yellow squash

FRUITS

- Apples
- Apricots
- Bananas
- Blackberries
- Blueberries
- Cantaloupe
- Cherries
- Clementines
- Cranberries
- Dates
- Figs
- Grapefruit
- Grapes
- Honeydew
- Kiwi
- Mangoes
- Nectarines
- Oranges
- Papayas
- Persimmons
- Peaches
- Pears
- Pineapple
- Plums
- Pomegranates
- Raspberries
- Strawberries
- Watermelon

MISCELLANEOUS

- Avocados
- Beverages:
    Coffee
    Sparkling water
    Tea, hot/iced
    Water
    Wine, red/white
- Butter from grass-fed cows
- Chia seeds
- Chocolate, dark
- Cocoa powder, unsweetened
- Coconut flakes, unsweetened
- Coconut milk, unsweetened
- Dried fruit, unsweetened
- Flaxseed, ground
- Hemp seeds
- Herbs and spices, fresh and dried
- Lemons/limes
- Miso paste
- Mustard
- Nutritional yeast
- Oils:
    Avocado
    Coconut
    Olive
    Sesame
- Olives
- Plant milk (with calcium and vitamin D)
- Seaweed:
    Dulse flakes
    Nori sheets
    Spirulina
- Sweeteners:
    Barley malt syrup
    Brown rice syrup
    Coconut sugar
    Date sugar
    Honey
    Maple syrup, pure
    Molasses
- Tamari, low sodium
- Vinegars

*Read labels: Choose "whole grains," or "sprouted" when possible. ** Starchy vegetable

EAT/AVOID

Eat more superfoods and less C.R.A.P., all while enjoying the flavors you crave.

EAT SUPERFOODS

✓ **Vegetables and fruits**

✓ **Beans and lentils**

✓ **Organic eggs**

✓ **Sustainable fish**

✓ **Yogurt and kefir, organic, 2%, plain**

✓ **Whole grains and potatoes**

✓ **Nuts and seeds**

✓ **Healthy fats**

✓ **Herbs and spices**

✓ **Eat, but limit, organic grass-fed beef, pasture-raised poultry and pork, and flavorful cheese**

✓ **Drink water, tea, and moderate coffee and alcohol**

AVOID C.R.A.P

You'll find **C.R.A.P.** mostly in overly processed packaged foods. **C.R.A.P.** is:

✖ **Chemicals you don't use in your own kitchen.**
Words like: azodicarbonamide, carrageenan, potassium bromate, soy isolate, brominated vegetable oil, and partially hydrogenated vegetable oil

✖ **Refined sugar and flour.**
Words like: refined flour, enriched wheat, high-fructose corn syrup, sugar, and anything ending in -ose

✖ **Artificial sweeteners, flavors, and colors.**
Words like: caramel coloring, saccharin, aspartame, acesulfame potassium, dyes, diacetyl, and just plain "artificial flavoring"

✖ **Preservatives.**
Words like: sodium nitrate/nitrite, BHA, TBHQ, BHT, heptyl paraben, and propyl gallate

SUPERSWAP
QUICKIES

Find your scene and take your pick.

START THE DAY RIGHT

DROP	☙ SUPERSWAP
TOAST with BUTTER	Toast with avocado
RAISIN BRAN	Oatmeal with raisins
LIGHT STRAWBERRY YOGURT	Plain yogurt with fresh strawberries
ENRICHED BAGEL	Sprouted whole-grain English muffin
STICK MARGARINE on your ENGLISH MUFFIN	Whipped butter or butter from grass-fed cows on your English muffin
FLAVORED COFFEE CREAMERS and SUGAR in your COFFEE	Cinnamon and coconut milk in your morning brew
PANCAKE SYRUP	Mashed berries with a touch of pure maple syrup

SURVIVE A SNACK ATTACK

DROP	✦ SUPERSWAP
CHOCOLATE CHIP COOKIE	Square of dark chocolate
ICE CREAM	Frozen banana slices
PROTEIN BAR	No-Bake Peanut Butter Cookies (page 121)
WHIPPED CREAM	Cashew Whip (page 159)
CHEESE-FLAVORED SNACK PUFFS	Cheezy Popcorn (page 164)
BEEF JERKY	Seaweed Snack Strips (page 165)
PRETZELS	Pistachios
GUMMY BEARS	Dried mango (no sugar added)
FRUIT SNACKS	Raisins
POPSICLES	Frozen grapes or Green Smoothie Ice Pops (page 160)

GET YOUR VEG ON

DROP	🌶 SUPERSWAP
TORTILLA WRAP	Collard Green Burrito (page 105)
FRIES	Parsnip Fries from Fish and Chips (page 197) or Carrot and Green Bean Fries (page 227)
NOODLES	Zoodles (page 111)
BAKED POTATO CHIPS	Spinach Chips (page 121)
LASAGNA NOODLES	Butternut Squash Lasagna (page 198)
CHEESE SAUCE	Sauce from Cauliflower Mac and Cheese (page 150)
FRUIT IN OATMEAL	Veggies in oatmeal from Carrot Cake Oats (page 135)
RICE	Coconut Curry and Super Rice (page 112) or Cauliflower Fried Rice Bowl (page 149)

CLASS UP THE JOINT

DROP	🌶 SUPERSWAP
PARTY MIX with M&M'S	Almond Joy Snack Mix (page 118)
PLASTIC GROCERY-STORE VEGGIE TRAY	Freshly cleaned veggies on a wooden cutting board
TAKEOUT straight from the CONTAINER	Takeout on a Green Base (see page 30)
BOXED RICE MIX	Brown rice with fresh parsley and lemon juice
CLUB SANDWICH with MAYO	Cashew Butter Club (page 143)
FROZEN VEGETABLES in the MICROWAVE	Frozen vegetables in a pan on the stovetop with olive oil and spices
SALTING FOOD before EATING	Light drizzle of vinegar (see page 236)

PUT A MEAL ON THE TABLE

DROP	➥ SUPERSWAP
FLOUR or CREAM to THICKEN SOUP	Pureed white beans to thicken soup
REFINED GRAINS	Soaked or sprouted whole grains
SEASONED GROUND BEEF	Seasoned lentils from Lentil Tacos (page 185)
VINAIGRETTE	Avocado or flavorful cheese plus vinegar
BREAD CRUMB COATING on FISH or CHICKEN	Chopped nut coating on fish or chicken
CROUTONS	Potato Croutons (page 225)
TURKEY SANDWICH	Avocado Tuna Sandwich (page 101)
CANNED BEANS	Slow cooker beans (see page 241)
BOXED VEGGIE BURGERS	Beet Burgers (page 153), Black Bean Burgers (page 147), or Kale Burgers (page 154)

FILL UP YOUR CUP

DROP	➥ SUPERSWAP
ENERGY DRINK	Super Latte (page 213), Matcha Jolt (page 212), or Green Bull Energy Drink (page 210)
JUICE as a SMOOTHIE BASE	Kefir as a smoothie base
DIET SODA	Super Soda (page 213)
CANNED GINGER ALE	Real Ginger Ale (page 214)
SUGARY COCKTAIL MIXERS	Kombucha
CHAI LATTE	Brewed chai tea

THE SUPERFOOD SWAP COOKBOOK

ABOUT THE RECIPES

READY, GET SET, SUPERSWAP!

Each recipe creates a complete, satisfying meal or perfectly portioned treat. For complete nutritional analysis for each meal, see pages 243 to 253.

EACH SUPERFOOD SWAP meal recipe contains about 400 calories in the ratios I recommend—heavy on the veg, with smaller amounts of protein, grain, fat, and fruit. Each Superfood Swap treat recipe contains 100 to 200 calories. Eating 3 meals and 2 treats each day adds up to 1,400 to 1,600 calories—the perfect amount for most women to fuel an active lifestyle and still lose weight. Guys need to double up on breakfast or lunch to bring their daily total closer to 1,800 or 2,000 calories.

Since each meal is 400 calories, feel free to mix it up—eat breakfast for dinner, dinner leftovers for lunch, or lunch for dinner—whatever is best for your lifestyle and preferences. The recipes make anywhere from 1 to 4 servings. If you are cooking for one, lucky you; extras make easy leftovers for the rest of the week. If you are cooking for a large family, no biggie; you can easily multiply any recipe to feed a crowd.

Calorie-conscious note: The treat recipes all make small batches, so you're not tempted to overdo it.

Keep in mind that you don't have to clean your plate, and you may not need the snacks every day. Our appetite isn't supposed to be the same day in and day out. Practice watching and listening to your body's cues to tell you when you're satisfied, not stuffed—take a pause or push back or put your fork down, and maybe the food stops tasting as good, or perhaps you feel a light pressure in your stomach. We were all born with internal cues for hunger and fullness, but we may have ignored them for so long that it will take some consistent practice reconnecting to and befriending them. Listening to your appetite is a beautiful thing.

SUPERFOOD
SWAP »
TRUTH

There is no bigger gesture of self-care and self-love than putting forth effort to prepare food and feed yourself well.

3 WAYS YOU CAN USE SUPERFOOD SWAP RECIPES:

1 **Try the recipes at your own pace.**
Start flipping around and sampling what sounds good to you. Go as fast or slow as you'd like. Make the dishes for yourself, serve them to your family, invite friends over to cook with you . . . whatever you do, just have fun!

2 **Design your own plan.**
Look through all the Superfood Swap recipes and pick 1 or 2 breakfasts, 1 or 2 lunches, 2 or 3 dinners, and a couple of snacks for the week. Repeat these same recipes for 7 days or more, basically until you feel like trying new stuff. Use the Meal-Planning Worksheet on page 230 to write down your choices and organize your shopping list.

This repetition creates what I call *delicious monotony*, getting you into a simple, satisfying groove. Fewer choices mean less planning, shopping, prepping, and waste. Plus, **repeating meals serves as a powerful strategy to keep you on track.** Researchers from the University of British Columbia found that having too many food choices leads to so-called decision fatigue. When

there are too many choices, your brain has to work overtime to choose the best option. Eventually, it leaves you with no resolve to make wise decisions.

3 **Follow a plan that I created.**
On pages 128 and 129, there are 2 weeks of meal plans that I created using the Express Recipes. I did the planning for you, so you can shop, cook, and enjoy.

RECIPE ICONS

The recipes in this book are a mix of vegetarian, vegan, and gluten-free friendly. Here are the codes:

(V) = vegetarian (includes dairy and/or eggs)

(V+) = naturally vegan*

(GF) = naturally gluten-free*

*Most of the Superfood Swap recipes can be easily made vegan or gluten-free. Check at the end of a recipe for "V+ Swap" or "GF Swap" suggestions on how to convert the recipe.

CHOP, CHOP!

FOLLOWING A PLAN LIKE this means eating a lot of veggies. These recipes have you covered when it comes to flavorful combinations and delicious seasonings—but there's another secret to enjoying vegetables, and that's prepping them properly. Cutting them well matters, and having the right tools makes this part of prep a snap. Here are some gadgets I use:

- **Cutting board.** I like eco-friendly wood boards like Epicurean brand. You can even wash them in the dishwasher—just make sure you buy a size that can fit without obstructing the spray arm (I like the 14.5-by-11.25-inch ones). To get the most from your board, put a wet cloth or paper towel underneath it during use to prevent wobbling. **My favorite tip:** Use only one side to cut and keep the other side free of knife marks and scratches so you can use it when you are entertaining as a stunning serving board and veggie platter.

- **5- to 7-inch Santoku-style knife.** In Japanese, *santoku* means "three virtues"—in this case, slicing, dicing, and mincing, the main techniques you need in the kitchen. The dimples on the edge of the blade allow food to slide off neatly as you slice. Plus, the medium size fits comfortably in your hand and handles tasks for which a paring knife's too small but a big chef's knife is overkill.

- **Food processor/blender** for making things like hummus, dressing, oat flour, and cookies. You'll see a food processor used in many Superfood Swap recipes because solid foods don't work as well in a tall, narrow blender cup. As for blenders, the smoothies in this book don't require a high-speed one, but I personally love mine. If you're in the market, consider a "kitchen system" that combines a high-power blender and a food processor attachment—a good investment, since it's two gadgets in one.

- **Spiralizer.** Turn veggies into long, beautiful strands of spaghetti noodles. You could use a julienne peeler instead, but spiralized noodles are more noodle-like.

- **Mandoline** to make perfect veggie chips, paper-thin raw beet slices for salad, or lasagna noodles from eggplant or squash. You can buy a decent Japanese-style slicer for $25.

GET THIS, NOT THAT: SKILLET EDITION

- **Get this: "green" cookware** with nonstick coatings made from porcelain enamel or ceramic. Several companies offer stainless-steel cookware with these better-for-you nonstick coatings. Or buy a well-seasoned cast-iron skillet. "Seasoning" means oil has baked into the iron, giving the pan a natural nonstick coating. I love cast iron; it holds heat well, so you rarely need to turn the burner up past medium.

- **Not that: traditional nonstick compounds** called PFOA (perfluorooctanoic acid) and PTFE (polytetrafluoroethylene). Not only do they harm the environment, but when heated to high temperatures, compounds can flake off these pans, smoke, and even form potentially cancer-causing chemicals.

SuperSwap your noodles for Pesto Zoodles (page III) with the spiralizer.

EXPRESS
RECIPES

(V+)

AVOCADO TOAST

A plain piece of toast grabbed when you're running out the door isn't a filling breakfast, but mashing an avocado on top gives you healthy fats and fiber, which together have major staying power. **MAKES 1 SERVING**

½ avocado, halved
2 slices sprouted whole-grain bread, toasted
½ tomato, sliced (4 slices)
2 tablespoons unsalted sunflower seeds (raw, if you can find them)
Crushed red pepper flakes
Sea salt

Mash half the avocado onto each piece of toast. Top each slice with 2 tomato slices, 1 tablespoon sunflower seeds, and crushed red pepper and salt to taste.

NUTRITION (1 SERVING): 390 calories, 21g total fat, 42g carbs, 13g fiber, 14g protein

OH YEAH, ONE MORE THING . . .

Store your avocado: The best way to prevent leftover avocado from going brown is to leave the pit in the remaining half and rub a little lime or lemon juice on the cut flesh. Wrap it tightly with plastic wrap, pressing out all the air. Use leftover avocado to make another avocado toast for breakfast tomorrow or as a snack with crackers like the Superseed Crackers on page 207.

Get eggy with it: Instead of the sunflower seeds, top one of the pieces of avocado toast with a cooked egg. Way better for you than a typical breakfast sandwich since you're getting a dose of superfoods—avocado and tomato.

(V+)

BETTERTELLA BREAKFAST

The popular jar of commercially sold chocolate hazelnut spread has sugar as the first ingredient, followed by palm oil, hazelnuts, cocoa, skim milk, reduced minerals, whey, lecithin, and artificial vanillin. We can do better. . . .

The almond butter with cocoa is not sweet, so topping it with the natural sweetness of fruit is key. To make the spread a little sweeter on its own, swap the water for pure maple syrup. **MAKES 1 SERVING**

2 tablespoons natural almond butter
1 teaspoon unsweetened cocoa powder (avoid Dutched versions)
1 teaspoon warm water
1 slice sprouted whole-grain bread, toasted
1 pear, sliced

In a small bowl, use a fork to mash the almond butter with the cocoa powder and water. Spread the mixture on the toast and top with the pear slices.

NUTRITION (1 SERVING): 380 calories, 19g total fat, 49g carbs, 12g fiber, 12g protein

OH YEAH, ONE MORE THING . . .

Time saver: Instead of mashing the almond butter with cocoa powder, spread the almond butter on toast and sprinkle it with the cocoa powder.

Get your learn on: Read more about cocoa powder and cacao powder on page 237.

CEREAL PUFF BOWL

Cold cereal usually isn't very filling, and many brands have C.R.A.P. ingredients. Plus, keeping an open box around the house can be an invitation to binge. Here, the SuperSwap is a bowl of protein- and probiotic-rich yogurt with berries and a topper of simple whole-grain puffs. **MAKES I SERVING**

I cup plain 2% Greek yogurt
I cup berries, such as sliced strawberries, raspberries, or blackberries
I cup puffed whole-grain cereal
2 tablespoons chopped almonds
Ground cinnamon or freshly grated nutmeg

In a bowl, layer the yogurt, berries, and almonds. Top with the puffed cereal to prevent it from getting soggy. Sprinkle with a little cinnamon or nutmeg for added flavor.

NUTRITION (I SERVING): 390 calories, IIg total fat, 5Ig carbs, IOg fiber, 25g protein

OH YEAH, ONE MORE THING . . .

GF Swap: If you follow a gluten-free diet, use gluten-free puffed cereal.

Puffed cereal: Read the ingredient list and choose a brand with only I simple ingredient, such as brown rice, quinoa, corn, or millet. Puffs usually have only 60 calories per cup (they are mostly air) and are a fun way to eat whole grains.

PEANUT BUTTER OATMEAL

I'm glad you can buy ready-to-eat cups of oatmeal at so many coffee shops, but making your own is quick and offers an ideal SuperSwap ratio: less oatmeal and more protein-rich nut butter and fresh fruit. **MAKES I SERVING**

¼ cup rolled oats
½ cup water
Pinch of sea salt
2 tablespoons natural peanut butter
I green apple, peeled, cored, and chopped (about I cup)
½ teaspoon ground cinnamon

I MAKE THE OATMEAL: In a medium microwave-safe bowl, stir together the oats, water, and salt. Microwave for 1 to 2 minutes, stopping and stirring once midway through.

2 STIR IN TOPPINGS: Stir in the peanut butter and top with the chopped apple and cinnamon. Yes, it will look more like an apple bowl than an oatmeal bowl. Nice.

NUTRITION (I SERVING): 380 calories, 18g total fat, 47g carbs, 9g fiber, IIg protein

OH YEAH, ONE MORE THING . . .

GF Swap: If you follow a gluten-free diet, use gluten-free oats.

SUPERFOOD SCRAMBLE BOWL

Skip the typical breakfast sandwich and SuperSwap to a breakfast bowl instead. Bowls are the fastest way to get a mega dose of veggies in the morning. **MAKES 1 SERVING**

2 organic eggs, beaten
1 teaspoon extra-virgin olive oil
2 cups baby spinach leaves or arugula
½ cup cooked quinoa
⅓ avocado, chopped
1 green onion, chopped
Juice of ½ lemon
Sea salt and freshly ground black pepper

1 **MAKE THE EGGS:** In a small pan, scramble the eggs in the olive oil over medium heat.

2 **ASSEMBLE THE BOWL:** Put the spinach in a medium bowl and top with the warm egg and the quinoa. The egg and quinoa will wilt the spinach. Top with the avocado, green onion, and lemon juice. Season with salt and pepper.

NUTRITION (1 SERVING): 410 calories, 23g total fat, 31g carbs, 9g fiber, 21g protein

OH YEAH, ONE MORE THING . . .

V+ Swap: Use tofu instead of the eggs. Here's how: Press the liquid out of a block of organic firm or extra-firm tofu, mash the tofu with a fork until it looks like scrambled eggs, and mix in a sprinkle of turmeric for an eggy hue. You can keep this in an airtight container in the freezer for up to 3 months. For every egg, use a quarter of the tofu mixture.

Time saver: Use frozen precooked quinoa, found in the freezer aisle of the grocery store. Or make a big batch of quinoa and freeze it in individual portions.

Super sipping: Use the other half of the lemon for a mug of hot lemon water.

No avocado, no problem: Swap the avocado for 2 tablespoons pine nuts or chopped walnuts.

GREEN OMELET

A typical omelet has more egg than greens. This recipe SuperSwaps that ratio to give you 4 times more greens than eggs. I wish all omelets looked like this! **MAKES I SERVING**

1½ teaspoons extra-virgin olive oil
½ teaspoon crushed red pepper flakes
2 kale leaves or your fave leafy greens, stemmed and thinly sliced (about 2 cups)
I garlic clove, minced (about ½ teaspoon)
2 organic eggs, beaten
Sea salt
⅓ avocado, diced
2 or 3 thin slices of red onion, or more to taste
½ grapefruit

I COOK THE KALE: In a 10-inch skillet, heat the oil and crushed red pepper over medium-low heat for 1 minute. Add the kale and cook for 3 minutes. Stir in the garlic and cook, stirring to prevent it from burning, for 2 minutes more.

2 POUR IN THE EGGS: Using a spatula, pat the kale flat enough to cover the bottom of the pan. Pour the eggs evenly over the kale. Cook, without stirring, until the egg is set, about 3 minutes. If the top is still wet, put the skillet under the broiler or flip the kale "pancake" over to set the top. Season with sea salt.

3 PLATE: Slide the omelet onto a plate. Put avocado and onion on top. Enjoy the grapefruit on the side.

NUTRITION (I SERVING): 380 calories, 27g total fat, 23g carbs, 7g fiber, 16g protein

OH YEAH, ONE MORE THING . . .

V+ Swap: Use tofu instead of the eggs. Here's how: Press the liquid out of a block of organic firm or extra-firm tofu, mash the tofu with a fork until it looks like scrambled eggs, and mix in a sprinkle of turmeric for an eggy hue. You can keep this in an airtight container in the freezer for up to 3 months. For every egg, use a quarter of the tofu mixture.

Protein plate: Another fast way to have a satisfying egg breakfast is a protein plate (375 calories): I hard-boiled organic egg plus ¼ cup raw walnuts plus I cup grapes. If you want a vegan version, swap the egg for 10 raw almonds. Mix everything in a zip-top bag, and enjoy "fresh grape trail mix."

Grapefruit slices: This is my favorite way to eat a grapefruit. Cut it in half through the end "spots" of the grapefruit. Set the halves cut sides down on a cutting board and make thick slices.

BELLY LOVE SMOOTHIE

Smoothies have gotten out of control—typical versions include too many fruits and other ingredients that make them high in calories and horrible for blood sugar. This SuperSwap version has good bacteria to aid digestion and follows the perfect smoothie ratio: protein base + 1 cup fruit + 1 to 2 cups vegetables + boost + flavor. **MAKES ONE 16-OUNCE SMOOTHIE**

8 ounces plain low-fat kefir
1 banana
2 cups baby spinach leaves
3 tablespoons chia seeds
½ teaspoon ground cinnamon
¼ cup ice water
¼ cup ice

In a blender, puree the kefir, banana, spinach, chia, and cinnamon until smooth. Add the ice water and ice and pulse to mix.

NUTRITION (1 SERVING): 390 calories, 12g total fat, 57g carbs, 17g fiber, 20g protein

OH YEAH, ONE MORE THING . . .

V+ Swap: Swap dairy kefir for unsweetened plant milk and add 1½ tablespoons almond butter and the contents of 1 probiotic capsule (empty the capsule right into blender).

Kefir: Kefir is a rock star in the dairy family. It has more strains of probiotics than yogurt, so there's a wider variety of good bacteria to help your digestive tract. Any time my stomach feels off or I have a client struggling with digestive issues, I prescribe kefir recipes to get back on track.

Smoothie bowls and pops: Hey, you don't only have to drink this smoothie! Pour half of it into a bowl and sprinkle ¼ cup granola on top, or freeze it into ice pops.

Kefir Shot and Berry Chaser: While we are on the topic of kefir, this is perfect for when you wake up, after a meal, or before a workout. Chug 4 ounces of plain 2% kefir and follow it with a handful of your favorite berries (about 70 calories total). The healthy carbs and protein offer steady energy.

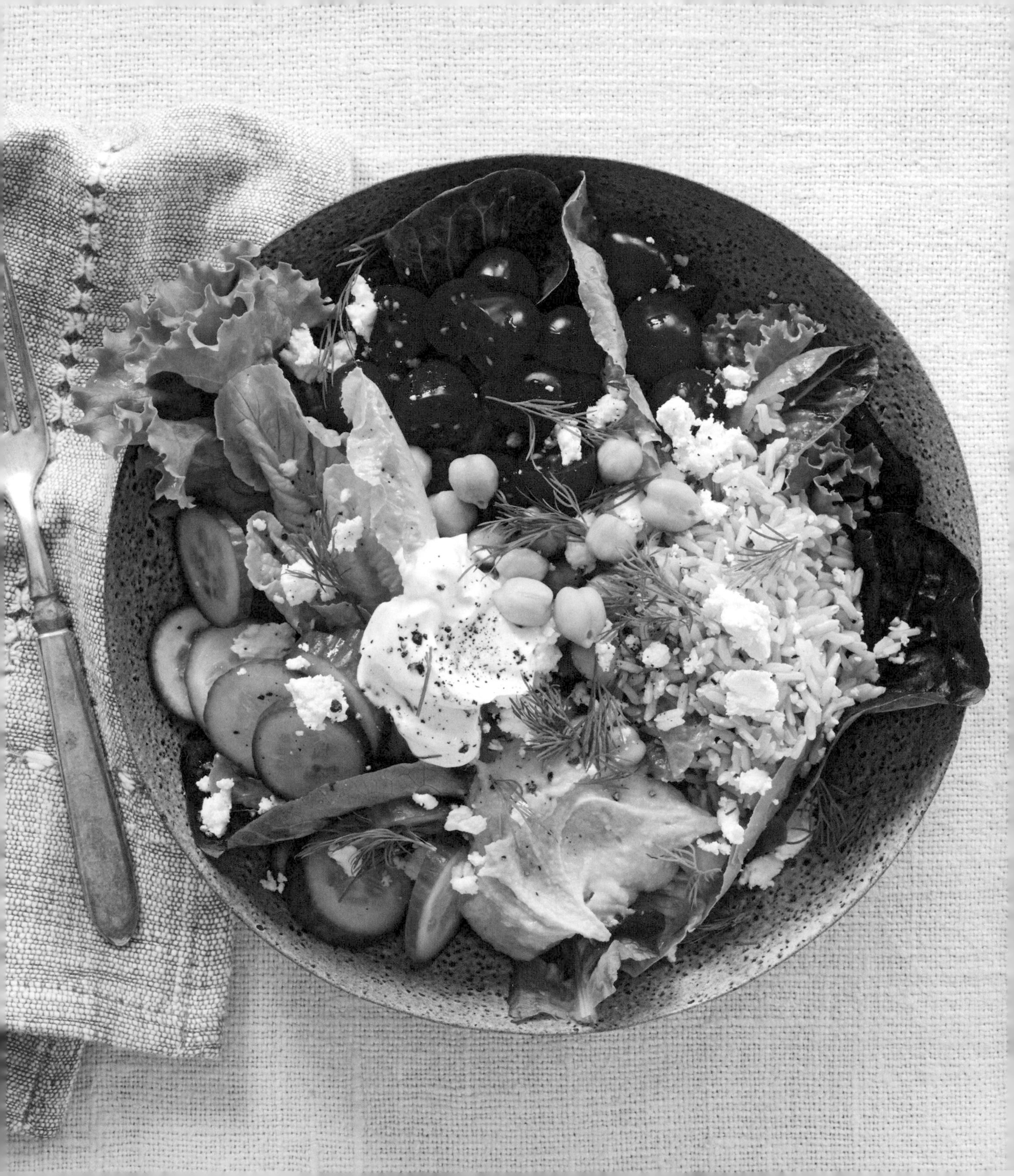

HUMMUS BOWL

This is one of my most popular recipes since it's incredibly convenient for a grab-and-go lunch. It's more meal assembly than cooking, and faster than waiting in line to order your lunch.

MAKES I SERVING

2 cups mixed greens
½ cup cooked brown rice, warmed
½ cucumber, sliced, or quartered lengthwise and chopped (about ½ cup)
½ cup grape tomatoes, halved
¼ cup canned chickpeas, drained and rinsed
¼ cup hummus
2 tablespoons crumbled feta cheese
2 tablespoons plain 2% Greek yogurt
⅛ teaspoon dried dill or ½ teaspoon fresh, plus more for garnish

Put the greens in a medium bowl and top with the rice, cucumber, tomatoes, chickpeas, hummus, feta, and yogurt. Sprinkle with the dill.

NUTRITION (I SERVING): 390 calories, I5g total fat, 52g carbs, 7g fiber, I7g protein

OH YEAH, ONE MORE THING . . .

V+ Swap: Use I tablespoon pine nuts instead of the feta cheese and yogurt.

Time saver: Use frozen precooked brown rice, found in the freezer aisle of the grocery store. Or make a big batch of brown rice yourself and freeze it in individual portions.

Extras: Artichoke hearts and red onion also taste great in this bowl.

DIY: Make your own delish Olive Oil Hummus using the recipe on page 224.

MEXICAN BURRITO BOWL

Typical burrito bowls don't have enough vegetables. This better bowl has double the ratio of veggies to beans and quinoa. Brown rice is good for you in burrito bowls, but quinoa is even better—it has about twice the protein and 1½ times more fiber than brown rice.

MAKES I SERVING

2 cups chopped romaine lettuce
I cup chopped bell pepper
½ cup canned black beans, drained, rinsed, and warmed
½ cup cooked quinoa, warmed
½ avocado, chopped
¼ cup pico de gallo or other fresh salsa

Put the lettuce in a medium bowl and top with the bell pepper, beans, quinoa, avocado, and pico de gallo.

NUTRITION (I SERVING): 420 calories, I3g total fat, 66g carbs, 20g fiber, I5g protein

OH YEAH, ONE MORE THING . . .

Cheese lovers: Swap the avocado for 3 tablespoons shredded cheddar cheese.

Better beans: Beans soaked and cooked from scratch are easier to digest and have more absorbable protein and minerals. Learn how to cook your own beans on page 24I.

Time saver: Use frozen precooked quinoa, found in the freezer aisle of the grocery store. Or make a big batch of quinoa yourself and freeze it in individual portions.

More, please: Check out the Sushi Bowl on page I4I.

(V+)

SUNFLOWER CAESAR

Classic Caesar dressing is mainly oil, with flavor coming from egg yolk, anchovies, and cheese. This SuperSwap has no oil and gets its fattiness and savory quality from whole sunflower seeds. Seems like a lot of dressing? Good, that's how I like it, and because it's a SuperSwap dressing, the big portion is allowed! **MAKES 1 SERVING (WITH EXTRA DRESSING)**

3 cups chopped romaine lettuce
1 cup grape tomatoes, halved
2 or 3 thin slices red onion, or more to taste
½ cup canned chickpeas, drained and rinsed
2 slices sprouted whole-grain bread, toasted and cut into crouton-size cubes
¼ cup Sunflower Caesar Dressing (recipe follows)

Toss the lettuce, tomatoes, onion, chickpeas, toast cubes, and dressing in a bowl.

NUTRITION (1 SERVING): 420 calories, 9g total fat, 65g carbs, 16g fiber, 21g protein

SUNFLOWER CAESAR DRESSING

MAKES 1 CUP

½ cup water
¼ cup sunflower seed butter (no sugar added)
¼ cup fresh lemon juice (from 1 to 2 lemons)
1 tablespoon Dijon mustard
1 garlic clove, minced (about ½ teaspoon)
Sea salt

In a lidded jar, combine the water, sunflower seed butter, lemon juice, mustard, garlic, and salt to taste and shake until smooth. Keep extra dressing in the fridge for up to 1 week.

NUTRITION (1 TABLESPOON): 25 calories, 1.5g total fat, 2g carbs, 1g fiber, 1g protein

OH YEAH, ONE MORE THING . . .

Hot Chickpeas: Adding something hot to a salad makes it seem even more like a meal. In a 10-inch skillet, heat 1 teaspoon oil over medium heat. Add the chickpeas and cook for 5 minutes, lightly smashing them with a fork. You can also add dried herbs and spices like oregano, ground cumin, crushed red pepper flakes, chili powder, or paprika.

Flavorize: Use other types of nut and seed butters like cashew, tahini, almond, or peanut to make this dressing. And if you don't have lemons, you can use red wine vinegar.

AVOCADO TUNA SANDWICH

Mashed avocado is the perfect superfood stand-in for mayo. Avocado has healthier fats than mayo and is packed with vitamins, minerals, and fiber. **MAKES I SERVING**

One 5-ounce can water-packed tuna, drained
¼ cup finely chopped celery
¼ cup finely chopped carrot
¼ cup finely chopped red onion
I tablespoon Dijon or grainy mustard
½ avocado, mashed
Juice of ½ lemon
½ teaspoon freshly ground black pepper
I small sprouted whole-grain roll (about I½ ounces)
2 romaine lettuce leaves

I MIX: In a medium bowl, mix together the tuna, celery, carrot, onion, mustard, avocado, lemon juice, and pepper.

2 SCOOP OUT THE BREAD AND ASSEMBLE: Scoop out most of the inside of the roll, leaving 2 little shells. Fill the shells with tuna salad. I suggest eating them open-faced with a piece of lettuce as the topper so they're easy to pick up.

NUTRITION (I SERVING): 390 calories, 14g total fat, 37g carbs, 10g fiber, 33g protein

OH YEAH, ONE MORE THING . . .

V+ Swap: Swap in ¾ cup lightly mashed cooked chickpeas for the tuna.

Tuna: Choose "light" tuna (skipjack, yellowfin, or tongol), which has lower levels of mercury than albacore or white tuna. Also look for brands labeled "sustainably caught."

Celery: I use a lot of celery in this recipe to add volume and because celery is a superfood. It's rich in vitamin K for healthy blood and bones. Plus, eating celery has been associated with lower blood pressure, thanks to compounds that relax the smooth muscles lining blood vessels.

Bread options: Instead of a roll, you can use I½ ounces sprouted whole-grain bread, baguette, hamburger bun, or hot dog bun. Whatever you choose, it should have about I00 calories.

ASIAN PEANUT BOWL

I love peanut sauce. Here it's a simple 3-ingredient recipe without the sugar you'll find in most versions—just natural peanut butter, lime juice, and soy sauce (with a little water to thin it out). You can use the sauce as a salad dressing or stir-fry sauce, too. **MAKES 1 SERVING**

2 cups shredded coleslaw mix (cabbage, carrots)
½ cup frozen edamame, thawed
½ cup cooked brown rice, warmed
1 green onion, chopped

PEANUT SAUCE
1½ tablespoons natural peanut butter
1 tablespoon water
Juice of ½ lime (about 1 tablespoon)
¼ teaspoon organic reduced-sodium gluten-free
    soy sauce

1 MIX: In a medium bowl, mix together the coleslaw mix, edamame, rice, and green onion.

2 MAKE THE PEANUT SAUCE: In a small bowl, whisk together the peanut butter, water, lime juice, and soy sauce. Drizzle the sauce over the coleslaw.

NUTRITION (1 SERVING): 410 calories, 16g total fat, 48g carbs, 11g fiber, 18g protein

OH YEAH, ONE MORE THING . . .

Time saver: Use frozen precooked brown rice, found in the freezer aisle of the grocery store. Or make a big batch of brown rice yourself and freeze it in individual portions.

Flavorize: Add cayenne, grated ginger, or chopped garlic to the basic peanut sauce recipe. You can also swap in coconut milk for the water to make it extra creamy.

LOX LUNCH PLATE

Here's the SuperSwap for your bagel with cream cheese and lox. Swap the processed and carb-y bagel for simple rye crackers, and kick the cream cheese to the curb. Use this simple avocado dill spread instead. **MAKES 1 SERVING**

AVOCADO DILL SPREAD
½ avocado
1 tablespoon fresh lemon juice
½ teaspoon dried dill

4 rye crisp crackers
½ cucumber, sliced (about 1 cup)
1 plum tomato, sliced
2 ounces wild lox or smoked salmon
2 or 3 thin red onion slices, or more to taste

1 MAKE THE SPREAD: In a small bowl, mash the avocado with the lemon juice and dill.

2 ASSEMBLE: Spread the avocado mixture on the rye crackers and top with the cucumber, tomato slices, lox, and onion. You won't be able to fit all the veggies on the crackers, so serve the extras on the side.

NUTRITION (1 SERVING): 400 calories, 18g total fat, 48g carbs, 15g fiber, 17g protein

OH YEAH, ONE MORE THING . . .

Rye crackers: Look for rye crackers with simple ingredients: whole-grain rye and salt. Rye contains a compound called resistant starch, which helps us feel full and supports gut health and steady blood sugar levels.

COLLARD GREEN BURRITO

Collard green leaves are nearly calorie-free, but even more important, they are packed with nutrition: antioxidant vitamins A, C, and E; blood builders iron and vitamin K; and bone builders calcium and magnesium. Make sure the beans and rice are warm when you make these so they slightly soften the wrap. **MAKES 1 SERVING (2 BURRITOS)**

2 collard green leaves
½ cup canned black beans, drained, rinsed, and warmed
½ cup cooked brown rice, warmed
½ avocado, sliced
4 tablespoons pico de gallo salsa

1 MAKE THE WRAPS: Cut the thick stems from the collard leaves with scissors or a knife so the leaves look like round tortillas. With a fork, mash the center veins to make them more pliable. (Mashing the center vein is the big secret to making collards into awesome wraps.)

2 ASSEMBLE: Fill each collard with ¼ cup of the beans, ¼ cup of the rice, half the avocado, and 2 tablespoons of the pico de gallo. Roll them to look like burritos.

NUTRITION (1 SERVING): 420 calories, 16g total fat, 63g carbs, 20g fiber, 13g protein

OH YEAH, ONE MORE THING . . .

Collard green wraps: You can prep a bunch of collard wraps and store them in a zip-top plastic bag in the fridge for up to 1 week for easy grab-and-go wraps.

Better beans: Beans soaked and cooked from scratch are easier to digest and have more absorbable protein and minerals. Learn how to cook your own beans on page 241.

Time saver: Use frozen precooked brown rice, found in the freezer aisle of the grocery store. Or make a big batch of brown rice yourself and freeze it in individual portions.

QUICK KALE PIZZA

Typical pizza is not a health food since it usually has a thick crust made from refined white flour, too much cheese, and not enough veggie toppings. This version uses a whole-grain tortilla for a thin crust, a dusting of cheese, and a heavy handful of flavorful kale. **MAKES I SERVING**

2 teaspoons extra-virgin olive oil
2 kale leaves, stemmed and chopped (about 2 cups)
I garlic clove, minced (about ½ teaspoon)
¼ teaspoon crushed red pepper flakes
One IO-inch sprouted whole-grain tortilla
¼ cup C.R.A.P.-free marinara sauce (or use the
    Supersauce Marinara on page 226)
¼ cup shredded Parmesan cheese

I COOK THE KALE: In a 10-inch skillet, heat the oil over medium heat. Add the kale, garlic, and crushed red pepper. Cook, stirring so the garlic doesn't burn, for about 4 minutes, until the kale is wilted. Transfer the cooked kale to a plate and set aside.

2 GET THE TORTILLA CRISP: Wipe out the skillet to remove the oil and set it over medium heat. Add the tortilla and heat for about 3 minutes, or until the bottom is crisp. Flip it over so the crisp side is facing up.

3 ADD THE TOPPINGS: Top the crisp side of the tortilla with the marinara sauce, kale, and cheese. Spread the cheese all the way to the edge of the skillet since the cheese around the edges gets nice and crisp. Cook for about 3 minutes more, until the cheese starts to melt and the bottom is crisp.

NUTRITION (I SERVING): 380 calories, 2Ig total fat, 34g carbs, 8g fiber, I6g protein

OH YEAH, ONE MORE THING...

V+ Swap: Swap the cheese for 2 tablespoons finely chopped walnuts or pine nuts.

Garden salad: I love hot pizza with a basic chopped salad made with chopped romaine lettuce, grape tomato halves, sliced red onion, red wine vinegar, sea salt, and pepper.

C.R.A.P.-free marinara sauce: Look for marinara with a simple ingredient list and no *added* sugar (it will have some natural sugar from the tomatoes).

GUAC AND GREENS TACOS

My husband and I make veggie tacos as our number-one go-to meal (#TacoObsessed). We make a million variations, but the main gist is corn tortillas, beans, and some kind of veggies. We never skip the avocado since it adds fatty decadence without having to rely on cheese or sour cream. **MAKES 2 SERVINGS (3 TACOS EACH)**

EASY GUAC

I avocado, chopped (I heaping cup)
Juice of ½ lime (about I tablespoon)
⅛ teaspoon sea salt

TACOS

I teaspoon extra-virgin olive oil
2 garlic cloves, minced (about I teaspoon)
I cup canned black beans, drained and rinsed
Hot sauce (optional)
6 organic sprouted corn tortillas
3 cups baby spinach leaves, cut into strips
½ cup chopped fresh cilantro

I PREP THE GUAC: In a small bowl, lightly mash together the avocado, lime juice, and salt.

2 MAKE THE TACOS: In a 10-inch skillet, heat the oil over medium-low heat. Add the garlic, beans, and hot sauce to taste (if using) and cook for about 4 minutes, slightly mashing the beans with a fork, until warm. While that's cooking, warm the tortillas directly on a stove burner over low heat. Use tongs to flip the tortillas from one side to the other. They get toasty and brown when you warm them this way, but they can easily burn—so watch them!

3 ASSEMBLE THE TACOS: Fill the warm tortillas with the smashed beans, spinach, and cilantro. Top with the guacamole.

NUTRITION (I SERVING): 430 calories, 16g total fat, 65g carbs, 19g fiber, 13g protein

OH YEAH, ONE MORE THING . . .

Better beans: Beans soaked and cooked from scratch are easier to digest and have more absorbable protein and minerals. Learn how to cook your own beans on page 241.

Leftovers: If you don't eat all the tacos, store the guacamole in the fridge in an airtight container for tomorrow. Before I close the container, I press plastic wrap directly against the surface of the guac to prevent it from turning brown.

BBQ SALMON AND CAULIFLOWER MASH

Compared to typical mashed potatoes, this version has 5 times fewer calories and 3½ times more vitamin C per cup. **MAKES 2 SERVINGS**

Two 6-ounce wild salmon fillets
2 tablespoons C.R.A.P.-free BBQ sauce (or use the Beet BBQ Sauce on page 222)
I head cauliflower, cut into small florets (about 6 cups)
Sea salt and freshly ground black pepper
2 cups Massaged Kale (recipe follows)

1 BROIL THE SALMON: Preheat the broiler. Place the salmon fillets skin side down on a rimmed baking sheet and spoon the BBQ sauce evenly over each piece. Broil for about 8 minutes per inch of thickness. I find it takes about 12 minutes for most fillets. You'll know it's done because it goes from translucent to opaque in color and easily flakes into moist pieces with a fork. You can use a thermometer to make sure you aren't under- or overcooking. The salmon is done when it registers 145°F on an instant-read thermometer in the thickest part.

2 STEAM AND MASH THE CAULIFLOWER: In a microwave-safe steamer (my preferred method) or in a steam basket set in a saucepan with 1 inch of simmering water, steam the cauliflower until tender. Transfer the cauliflower to a large bowl and, using a potato masher or immersion blender, puree it until smooth. Season with salt and pepper.

3 SERVE: On each plate, serve 1 cup of the massaged kale, 1 salmon fillet, and half the mashed cauliflower.

NUTRITION (I SERVING): 390 calories, 14g total fat, 24g carbs, 7g fiber, 44g protein

MASSAGED KALE

Raw kale is delicious but a little tough. Here's how to make it tender. **MAKES ABOUT 4 CUPS**

I bunch kale, stemmed and leaves thinly sliced (about 8 cups)
Juice of I lemon (about 3 tablespoons)
I tablespoon extra-virgin olive oil
Sea salt

In a large bowl, combine the kale, lemon juice, olive oil, and salt to taste. Use your hands to massage everything together until the kale is bright green and has shrunk down to 4 cups. Massaged kale will keep for up to 3 days in the fridge. It's good as is or with shredded Parmesan or chopped walnuts sprinkled on top.

OH YEAH, ONE MORE THING . . .

Salmon: Read Go Fish on page 29 or visit seafoodwatch.org to find the many other sustainable fish options.

C.R.A.P.-free BBQ sauce: When choosing store-bought BBQ sauce, look for brands with tomatoes as the first ingredient and no high-fructose corn syrup.

PESTO ZOODLES WITH GARLIC BREAD

Zucchini sliced into the shape of a noodle = zoodles. They taste as fun as they sound. Compared to usual pasta, zoodles have 9 times fewer calories per 1 cup cooked pasta (20 cals versus 180 cals). The pesto is made with a base of pureed white beans for extra protein and fiber. I never serve garlic bread with pasta—that's a double starchy carb no-no—but since these noodles are actually veggies, the bread is the perfect addition. **MAKES 2 SERVINGS**

PESTO
One 15-ounce can white beans, drained and rinsed (1½ cups)
1 cup fresh basil
Juice of ½ lemon (about 1½ tablespoons)
1½ tablespoons extra-virgin olive oil
3 tablespoons water
½ teaspoon sea salt

2 zucchini
1 pint grape tomatoes (about 2 cups), halved
2 small sprouted whole-grain rolls (1½ ounces/100 calories each), toasted
1 garlic clove

1 MAKE THE PESTO: In a food processor, combine the beans, basil, lemon juice, olive oil, water, and salt and puree until smooth.

2 MAKE THE ZOODLES: Using a spiralizer (my preference; see page 84) or vegetable peeler, slice the zucchini into noodle shapes.

3 COMBINE: In a large bowl, toss the pesto with the zoodles and tomatoes and serve at room temperature. If you prefer this warm, toss the noodles, pesto, and tomatoes in a 12-inch pan over medium heat for a few minutes.

4 SERVE: Halve the rolls, toast them, and rub the garlic over the cut sides. Serve the warm garlic bread on the side.

NUTRITION (1 SERVING): 410 calories, 14g total fat, 58g carbs, 15g fiber, 18g protein

OH YEAH, ONE MORE THING . . .

Better beans: Beans soaked and cooked from scratch are easier to digest and have more absorbable protein and minerals. Learn how to cook your own beans on page 241.

Bread options: Instead of a roll, you can use 1½ ounces of sprouted whole-grain bread, baguette, hamburger bun, or hot dog bun. The piece of bread should have about 100 calories.

COCONUT CURRY AND SUPER RICE

If you're a rice lover, you'll love this SuperSwap trick. Buy shredded coleslaw mix (cabbage and carrots) and chop it up to look like rice. When you warm and toss it with brown rice, it looks like a huge amount of rice, even though it's really mostly veggies. **MAKES 2 SERVINGS**

¾ cup canned coconut milk
2 teaspoons curry powder
2 cups broccoli florets
2 tablespoons raisins
2 cups shredded coleslaw mix (cabbage, carrots)
I cup cooked brown rice
4 tablespoons chopped raw cashews
2 green onions, chopped
Sea salt

I MAKE THE CURRY: In a 12-inch skillet, warm the coconut milk and curry powder over medium heat for 2 minutes. Add the broccoli and raisins and cook for 5 minutes more, until the broccoli is tender.

2 MAKE THE SUPER RICE: Chop the coleslaw to make it look like rice. In a microwave-safe bowl or a small saucepan, mix it with the cooked brown rice. Heat it in the microwave or over medium heat until warm.

3 SERVE: Top the super rice with the coconut curry mixture. Sprinkle with cashews and green onions and season with salt.

NUTRITION (I SERVING): 400 calories, 20g total fat, 47g carbs, 8g fiber, IOg protein

OH YEAH, ONE MORE THING...

Time saver: Use frozen precooked brown rice, found in the freezer aisle of the grocery store. Or make a big batch of brown rice yourself and freeze it in individual portions.

OLIVE OIL PASTA

Even without meat or poultry, this dish has 16 grams of plant protein per serving, not only from nuts, but also from the pasta and abundant kale.

MAKES 2 SERVINGS

3 ounces uncooked quinoa pasta or your favorite type of whole-grain pasta

2 tablespoons extra-virgin olive oil

¼ teaspoon crushed red pepper flakes

I bunch kale, stemmed and leaves cut into thin strips (about 8 cups)

2 garlic cloves, minced (about I teaspoon)

3 tablespoons chopped walnuts

Sea salt and freshly ground black pepper

I COOK THE PASTA AND KALE: Cook the pasta according to the package directions. In a 12-inch skillet, heat the oil and crushed red pepper over medium heat for 1 minute. Add the kale and cook for 7 minutes. Stir in the garlic and cook for 3 minutes more.

2 TOSS: In a large bowl, toss the pasta with the kale and walnuts and season with salt and pepper.

NUTRITION (I SERVING): 380 calories, 23g total fat, 43g carbs, 6g fiber, 8g protein

OH YEAH, ONE MORE THING . . .

Marinara lovers: Add ¼ cup C.R.A.P.-free marinara or Supersauce Marinara (page 226) to each serving of hot pasta.

CHEDDAR GRITS WITH BEANS AND GREENS

This SuperSwap uses whole-grain cornmeal instead of the refined, degermed corn often used as grits. Traditionally, the greens are cooked and cooked and cooked some more, but this "Southern comfort" recipe coaxes out their flavor in under 10 minutes so they retain more of their leafy-green nutrition. **MAKES 4 SERVINGS**

4 cups water

1¼ teaspoons sea salt

1 cup organic finely ground whole-grain cornmeal

1 cup shredded cheddar cheese

1½ tablespoons extra-virgin olive oil

2 garlic cloves, minced (about 1 teaspoon)

1 bunch collard greens, stemmed and leaves chopped (about 6 cups)

One 15-ounce can pinto beans, drained and rinsed (1½ cups)

Hot sauce (optional)

1 MAKE THE GRITS: In a 3-quart pot, bring the water and 1 teaspoon of the salt to a boil. Slowly stir in the cornmeal. Reduce the heat to low and simmer for 20 minutes, stirring every couple of minutes. Stir in the cheese.

2 MAKE THE GREENS, HEAT THE BEANS, AND SERVE: In a 12-inch skillet, heat the oil over medium heat. Add the garlic, collards, and remaining ¼ teaspoon salt and cook, stirring occasionally, for 4 minutes. Add the beans and cook for 5 minutes more, until the beans are hot. Serve the grits with greens, beans, and hot sauce to taste, if desired.

NUTRITION (1 SERVING): 380 calories, 17g total fat, 44g carbs, 12g fiber, 16g protein

OH YEAH, ONE MORE THING . . .

V+ Swap: In the grits, swap out the cheddar cheese for ¼ cup nutritional yeast and 1½ tablespoons extra-virgin olive oil.

Better beans: Beans soaked and cooked from scratch are easier to digest and have more absorbable protein and minerals. Learn how to cook your own beans on page 241.

5-MINUTE CHOCOLATE

Research shows that when you put in the effort to prepare your own food, you naturally eat less but enjoy it more. So put 5 minutes of effort into making homemade chocolate for built-in portion control—way better than any store-bought chocolate bar or bag of chocolate chips. I prefer it with brown rice syrup, but maple syrup or honey works, too. **MAKES THREE 3-BY-2-INCH PIECES**

2 tablespoons unsweetened cocoa powder (avoid Dutched versions)
2 tablespoons coconut oil
1 tablespoon brown rice syrup, pure maple syrup, or honey
Optional toppings: sea salt, cayenne, slivered almonds, unsweetened coconut flakes, ground cinnamon, goji berries, hemp seeds, etc.
5 medium strawberries (optional)

1 HEAT: In a small saucepan, combine the cocoa powder, coconut oil, and brown rice syrup and heat over medium-low heat, stirring, just until the mixture begins to bubble, about 1 minute.

2 POUR: Pour the chocolate onto a parchment paper–lined baking sheet or plate that will fit in the freezer. Aim to pour it into a 3-by-6-inch rectangle. It tastes great just as is, but you can sprinkle on your favorite toppings at this point—I love sea salt and cayenne.

3 SET: Freeze the chocolate for about 5 minutes, until set. Break it into 3 pieces. This DIY chocolate melts easily, so store the leftovers in the fridge.

4 SERVE: For a more filling snack, eat a 3-by-2-inch piece with the strawberries.

NUTRITION (1 PIECE, NO BERRIES): 110 calories, 10g total fat, 8g carbs, 1g fiber, 1g protein **NUTRITION (1 PIECE W/ BERRIES):** 130 calories, 10g total fat, 12g carbs, 2g fiber, 1g protein

OH YEAH, ONE MORE THING . . .

Coconut oil cubes: Measuring coconut oil can make a mess. My solution: coconut oil cubes. To make them, fill the indentations of a silicone ice-cube tray with 1½ teaspoons (60 calories) melted coconut oil. Freeze for 5 minutes to let the oil harden, then pop the cubes out. Store in the fridge in an airtight container.

Get your learn on: Read more about cocoa powder and cacao powder on page 237.

ALMOND JOY SNACK MIX

There are over 20 ingredients in an Almond Joy candy bar, and corn syrup tops the list, followed by other C.R.A.P. such as partially hydrogenated vegetable oil and artificial flavor. This SuperSwap has just 3 wholesome ingredients and zero sugar. Oh, joy! **MAKES 2 SERVINGS**

¼ cup raw almonds
2 tablespoons unsweetened coconut flakes
1 tablespoon cacao nibs

Mix all the ingredients together and divide the snack mix into 2 servings.

NUTRITION (1 SERVING): 200 calories, 17g total fat, 10g carbs, 4g fiber, 5g protein

OH YEAH, ONE MORE THING . . .

Get your learn on: Read more about cacao nibs on page 238.

FREEZER FUDGE

Some people call this "magic" fudge because it satisfies your sweet tooth, but has *no sugar.* It contains bone-building magnesium, anti-inflammatory fats, skin-boosting vitamin E, filling fiber, and plant protein. It's called "freezer" fudge because it needs to be kept cool—these fudgy squares get melty! **MAKES 4 SERVINGS**

¼ cup natural peanut or almond butter
1 tablespoon coconut oil, melted
⅛ teaspoon sea salt
½ tablespoon unsweetened cocoa powder (avoid Dutched versions)
1 tablespoon cacao nibs (optional)

1 STIR, POUR, AND SPRINKLE: Stir together the peanut butter, coconut oil, and salt. Pour into a small, parchment paper–lined container so it's ¾ to 1 inch thick. Sprinkle with cocoa powder and cacao nibs, if desired.

2 FREEZE: Freeze for at least 4 hours. Lift the fudge from the container and cut it into 4 small squares. Store in a sealed container in the freezer for up to 3 months.

NUTRITION (1 PIECE): 130 calories, 11g total fat, 4g carbs, 1g fiber, 4g protein

BANANA SKINNIES

When I'm looking for a little something sweet after dinner, skinny slices of frozen banana with a sprinkle of unsweetened cocoa powder are my go-to. **MAKES 2 SERVINGS**

I ripe banana
2 tablespoons natural almond butter
Unsweetened cocoa powder (avoid Dutched versions)

I CUT AND FREEZE: Cut the banana into 20 thin slices. Arrange them in a single layer in a plastic sandwich bag and freeze for at least 2 hours. Store in the freezer for up to 3 months.

2 SPREAD AND SPRINKLE: When you are ready to eat the bananas, spread a teeny-tiny amount of almond butter (about ¼ teaspoon) on each frozen piece and sprinkle with cocoa powder to taste.

NUTRITION (I SERVING): 150 calories, 9g total fat, 17g carbs, 3g fiber, 4g protein

OH YEAH, ONE MORE THING . . .

Extra skinny: Omit the almond butter for a straight chocolaty banana treat.

Flavorize: You can use ground cinnamon or ground vanilla beans instead of cocoa powder. Learn about ground vanilla beans on page 236.

Nice cream: You can also turn frozen bananas into Nice Cream (the SuperSwap version of ice cream). Learn how on page 163.

CHOCOLATE YOGURT MOUSSE

Typical mousses are made with heavy cream and eggs, but this SuperSwap uses 2% Greek yogurt instead. Skip the no-fat yogurt, since a little milk fat decreases the sourness of yogurt and contains a healthy compound called conjugated linoleic acid (CLA), which may help decrease body fat. **MAKES 2 SERVINGS**

One 6-ounce container plain 2% Greek yogurt
I tablespoon unsweetened cocoa powder (avoid Dutched versions)
I tablespoon honey
½ cup fresh or thawed frozen raspberries or sliced strawberries (unsweetened)

In the yogurt container or a small bowl, stir together the yogurt, cocoa powder, and honey. Divide the mixture between two bowls and top each with ¼ cup of the berries.

NUTRITION (I SERVING): 110 calories, 2g total fat, 17g carbs, 3g fiber, 8g protein

OH YEAH, ONE MORE THING . . .

Chocolate mousse morning: This recipe is healthy enough to have for breakfast. To make it a meal, eat both servings at once, add ¼ cup more fruit, and top with 2 tablespoons rolled oats.

Chia Pudding [V+, GF]: With a fork, stir together ¼ cup chia seeds and I cup unsweetened vanilla plant milk, such as soy or almond. Pour evenly into two small, single-serving airtight containers, cover, and refrigerate for at least 20 minutes or overnight until thick. Store in the fridge for up to 5 days. Top with peaches and ground ginger; blueberries and lemon zest; banana and freshly grated nutmeg; strawberries and unsweetened cocoa powder; or mango and unsweetened coconut flakes.

(V+)

NO-BAKE PEANUT BUTTER COOKIES

This is an easy, no-bake way to take healthy fats and protein with you when you're on the go. Eat these instead of protein bars since most bars on the market are loaded with sugar. These have no added sugar! **MAKES 2 SERVINGS**

3 tablespoons rolled oats
2 tablespoons natural peanut butter
1 tablespoon ground flaxseeds

1 STIR AND PORTION: In a small bowl, mix the oats, peanut butter, and flaxseeds. The mixture will be super thick. Portion it out into 4 tablespoon-size bites and roll each in your hands to form a ball. Smash each lightly with a fork to form a thick cookie shape.

2 STORE: Store the cookies in an airtight container in the fridge for up to 1 week. You can make extras and freeze them for up to 3 months. Pop them into unbleached paper sandwich bags to take with you. If you don't have these bags, get them in health-food stores or online.

NUTRITION (1 SERVING): 140 calories, 10g total fat, 9g carbs, 3g fiber, 6g protein

OH YEAH, ONE MORE THING . . .

GF Swap: Use gluten-free oats or quinoa flakes.

Flavorize: Change up the cookies by adding 2 teaspoons cacao nibs (nature's unsweetened chocolate chips).

(V+) (GF)

SPINACH CHIPS

This SuperSwap is in honor of chip lovers everywhere. The tahini makes them heartier and more savory than a typical veggie chip and is a great flavor swap for anyone who loves sesame stick crackers, which are made with refined white flour. **MAKES 2 SERVINGS**

4 cups baby spinach leaves
2 tablespoons tahini (sesame seed paste)
Sea salt

1 PREHEAT THE OVEN AND TOSS: Preheat the oven to 300°F. In a medium bowl, use your hands to toss the baby spinach and tahini.

2 PLACE AND BAKE: Put the tahini-coated leaves on two parchment paper–lined baking sheets in a single layer. If they overlap, they won't get crisp. Sprinkle with salt to taste and bake for 15 minutes, or until crisp. Remove from the oven and let cool for 5 minutes.

NUTRITION (1 SERVING): 120 calories, 8g total fat, 7g carbs, 3g fiber, 5g protein

OH YEAH, ONE MORE THING . . .

Happy bones: Both spinach and sesame seeds are rich in bone-building calcium.

SESAME SEAWEED POPCORN

Popcorn is naturally good for you because it's a whole grain. Just swap the usual butter topping for savory, mineral-rich seaweed. **MAKES 2 SERVINGS**

4 cups air-popped popcorn (from 3 tablespoons
    unpopped kernels)
2 sheets toasted nori seaweed, crumbled
2 tablespoons sesame seeds
I tablespoon dark sesame oil

Put the popcorn in a large bowl and sprinkle with the seaweed, sesame seeds, and sesame oil. Toss for a couple of minutes to combine evenly.

NUTRITION (I SERVING): 180 calories, 12g total fat, 16g carbs, 4g fiber, 5g protein

OH YEAH, ONE MORE THING . . .

Seaweed seasoning: Pretoasted nori seaweed sheets (the seaweed used to make sushi) can be found in the international aisle of the grocery store. To crumble, put the sheets into a plastic sandwich bag and squeeze or twist it for a couple of minutes until the sheets become small, crumbly pieces.

Dulse: Another type of seaweed you can use on popcorn is dulse. I buy it already ground in a convenient shaker bottle at health food stores or online at sites like amazon.com.

Sesame seeds: These little seeds have a hefty dose of calcium for strong bones.

Air popper: I love my air popper. I put the oil and seasonings in a large bowl, pop the corn right into the bowl . . . and then toss.

SUPERFOOD PARTY MIX

The typical party mix has butter, salt, and too much refined white flour in the pretzels and cereal. This SuperSwap features whole-grain cereal, healthy fats from nuts, and the superfood spice turmeric, the primary ingredient in curry powder and a powerful inflammation fighter.

MAKES 4 SERVINGS

I cup organic whole-grain flake cereal
¼ cup raw cashews
¼ cup raw peanuts
I tablespoon avocado oil
2 teaspoons curry powder
¼ teaspoon cayenne
¼ teaspoon sea salt
¼ cup freeze-dried edamame

Preheat the oven to 375°F. In a medium bowl, toss the cereal, cashews, peanuts, oil, curry powder, cayenne, and salt. Pour onto a parchment paper–lined baking sheet and bake for about 8 minutes, stirring once halfway through. Toss with the edamame and serve.

NUTRITION (I SERVING): 170 calories, IIg total fat, 13g carbs, 2g fiber, 5g protein

OH YEAH, ONE MORE THING . . .

GF Swap: Use gluten-free cereal.

Get your learn on: Read more about avocado oil on page 238.

10 BASIC SNACKS

Sometimes you just want a basic snack that has the function of bridging your appetite from one meal to the next. I like to snack on a combo of produce and protein. The produce is loaded with energizing nutrients and hydrating water, while the protein has staying power. Here are 10 of my favorites.

1   Apple + almonds (10)
2   Pear + edamame (¼ cup)
3   Carrots + hummus (¼ cup)
4   Tomatoes + string cheese (1 ounce)
5   Grapes + roasted chickpeas (¼ cup)
6   Orange + pistachios (30)
7   Cucumber + hard-boiled egg (1)
8   Celery + nut butter (1½ tablespoons)
9   Berries + plain 2% yogurt or kefir (½ cup)
10 Banana + pumpkin seeds (¼ cup)

OH YEAH, ONE MORE THING...

Calories: Each one of these combos is about 150 calories.

2 WEEKS OF
EXPRESS-MEAL PLANS

Use any express recipe you want, anytime. Or you can follow this 2-week plan for a more focused approach.

WEEK 1

	MONDAY	TUESDAY	WEDNESDAY	THURSDAY	FRIDAY	SATURDAY	SUNDAY
BREAKFAST	Green Omelet (page 95)	Peanut Butter Oatmeal (page 92)	Avocado Toast (page 91)	Green Omelet (page 95)	Peanut Butter Oatmeal (page 92)	Avocado Toast (page 91)	Belly Love Smoothie (page 96)
LUNCH	Sunflower Caesar (page 100)	Hummus Bowl (page 99)	Mexican Burrito Bowl (page 99)	Sunflower Caesar (page 100)	Hummus Bowl (page 99)	Mexican Burrito Bowl (page 99)	Lox Lunch Plate (page 102)
DINNER	Quick Kale Pizza (page 106)	Guac and Greens Tacos (page 107)	BBQ Salmon and Cauliflower Mash (page 108)	Quick Kale Pizza (page 106)	Guac and Greens Tacos (page 107)	BBQ Salmon and Cauliflower Mash (page 108)	Olive Oil Pasta (page 115)

SNACKS AND TREATS (MAX OF 2 PER DAY, TOTAL): No-Bake Peanut Butter Cookies (page 121), Spinach Chips (page 121), 5-Minute Chocolate (page 117), Superfood Party Mix (page 125), or any of the "10 Basic Snacks" (page 126)

WEEK 2

	MONDAY	TUESDAY	WEDNESDAY	THURSDAY	FRIDAY	SATURDAY	SUNDAY
BREAKFAST	Cereal Puff Bowl (page 92)	Superfood Scramble Bowl (page 93)	Bettertella Breakfast (page 91)	Cereal Puff Bowl (page 92)	Superfood Scramble Bowl (page 93)	Bettertella Breakfast (page 91)	Belly Love Smoothie (page 96)
LUNCH	Avocado Tuna Sandwich (page 101)	Asian Peanut Bowl (page 102)	Collard Green Burrito (page 105)	Avocado Tuna Sandwich (page 101)	Asian Peanut Bowl (page 102)	Collard Green Burrito (page 105)	Lox Lunch Plate (page 102)
DINNER	Coconut Curry and Super Rice (page 112)	Pesto Zoodles with Garlic Bread (page 111)	Cheddar Grits with Beans and Greens (page 116)	Coconut Curry and Super Rice (page 112)	Pesto Zoodles with Garlic Bread (page 111)	Cheddar Grits with Beans and Greens (page 116)	Olive Oil Pasta (page 115)

SNACKS AND TREATS (MAX OF 2 PER DAY, TOTAL): Banana Skinnies (page 120), Sesame Seaweed Popcorn (page 122), Freezer Fudge (page 118), Almond Joy Snack Mix (page 118), or any of the "10 Basic Snacks" (page 126)

SPRING/SUMMER
RECIPES

LEAFY OMELET ROLL-UP

What I'm doing here is sneaking in a salad at breakfast with something that feels like a sandwich wrap. **MAKES 1 SERVING**

2 organic eggs
½ cup cooked quinoa
1½ teaspoons extra-virgin olive oil
Sea salt and freshly ground black pepper
2 cups mixed salad greens
2 or 3 thin slices red onion, or more to taste
2 tablespoons crumbled goat cheese, or 1 tablespoon pine nuts

1 WHISK AND COOK THE EGGS: In a small bowl, whisk together the eggs and quinoa. In a 10-inch nonstick skillet, heat the oil over medium-low heat. Add the egg mixture and, without stirring, let the egg cook. It is thin, so it will cook in 1 or 2 minutes.

2 REMOVE THE EGG AND ASSEMBLE: With a spatula, scrape or push the egg onto a large cutting board (it will look like a thin crepe or tortilla wrap). Season with salt and pepper, then fill the egg wrap with the greens, onion, and cheese and roll it up.

NUTRITION (1 SERVING): 390 calories, 22g total fat, 27g carbs, 6g fiber, 21g protein

OH YEAH, ONE MORE THING . . .

Roll-up swap: Don't want to deal with an egg roll-up? Just have a simple breakfast of 2 eggs seasoned with salt and pepper on 2 pieces of sprouted whole-grain toast. Serve a simple mixed green salad dressed with red wine vinegar alongside. Salad for breakfast is the lesson here! Check out the egg-cooking tips on page 239.

Time saver: Use frozen precooked quinoa, found in the freezer aisle of the grocery store. Or make a big batch of quinoa yourself and freeze it in individual portions.

(V) (GF)

GOLDEN SMOOTHIE BOWL

Who says you have to drink smoothies? Pour a smoothie into a bowl and add satisfying toppings. It's even more filling than sipping one through a straw. **MAKES I SERVING**

8 ounces plain low-fat kefir
I banana
½ teaspoon ground turmeric
2 tablespoons chopped raw walnuts
2 tablespoons unsweetened coconut flakes
¼ teaspoon ground cinnamon

In a blender, puree the kefir, half the banana, and the turmeric. Slice the remaining half of the banana. Pour the kefir mixture into a bowl and top it with the banana slices, walnuts, coconut, and cinnamon.

NUTRITION (I SERVING): 390 calories, 19g total fat, 44g carbs, 6g fiber, 15g protein

OH YEAH, ONE MORE THING . . .

Turmeric: This golden-yellow spice has superfood powers to help decrease inflammation, which is good news for joint and heart health. Plus, early research suggests it may help decrease your risk of cancer.

No sugar added: There's no added sugar in this recipe since natural sweetness comes from the banana, coconut flakes, and cinnamon. If you would like a little more sweetness, drizzle the smoothie with I teaspoon honey.

(V+) (GF)

CHOCOLATE BEETBERRY SMOOTHIE

This smoothie starts with a base of plant-based milk and cashews instead of sugary juice—and adds no sweeteners. Each serving has 1 whole fruit serving and a dose of beets, which energize you by shuttling more oxygen to your brain and muscles. Drink this before your workout for a noticeable improvement! **MAKES 2 SERVINGS**

I beet, peeled and chopped (about I cup)
I cup strawberries
I banana
1½ cups unsweetened plant milk, such as almond or hemp milk
¾ cup raw cashews
1½ tablespoons unsweetened cocoa powder (avoid Dutched versions)
½ cup ice cubes

In a blender, combine the beet, berries, banana, milk, cashews, and cocoa powder and puree. Add the ice and blend until smooth. If you're making this for one, the extra serving can be stored in an airtight container in the fridge for up to 2 days.

NUTRITION (I SERVING): 380 calories, 22g total fat, 41g carbs, 8g fiber, 11g protein

OH YEAH, ONE MORE THING . . .

Dessert Pops: This smoothie makes great ice pops. Pour it into molds and freeze.

Peeling beets: Cut off both ends of the beet. Under cold running water (this helps keep the beet from staining your hands), use a vegetable peeler to easily remove the skin.

CARROT CAKE OATS

Typically, you'll find oatmeal piled in a big bowl and sprinkled with dried fruit and nuts. This SuperSwap gives you a dose of veggies as well as fruit and nuts in the a.m. **MAKES 2 SERVINGS**

¾ cup rolled oats
1½ cups unsweetened plant milk, such as almond or hemp milk
¼ teaspoon freshly grated nutmeg
2 carrots, grated (about 1 cup)
¾ cup chopped pecans
¼ cup raisins
Pure maple syrup (optional)

In a medium bowl, combine the oats, milk, and nutmeg. Cover and refrigerate for at least 4 hours or up to overnight. Stir in the carrots, pecans, and raisins and serve the oatmeal cold. The raisins sweeten this naturally, but if you'd like, add 1 teaspoon maple syrup per serving.

NUTRITION (1 SERVING): 380 calories, 19g total fat, 45g carbs, 8g fiber, 9g protein

OH YEAH, ONE MORE THING . . .

GF Swap: Use gluten-free oats.

Some like it hot: Instead of letting the oatmeal soak in the fridge and serving it cold, cook it in the microwave or on the stovetop according to the package directions before mixing in the other ingredients. Serve warm.

Flavorize: Here are some other good oatmeal combos:

- **Pumpkin pie:** pure canned pumpkin, pumpkin pie spice, and pecans

- **Sugar plum spice:** plums, candied ginger, and cashews

- **Chocolate banana bread:** banana, unsweetened cocoa powder, and walnuts

- **Zucchini bread:** grated zucchini, pure maple syrup, and sunflower seeds

- **PB&J:** grapes, ground flaxseed, and natural peanut butter

ALMOND BUTTER AND CHIA JAM SANDWICH

Not the same PB&J you packed in your school lunchbox, this has better-for-you bread, no-C.R.A.P. nut butter, and jam with healthy fiber and fat. **MAKES 1 SERVING, WITH EXTRA JAM**

2 tablespoons natural almond butter
2 slices sprouted whole-grain bread, toasted
2 tablespoons Chia Jam (recipe follows)

Spread the almond butter on the toast and top with the jam. Serve open-faced so it feels like 2 sandwiches.

NUTRITION (1 SERVING): 380 calories, 20g total fat, 40g carbs, 11g fiber, 15g protein

---

CHIA JAM

Typical jams have added sugars, but this SuperSwap version needs none, thanks to the natural sugars in the fruit. Chia seeds not only thicken the jam, but also add healthful fats, fiber, and protein. The fig version is especially good on a cheese board. **MAKES 1 HEAPING CUP**

2 cups fresh or unsweetened frozen fruit (such as berries, grapes, or figs)
2 tablespoons chia seeds

In a small pot, heat the fruit over medium heat, mashing until smooth, about 5 minutes. Stir in the chia seeds. Store in a lidded jar in the refrigerator for up to 2 weeks.

NUTRITION (1 TABLESPOON): 10 calories, 0.5g total fat, 2g carbs, 1g fiber, 0g protein

OH YEAH, ONE MORE THING . . .

Chia Jam Parfait: Use the jam in a parfait! Top a 6-ounce container of plain 2% Greek yogurt with ¼ cup Chia Jam, ¼ cup rolled oats, and ¼ cup slivered almonds.

NO-SUGAR GRANOLA PARFAIT

A typical parfait contains sweetened yogurt, artificially flavored fruit filling, and a sugary granola on top. This SuperSwap version has none of that C.R.A.P. **MAKES I SERVING, WITH EXTRA GRANOLA**

¼ cup No-Sugar Granola (recipe follows)
I cup fresh berries, such as raspberries, blackberries, or strawberries
One 6-ounce container plain 2% Greek yogurt

Layer the yogurt, berries, and granola in a bowl.

NUTRITION (I SERVING): 390 calories, 16g total fat, 41g carbs, 6g fiber, 22g protein

---

NO-SUGAR GRANOLA

Store-bought granola is usually su-gar-eee! You won't miss the sugar in this SuperSwap version, since cinnamon, coconut oil, and coconut flakes all have natural sweetness. Plus, the hemp seeds give the granola a protein boost. **MAKES 2 CUPS**

I tablespoon coconut oil
I cup rolled oats
½ cup hemp seeds
½ cup unsweetened coconut flakes
I teaspoon ground cinnamon
⅛ teaspoon sea salt

In a 12-inch skillet, heat the coconut oil over medium-low heat. Add the oats, hemp seeds, coconut, cinnamon, and salt and stir until well coated with the oil. Cook, stirring occasionally, for 8 minutes, until golden. Let cool for 5 minutes. Store any extra granola in an airtight container at room temperature for up to 5 days.

NUTRITION (¼ CUP GRANOLA): 150 calories, 10g total fat, 10g carbs, 2g fiber, 5g protein

OH YEAH, ONE MORE THING . . .

GF Swap: Swap out the regular rolled oats for gluten-free oats or quinoa flakes.

Activated lentils: Want to take your granola game up a notch? Add activated lentils to the mix. Activated lentils have been soaked to make them more digestible and increase the amount of protein and minerals our body can absorb. This is easy, but a wee bit time intensive. Soak I cup red lentils in 3 cups water in a large bowl covered with a kitchen towel for 12 hours at room temperature. Drain, rinse, and spread on a parchment paper–lined baking sheet. Roast in a preheated 325°F oven for 30 minutes, until crunchy. Stir into the cooled granola.

SUSHI BOWL

A quick sushi bowl made with brown rice ranks as far superior to an order of white rice sushi with spicy mayo or tempura. **MAKES 2 SERVINGS**

Juice of I orange (about ¼ cup)
2 teaspoons organic reduced-sodium gluten-free soy sauce
½ teaspoon minced fresh ginger
I cup cooked brown rice, warmed
I cup shelled edamame, warmed
2 carrots, cut into matchsticks (about I cup)
I cucumber, cut into matchsticks (about 2 cups)
½ avocado, cut into ½-inch cubes
2 sheets toasted nori seaweed, cut into ¼-inch-wide strips
I tablespoon sesame seeds

1 MIX THE DRESSING: In a small bowl, stir together the orange juice, soy sauce, and ginger.

2 ASSEMBLE THE BOWL: In a medium bowl, toss the rice, edamame, carrots, cucumber, and avocado. Drizzle with the dressing and top with the nori strips and sesame seeds.

NUTRITION (I SERVING): 390 calories, 14g total fat, 53g carbs, 13g fiber, 16g protein

OH YEAH, ONE MORE THING . . .

Time saver: Use frozen precooked brown rice, found in the freezer aisle of the grocery store. Or make a big batch of brown rice yourself and freeze it in individual portions.

BBQ SANDWICH AND COLLARD CHIPS

When you find yourself in the mood for BBQ, know that you have an alternative to meat on the grill. SuperSwap to tempeh, high in plant-based protein with a hearty meat texture. Steaming plumps up the tempeh and reduces any bitterness. I used to skip this step, but it's worth the extra time. **MAKES 2 SERVINGS**

COLLARD CHIPS

1 bunch collard greens (about 7 leaves)
2 teaspoons extra-virgin olive oil
½ teaspoon sea salt

½ package (4 ounces) organic tempeh, halved crosswise
1½ teaspoons avocado oil
¼ cup C.R.A.P.-free BBQ sauce (or use the Beet BBQ Sauce on page 222)
½ avocado, mashed
2 sprouted whole-grain English muffins, toasted
1 tomato, cut crosswise into 8 slices
¼ red onion, sliced (about ¼ cup)

1 MAKE THE COLLARD CHIPS: Preheat the oven to 300°F. Line two baking sheets with parchment paper. Remove the collard stems and tear the leaves into chiplike pieces. In a large bowl, toss the collard pieces with the olive oil. Spread them in a single layer on the baking sheets (it all usually fits on two sheets—use a third, if you need to, to avoid overcrowding). Sprinkle with the salt and bake for about 18 minutes, until crisp—keep a close eye on them to prevent burning.

2 PREP THE TEMPEH: Meanwhile, steam the tempeh in a microwave-safe steamer (my preferred method) for 4 minutes, or in a stovetop steamer basket set in a saucepan with 1 inch of simmering water for 8 minutes.

3 GRILL: Heat a grill to medium heat or heat a grill pan over medium-high heat. Brush the steamed tempeh with avocado oil and grill for about 5 minutes on each side. Midway through grilling, brush BBQ sauce on both sides of the tempeh.

4 SERVE: Spread the mashed avocado on the English muffins and top with tomato slices, red onion, and BBQ tempeh. Serve with the collard chips.

NUTRITION (1 SERVING): 410 calories, 14g total fat, 56g carbs, 17g fiber, 21g protein

OH YEAH, ONE MORE THING . . .

C.R.A.P.-free BBQ sauce: When choosing store-bought BBQ sauce, look for brands with tomatoes as the first ingredient and no high-fructose corn syrup.

Leftover tempeh: Freeze any extra tempeh in an airtight container for up to 3 months.

CASHEW BUTTER CLUB

There are 3 steps to SuperSwapping your sandwich: 1) ditch processed lunch meat; 2) pile on veggies; and 3) eat it open-faced.

MAKES I SERVING, WITH EXTRA PICKLED ONION

I red onion, cut into ⅛-inch-thick rounds (about I cup)
½ cup boiling water
¼ cup apple cider vinegar
I tablespoon coconut sugar
¼ teaspoon sea salt
2 tablespoons natural cashew or almond butter
2 slices sprouted whole-grain bread, toasted
I cup watercress

I QUICK-PICKLE THE RED ONION: In a glass container with an airtight lid (like a Mason jar), combine the onion, boiling water, vinegar, sugar, and salt. Put the lid on and let the mixture sit for 5 minutes, shaking the jar periodically. Pull out the onions you want for your sandwich and refrigerate the rest in their liquid for up to 2 weeks, occasionally shaking the container to make sure none of the onions dry out. Having extra pickled onions makes it easy to repeat this sandwich anytime.

2 ASSEMBLE THE SANDWICH: Spread 1 tablespoon of the cashew butter on each slice of toast and top them evenly with the watercress and pickled onion. Serve the sandwich open-faced to feel like you have 2 sandwiches.

NUTRITION (I SERVING): 380 calories, I8g total fat, 45g carbs, 8g fiber, I3g protein

OH YEAH, ONE MORE THING . . .

Watercress: Watercress is a nutrition rock star and, in fact, was listed as the most nutrient-packed superfood on a list published in the Centers for Disease Control and Prevention journal *Preventing Chronic Disease.* If you don't have watercress, baby spinach works, too—it was number 5 out of 4I on the list of powerhouse produce.

Pickled red onion: The vinegar tones down the onion flavor so you won't have overly oniony breath. Not to mention that vinegar may keep food in your stomach longer to help you feel more satisfied. Oh, and pickled onions are versatile! Try them on sandwiches, tacos, and burgers and in salads.

FAST FALAFEL BOWL

Typical falafel is deep-fried, but for this SuperSwap, it's just lightly panfried. The secret to holding the patties together lies with the ground flaxseed. No need for an egg or bread crumbs. Oh, and don't for a second try to skip the fresh mint—it adds big-time flavor. P.S.: Use this tahini dill dressing as a quick veggie dip anytime. **MAKES 2 SERVINGS**

FALAFEL

One 15-ounce can chickpeas, drained and rinsed (1½ cups)
¼ red onion, finely chopped (about ¼ cup)
Juice of 1 lemon (about 3 tablespoons)
2 tablespoons ground flaxseed
¼ teaspoon ground cumin
¼ teaspoon sea salt
⅛ teaspoon cayenne
2 tablespoons chopped fresh flat-leaf parsley
2 tablespoons chopped fresh mint
1½ tablespoons extra-virgin olive oil

TAHINI DILL DRESSING

2 tablespoons tahini (sesame seed paste)
3 tablespoons water
⅛ teaspoon dried dill
⅛ teaspoon sea salt

SALAD

5 cups chopped romaine lettuce
2 tablespoons chopped fresh flat-leaf parsley
2 tablespoons chopped fresh mint

1 MAKE THE FALAFEL: In a food processor or blender, combine half the chickpeas, the onion, lemon juice, flaxseed, cumin, salt, and cayenne and pulse until mostly smooth. Add the remaining chickpeas, the parsley, and the mint. Pulse again just until slightly chunky. Form the chickpea mixture into 6 patties and freeze them for 10 minutes to firm up.

2 COOK THE FALAFEL: In a 12-inch skillet, heat the oil over medium heat. Add the patties and cook for about 4 minutes on each side, until golden.

3 MAKE THE DRESSING: In a small bowl, stir together the tahini, water, dill, and salt until well mixed.

4 ASSEMBLE THE SALAD: In a large bowl, toss together the lettuce, parsley, and mint. Divide the salad between two plates and top each with 3 falafel patties and drizzles of the dressing.

NUTRITION (1 SERVING): 420 calories, 24g total fat, 41g carbs, 15g fiber, 16g protein

OH YEAH, ONE MORE THING . . .

Better beans: Beans soaked and cooked from scratch are easier to digest and have more absorbable protein and minerals. Learn how to cook your own beans on page 241.

Sliders: These falafel patties also make awesome sliders on sprouted whole-grain dinner rolls. Use the dressing as a spread for the sliders.

SEA CAKES AND SALAD

A good crab cake with a basic garden salad is a go-to restaurant meal for me. This is my SuperSwap plant-based version, packed with beans and veggies. When I put in the time to make super-flavorful sea cakes, I keep the salad simple, but you can add any other veggies you'd like. **MAKES 2 SERVINGS**

2 sheets toasted nori seaweed
One 15-ounce can chickpeas, drained and rinsed (1½ cups)
Zest of 1 lemon (about 1 tablespoon)
Juice from 1 lemon (about 3 tablespoons, 1 squeeze reserved for serving)
1 teaspoon Old Bay seasoning
2 garlic cloves, minced (about 1 teaspoon)
1 teaspoon Dijon mustard
½ red onion, finely chopped (about ½ cup)
½ zucchini, grated (about ½ cup)
1 celery stalk, finely chopped (about ½ cup)
16 brown rice crackers, crushed (about ½ cup)
1½ tablespoons extra-virgin olive oil
½ teaspoon smoked paprika
Pinch of cayenne
Sea salt
4 cups salad greens

1 MAKE THE SEA CAKES: Using kitchen scissors, cut the nori sheets into quarters, stack them, and then cut them into threads. In a food processor, puree the beans, lemon zest, lemon juice, Old Bay seasoning, garlic, and mustard until about 75% smooth. Add the nori, onion, zucchini, and celery and combine with a few short pulses. Stir in the crushed crackers. Form the mixture into 6 patties.

2 COOK AND SERVE: In a large skillet, heat the oil, paprika, and cayenne over medium heat. Add the sea cakes and cook for 4 minutes on each side. Season with salt. Divide the salad greens between two plates and top each with 3 sea cakes. Finish with a squeeze of lemon juice.

NUTRITION (1 SERVING): 410 calories, 14g total fat, 58g carbs, 14g fiber, 14g protein

OH YEAH, ONE MORE THING . . .

Better beans: Beans soaked and cooked from scratch are easier to digest and have more absorbable protein and minerals. Learn how to cook your own beans on page 241.

Stock up: You can always double the sea cake recipe and freeze the extras for up to 6 months. I always eat healthier when I have easy-to-grab goodies like these in the freezer.

(V+) (GF)

BLACK BEAN BURGERS

Boxed veggie burgers often contain stuff that your body doesn't need, such as soy protein concentrate, hydrolyzed vegetable protein, disodium inosinate, caramel color, wheat gluten, and artificial flavors. This SuperSwap is just beans, veggies, and a few simple corn chips to hold it all together. **MAKES 2 SERVINGS, WITH 6 EXTRA BURGERS**

BURGERS

I tablespoon avocado oil, plus extra for brushing

I red onion, chopped (about I cup)

2 garlic cloves, minced (about I teaspoon)

I poblano pepper, seeded and diced (about I cup)

2 carrots, grated (about I cup)

2 tablespoons taco seasoning

One 15-ounce can vegetarian refried beans

One 15-ounce can black beans, drained and rinsed (1½ cups)

2 ounces organic corn tortilla chips, crushed (about I cup), plus extra as needed

4 organic sprouted corn tortillas, warmed

I cup loosely packed baby spinach leaves

½ avocado, sliced

1 MAKE THE BURGERS: In a 12-inch skillet, heat the avocado oil over medium heat. Add the onion, garlic, poblano pepper, carrots, and taco seasoning and cook for about 8 minutes, until the vegetables are tender. Stir in the refried beans, black beans, and crushed chips. If the mixture is too wet, add more crushed chips. Remove from the heat and set aside until cool enough to handle, then form the mixture into 10 patties.

2 COOK AND SERVE THE BURGERS: Brush 4 of the patties with avocado oil. In a large skillet, brown the patties over medium heat for about 4 minutes on each side. Serve the burgers in tortillas, topped with spinach and avocado slices.

3 STORE THE EXTRAS: Put the 6 remaining uncooked patties in an airtight container, stacking them with a sheet of parchment paper between each one to prevent sticking. Store in the freezer for up to 3 months. When you're ready to eat, brush a frozen patty with avocado oil and grill for 4 minutes on each side, until the center is hot.

NUTRITION (I SERVING): 420 calories, 13g total fat, 67g carbs, 17g fiber, 15g protein

OH YEAH, ONE MORE THING . . .

On the side: Peel jicama and cut it into sticks, sprinkle the sticks with chili powder, and squeeze on fresh lime juice.

Taco seasoning: Look for brands that contain just spices, without stuff like dextrose, hydrolyzed soy protein, caramel color, potato starch, whey, or MSG. Or make your own by mixing chili powder, ground cumin, smoked paprika, sea salt, and pepper.

Warm the tortillas: Warm the tortillas directly on an electric or gas stove burner over low heat. Use tongs to flip the tortillas from one side to the other. They get toasty and brown when you warm them this way, but they can easily burn—so watch them!

CAULIFLOWER FRIED RICE BOWL

SuperSwap regular rice to cauliflower rice for one-fifth the calories and a heartier dose of vegetable nutrients, including immune-boosting vitamin C. **MAKES 2 SERVINGS**

1 head cauliflower, cut into florets (about 6 cups)
1 tablespoon dark sesame oil
2 teaspoons minced fresh ginger
2 garlic cloves, minced (about 1 teaspoon)
⅛ teaspoon cayenne
½ cup frozen green peas, thawed
½ teaspoon olive oil
2 organic eggs
2 green onions, sliced
½ cup chopped raw cashews
2 teaspoons organic reduced-sodium gluten-free soy sauce
2 lime wedges

1 MAKE THE CAULIFLOWER RICE: Place about a third of the cauliflower into a food processor and pulse until the cauliflower has the texture of rice. Set aside and repeat with the remaining cauliflower. (I do it in batches because if there's too much in the processor at once, the cauliflower doesn't break down to the right consistency.)

2 PANFRY THE RICE AND PEAS: In a 12-inch skillet, heat the sesame oil over medium-high heat. Add the ginger, garlic, and cayenne and cook for 1 minute. Add the cauliflower rice and peas and cook for 4 minutes more.

3 COOK THE EGGS: In a separate skillet, heat the olive oil over medium heat. Add the eggs and cook, turning them once for over easy.

4 SERVE: Top each serving of rice with a fried egg, green onions, cashews, a drizzle of soy sauce, and a lime wedge for squeezing on top before eating.

NUTRITION (1 SERVING): 410 calories, 25g total fat, 31g carbs, 9g fiber, 20g protein

OH YEAH, ONE MORE THING . . .

V+ Swap: Swap the 2 eggs for ½ cup organic tofu cut into ¼-inch cubes. Cook the tofu as instructed for the eggs.

CAULIFLOWER MAC AND CHEESE

Buy mac and cheese in a box and you are getting refined-white-flour pasta with artificial ingredients. This SuperSwap uses less cheese than other homemade versions and amps up the nutrition by adding creamy pureed cauliflower. You could use an equal amount of pureed butternut squash instead of the cauliflower, too. **MAKES 6 SERVINGS**

MAC AND CHEESE

8 ounces uncooked quinoa elbow noodles or brown rice elbow noodles
½ head cauliflower, chopped into florets (about 3 cups)
½ cup unsweetened plant milk, such as soy or almond milk
8 ounces shredded 2% sharp cheddar cheese
½ teaspoon sea salt

SIDES

2 pounds green beans (about 6 cups), steamed and sprinkled with sea salt
BBQ Tofu (recipe follows)

1 PREP THE PASTA: Cook the pasta according to the package directions.

2 MAKE THE CHEESE SAUCE: Meanwhile, steam the cauliflower until tender in a microwave-safe steamer (my preferred method) for 6 to 8 minutes, or in a stovetop steamer basket set in a saucepan with 1 inch of simmering water for 8 to 10 minutes. With an immersion blender, puree the cauliflower and milk in a large bowl until creamy. Stir in the cheese and salt until the sauce is smooth.

3 COMBINE: Drain the pasta and return it to the pot. Add the sauce and gently stir until the pasta is coated.

4 SERVE: Plate the mac and cheese with the green beans and BBQ tofu alongside. Portion any extra individual servings and freeze them in individual airtight containers for up to 3 months, for a SuperSwap of boxed frozen meals.

NUTRITION (1 SERVING; INCLUDING SIDES): 370 calories, 13g total fat, 47g carbs, 7g fiber, 22g protein

---

BBQ TOFU

MAKES 6 SERVINGS

One 14-ounce package organic extra-firm (not silken) tofu
4 tablespoons C.R.A.P.-free BBQ sauce (or use the Beet BBQ Sauce on page 222)

1 PRESS THE EXCESS WATER OUT OF THE TOFU: Set the tofu block on several paper towels and top it with several more, then set a stack of heavy salad plates on top. Press the tofu for 10 to 15 minutes, then cut the block into 6 pieces, each about ¾ inch thick. Cut each piece diagonally into 2 triangles.

2 COOK THE TOFU: In a medium bowl, toss the tofu with 2 tablespoons of the BBQ sauce. Set on a pan and broil for 4 minutes on each side, until warm and slightly golden. Toss the hot tofu with the remaining 2 tablespoons BBQ sauce.

OH YEAH, ONE MORE THING . . .

C.R.A.P.-free BBQ sauce: When choosing store-bought BBQ sauce, look for brands with tomatoes as the first ingredient and no high-fructose corn syrup.

FISH TACOS WITH CRUNCHY CABBAGE SLAW

I go loco for tacos, especially fish tacos. The fish gets its flavor from chili powder instead of fried batter. The slaw topping is made mainly with cabbage—a cancer-fighting superfood that works hard to keep cells healthy. **MAKES 2 SERVINGS**

8 ounces white fish fillets, such as catfish or tilapia
1 tablespoon chili powder

SLAW
½ head cabbage, shredded (about 4 cups)
½ cup thinly sliced red onion
½ cup chopped fresh cilantro
1 jalapeño, seeded and diced (about 2 tablespoons)
Juice of 1 lime (about 2 tablespoons)
½ teaspoon sea salt

6 organic sprouted corn tortillas, warmed
½ avocado, sliced

1 BROIL THE FISH: Heat the broiler. Put the fish on a parchment paper–lined baking sheet and sprinkle with the chili powder. Broil about 4 inches away from heat for about 10 minutes. The general rule of thumb is to cook fish for 8 minutes per inch of thickness. The fish is done when it's opaque and registers 145°F on an instant-read thermometer in the thickest part. Break or cut the fish into bite-size pieces.

2 MAKE THE SLAW: Toss together the cabbage, onion, cilantro, jalapeño, lime, and salt.

3 ASSEMBLE: Serve the fish in warm tortillas, topped with avocado and slaw. Enjoy any slaw that won't fit on the tacos as a side salad.

NUTRITION (1 SERVING): 410 calories, 10g total fat, 54g carbs, 14g fiber, 31g protein

OH YEAH, ONE MORE THING . . .

V+ Swap: Use 1½ cups cooked black beans (one 15-ounce can) instead of the fish.

Warm tortillas: Warm the tortillas directly on an electric or gas burner over low heat. Use tongs to flip the tortillas from one side to the other. They get toasty and brown when you warm them this way, but they can easily burn— so watch them!

Time saver: Use preshredded coleslaw mix instead of cutting your own cabbage.

Special slaw: This slaw is one of my go-to side salads. It's great with grilled foods such as burgers, steak, and hot sauce chicken!

(V+)

BEET BURGERS AND
15-MINUTE PICKLES

I love burgers, and beets make these energizing. The water content of the cucumbers and the magic powers of vinegar keep you feeling full longer. **MAKES 2 SERVINGS, WITH 2 EXTRA BEET BURGERS**

BEET BURGERS

1 tablespoon ground flaxseed
1 tablespoon warm water
½ cup rolled oats
One 15-ounce can black beans, drained and rinsed (1½ cups)
1 medium beet, peeled and grated (about 1 cup)
½ red onion, chopped (about ½ cup)
1 tablespoon chili powder
½ teaspoon sea salt
1½ teaspoons avocado oil

15-MINUTE PICKLES

1 English cucumber, unpeeled, thinly sliced (about 2 cups)
½ cup boiling water
½ cup apple cider vinegar
2 tablespoons coconut sugar
¼ teaspoon sea salt

2 sprouted whole-grain vegan English muffins, toasted
4 romaine or large Bibb lettuce leaves

1 MAKE THE BURGERS: In a small bowl, mix the flaxseed and water and let it sit for about 5 minutes until thick. In a food processor, pulse the oats until they have a flourlike texture. Pulse in the flaxseed mixture, beans, beets, onion, chili powder, and salt. Leave it chunky, not totally smooth. Form the mixture into 6 patties and freeze them for 15 minutes to firm up.

2 GRILL THE BURGERS: Heat a grill to medium or heat a grill pan over medium-high heat. Brush 4 of the burgers with avocado oil and grill them for about 4 minutes on each side. Pack the remaining 2 burgers in an airtight container separated by a piece of parchment paper and freeze for up to 3 months.

3 MAKE THE PICKLES: In a lidded glass jar (such as a Mason jar), combine the cucumber, boiling water, vinegar, sugar, and salt. Put the lid on and let the pickles sit for 15 minutes in the fridge, shaking the jar occasionally.

4 ASSEMBLE: Top each English muffin half with lettuce and a burger. Serve open-faced, with pickles on the side. Store any leftover pickles in the fridge for up to 1 week.

NUTRITION (1 SERVING): 380 calories, 6g total fat, 68g carbs, 19g fiber, 19g protein

OH YEAH, ONE MORE THING . . .

GF Swap: If you follow a gluten-free diet, use gluten-free oats and English muffins.

Better beans: Beans soaked and cooked from scratch are easier to digest and have more absorbable protein and minerals. Learn how to cook your own beans on page 241.

Optional topping: Add Cashew Mayo (page 224) to your burger.

KALE BURGERS AND VEGGIE DIPPERS

This vegan veggie burger is basically just kale and white beans. It's unlike many boxed veggie burgers that barely have any vegetables and are mostly protein isolates, grains, and cheese. Any time you are looking for a quick side for burgers or sandwiches, serve veggie dippers—the SuperSwap name for cut-up vegetables and your fave C.R.A.P.-free salad dressing. **MAKES 2 SERVINGS, WITH 2 EXTRA BURGERS**

2 Kale Burgers (recipe follows)
2 sprouted whole-grain vegan English muffins, toasted
½ avocado, sliced
I tomato, sliced
I cup cut veggies, such as broccoli, celery, and carrot sticks
2 tablespoons of your favorite salad dressing (100 calories)

Set 1 burger on the bottom half of each English muffin. Top each with half the avocado and tomato slices, and the top of the English muffin. Serve the veggie dippers and dressing on the side.

NUTRITION (I SERVING): 400 calories, 15g total fat, 54g carbs, 13g fiber, 16g protein

KALE BURGERS

MAKES 4 BURGERS

I tablespoon extra-virgin olive oil, plus a little for brushing
¼ teaspoon crushed red pepper flakes
¼ teaspoon sea salt
I bunch kale, stemmed, leaves finely chopped (about 8 cups)
2 garlic cloves, minced (about I teaspoon)
One 15-ounce can white beans, drained and rinsed (1½ cups)
¼ cup rolled oats

I MAKE THE BURGERS: In a 12-inch skillet, heat the oil, crushed red pepper, and salt over medium heat for 1 minute. Add the kale and garlic and cook for about 7 minutes, until the kale has totally wilted. Transfer the kale to a food processor or blender, add the beans and oats, and pulse until well combined. Form the mixture into 4 patties and freeze for 10 minutes to firm up.

2 GRILL THE BURGERS: Heat a grill to medium or heat a grill pan over medium-high heat. Brush the patties with oil and grill or broil for 4 minutes on each side, until golden.

3 STORE: Freeze any extra burgers in an airtight container, separated by pieces of parchment paper, for up to 3 months; reheat in a pan or on the grill for about 5 minutes on each side.

OH YEAH, ONE MORE THING . . .

GF Swap: Use gluten-free oats and English muffins.

Hand-mash: You can make the burgers by hand: Cut the kale leaves into fine pieces and cook as directed. Mash the cooked kale, beans, and oats together using a potato masher.

(V)

SPROUTED PIZZA

This crust is better for you than typical versions, since the sprouted grains are easier to digest and have more absorbable proteins and minerals. I used to be intimidated by making my own crust, but this recipe is simple, pinky swear! **MAKES TWO 12-INCH PIZZAS (8 SERVINGS)**

DOUGH
3 cups organic sprouted whole wheat flour
One ¼-ounce packet instant yeast (2¼ teaspoons)
2 tablespoons honey
2 teaspoons sea salt
1½ cups warm water
4 tablespoons extra-virgin olive oil

TOPPINGS (PER EACH PIZZA)
¾ cup shredded cheese of your choice
1½ cups thinly sliced raw veggies of your choice, such as fennel, spinach, broccoli, onions, zucchini, bell peppers, or mushrooms

1 MAKE THE DOUGH: In a food processor—or even by hand, if you prefer—mix the flour, yeast, honey, salt, and warm water (it should be slightly warmer than your body temp; if the water is too hot, the yeast will die) for about 5 minutes.

2 LET THE DOUGH RISE: Split the dough in half and shape each half into a ball. Pour 1 tablespoon of the oil into the bottom of each of two bowls. Place 1 dough ball in each bowl. Place a clean kitchen towel over the bowls and let the dough sit for 30 minutes in a warm spot. While you are waiting, get your toppings ready. After 30 minutes, you can use the dough immediately or wrap it in plastic wrap, place it in a zip-top bag, and freeze it for up to 3 months. Leave it in the fridge overnight to thaw before using.

3 BAKE THE CRUST: Preheat the oven to 425°F. On a sheet of parchment paper, press 1 dough ball into a 12-inch circle. Use a gentle touch here—if you overwork the dough, you'll deflate the air the yeast created and you'll have a flat crust. Repeat with the second ball of dough on a separate piece of parchment paper.

4 TOP, BAKE, AND SLICE THE PIZZA: Top the pizzas as you like. One at a time, slide the pizza (including the parchment paper) into the oven. I use a cutting board to make it easy to slide the parchment on and off the oven racks. Bake for about 18 minutes, until the crust is crisp and golden. Slice each pizza into 8 pieces.

NUTRITION (2 SLICES WITH TOPPINGS): 380 calories, 15g total fat, 50g carbs, 7g fiber, 14g protein

OH YEAH, ONE MORE THING . . .

V+ Swap: Use pure maple syrup instead of honey and ¼ cup finely chopped walnuts instead of cheese.

Yeast: All these will work for this dough: **instant yeast = quick yeast = fast-rising yeast = rapid-rise active dry yeast = quick-rise active dry yeast = fast-rising active dry yeast = bread machine yeast.**

Pizza PRONTO: Hey! If you don't want to make your own crust, check out the Quick Kale Pizza on page 106 or buy premade sprouted whole-grain pizza dough at the health food store.

CASHEW ALFREDO

Classic Alfredo contains butter, heavy cream, and cheese. SuperSwap to a creamy sauce made from raw cashews and packed with minerals, protein, and healthy fat. **MAKES 2 SERVINGS**

CASHEW ALFREDO SAUCE

¼ cup raw cashews

6 tablespoons almost-boiling water

2 teaspoons fresh lemon juice

I garlic clove, minced (about ½ teaspoon)

2 tablespoons nutritional yeast

¼ teaspoon sea salt

¼ teaspoon freshly ground black pepper

PASTA AND VEGGIES

4 ounces uncooked quinoa pasta or other whole-grain pasta (linguine shape works best)

2 teaspoons extra-virgin olive oil

I garlic clove, minced (about ½ teaspoon)

¼ teaspoon crushed red pepper flakes

I bunch asparagus, cut into I-inch pieces (about 2 cups)

½ cup frozen green peas

2 tablespoons chopped fresh chives

1 MAKE THE SAUCE: In a food processor, combine the cashews, water, lemon juice, garlic, nutritional yeast, salt, and black pepper and puree until smooth.

2 MAKE THE PASTA AND VEGGIES: Cook the pasta according to the package directions. In a medium skillet, heat the oil over medium heat. Add the garlic and crushed red pepper and cook for 30 seconds. Add the asparagus and peas and cook for about 8 minutes, until the peas are hot and the asparagus is tender.

3 COMBINE: Drain the pasta and return it to the pot. Add the Alfredo sauce and the veggies and toss to coat.

4 SERVE: Divide between two plates and top with the chives.

NUTRITION (I SERVING): 4IO calories, I2g total fat, 64g carbs, IIg fiber, I6g protein

OH YEAH, ONE MORE THING . . .

Get your learn on: Read more about nutritional yeast on page 235. If you don't want to use nutritional yeast, you can use 2 tablespoons shredded Parmesan cheese instead.

Flavorize: I love this with asparagus and peas, but you can change up the veggies. Try broccoli, zucchini, or red peppers.

BROWNIE BITES

Brownie taste without flour, sugar, or butter: a clear SuperSwap. Put them in a cute box and use as a hostess or holiday gift—much better than a box of store-bought candy. **MAKES 4 SERVINGS**

6 Medjool dates, pitted
3 tablespoons almost-boiling water
2 tablespoons unsweetened cocoa powder (avoid Dutched versions), plus extra for rolling
¼ cup raw walnuts
I tablespoon chia seeds
Sea salt

1 MAKE THE BROWNIE DOUGH: In a food processor, puree the dates and water until a sticky paste forms and balls up on the blade. Add the cocoa powder, walnuts, and chia seeds and pulse until a solid dough forms.

2 MAKE THE BALLS AND SET: With a 1-tablespoon cookie scoop, form the dough into 8 round balls, setting them on a plate as you work. Refrigerate for 30 to 60 minutes to set. Roll each ball in cocoa powder to coat lightly and sprinkle with salt. Serve or refrigerate in an airtight container for up to 7 days.

NUTRITION (I SERVING): 150 calories, 6g total fat, 27g carbs, 5g fiber, 3g protein

OH YEAH, ONE MORE THING . . .

Hot tip: Add spice to the mix—try cayenne, ground ginger, or ground cinnamon.

(V+) (GF)

CASHEW WHIP AND BERRIES

This SuperSwap whipped cream has more healthy fat and protein than the classic dessert topping—and berries always provide a boost of disease-fighting antioxidants. **MAKES 2 SERVINGS**

½ cup raw cashews
6 tablespoons almost-boiling water
I teaspoon pure maple syrup
¼ teaspoon ground vanilla beans (optional, but recommended!)
I cup berries, such as strawberries, raspberries, or blackberries

In a food processor, blend the cashews, water, maple syrup, and vanilla (if using). Serve with the berries.

NUTRITION (I SERVING): 190 calories, 12g total fat, 16g carbs, 3g fiber, 6g protein

OH YEAH, ONE MORE THING . . .

More fun: Spoon a dollop of cashew whip on a cup of coffee or tea or stir it into oatmeal for breakfast.

Get your learn on: Read more about ground vanilla beans on page 236.

DARK CHOCOLATE CHERRY MILK SHAKE

What?! A milk shake with no added sugar? Yes! A typical 12-ounce chocolate milk shake is loaded with C.R.A.P. and has 560 empty calories and about 6 tablespoons (70+ grams) of added sugar. Not this one! **MAKES I SERVING**

I cup unsweetened plant milk, such as almond or hemp milk
I cup frozen unsweetened tart red cherries
2 tablespoons unsweetened cocoa powder (avoid Dutched versions)

In a blender, puree the milk, cherries, and cocoa powder until smooth.

NUTRITION (I SERVING): 140 calories, 6g total fat, 24g carbs, 7g fiber, 4g protein

OH YEAH, ONE MORE THING . . .

Choose tart: Look for the word "tart" on the label for tart cherries. Also make sure there's no added sugar in the ingredients. Tart cherries have been shown to help muscle and joint soreness and promote heart health.

GREEN SMOOTHIE ICE POPS

Just about any smoothie can be made into a great ice pop! These are so good for you, you'll want to enjoy them two at a time! **MAKES 8 ICE POPS**

2 cups unsweetened plant milk, such as almond or hemp milk
2 tablespoons natural almond butter
2 ripe bananas
2 cups chopped kale or baby spinach leaves

In a blender, puree the milk, almond butter, bananas, and kale or spinach until smooth. Pour into ice pop molds and freeze for at least 4 to 5 hours.

NUTRITION (2 ICE POPS): 130 calories, 6g total fat, 17g carbs, 3g fiber, 3g protein

OH YEAH, ONE MORE THING . . .

You can switch up the flavors if you like:

- **Energy Pops:** For an energy boost, add I teaspoon matcha green tea powder to the recipe before freezing.

- **Carrot-Mango Pops:** Blend 2 cups unsweetened plant milk, such as almond or hemp milk; 2 tablespoons natural almond butter; 2 cups frozen unsweetened mango chunks; I cup shredded carrots; and I teaspoon ground cinnamon.

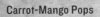
Carrot-Mango Pops

MINI YOGURT CHEESECAKE

No white sugar, white flour, or butter in this SuperSwap crust. And the cheesecake filling? Well, it's mostly belly-soothing, protein-rich yogurt. **MAKES 4 SERVINGS**

CRUST

3 tablespoons ground flaxseed

1 tablespoon coconut sugar

¼ teaspoon ground cinnamon

1 teaspoon coconut oil, melted

FILLING

½ cup plain 2% Greek yogurt

1 organic egg, lightly beaten

1 tablespoon coconut sugar

4 pitted fresh or unsweetened frozen cherries (optional)

1 PREHEAT THE OVEN AND MAKE THE CRUST: Preheat the oven to 325°F. In a small bowl, stir together the flaxseed, coconut sugar, and cinnamon. Coat four cups of a muffin tin with the coconut oil. Sprinkle 1 heaping tablespoon of the flaxseed mixture evenly into each cup.

2 STIR THE BATTER, POUR, AND BAKE: In a medium bowl, stir together the yogurt, egg, and coconut sugar until smooth. Slowly pour 2 heaping tablespoons on top of the flaxseed mixture in each cup. Bake for about 35 minutes, until the filling is nearly set. Remove from the oven and let cool for 10 minutes. Refrigerate for at least 30 minutes to set completely. Run a butter knife around each cheesecake to pop it out of the tin. Top each with a cherry, if desired.

NUTRITION (1 SERVING): 90 calories, 4.5g total fat, 9g carbs, 2g fiber, 5g protein

OH YEAH, ONE MORE THING . . .

Get your learn on: Read about baking flaxseeds on page 239.

More: Of course you can make more than 4 cheesecakes at a time, but I like to make desserts in small batches so I'm not tempted to overdo it.

NICE CREAM

This is a perfect use for those extra bananas that are almost too ripe. The soft-serve treat is loaded with potassium, vitamin C, fiber, and even biotin for healthy hair, skin, and nails. I like topping it with nuts or seeds to add a little plant protein and fat. **MAKES 2 SERVINGS**

2 ripe bananas, sliced and frozen

2 tablespoons unsweetened plant milk, such as almond or hemp milk

2 tablespoons chopped walnuts or your favorite nut or seed

1 BLEND: In a food processor (my choice) or blender, puree the bananas and milk until smooth. Don't use more than a splash of milk or your nice cream will be soupy. You'll have to work with this a bit to get it smooth by blending, scraping, blending, stirring, and blending. With a little effort, this will have a creamy soft-serve texture.

2 TOP, EAT, AND STORE: Scrape the nice cream into two bowls and sprinkle the walnuts on top. Eat immediately or freeze in an airtight container for up to 1 month—let it thaw for a few minutes before eating.

NUTRITION (½ CUP; 1 SERVING): 160 calories, 5g total fat, 28g carbs, 4g fiber, 2g protein

OH YEAH, ONE MORE THING . . .

Freezing tip: This works best when the bananas aren't all stuck together. I cut the bananas, spread them out evenly on a parchment paper–lined baking sheet, and freeze them. Once they're frozen, I toss them into a zip-top bag for longer storage.

Flavorize: Experiment with different flavors by blending the cream with unsweetened cocoa powder, ground cinnamon, freshly grated nutmeg, shredded unsweetened coconut, natural peanut butter, strawberries, etc. One of my favorites is adding ground vanilla beans. Check out page 236 for more info on this awesome addition to your spice rack.

CHEEZY POPCORN

Popcorn makes a smart snack when you get a carb craving—it's a nutritious whole grain, and you get 3 heaping cups of the air-popped version for a mere 90 calories. Many brands of microwave popcorn, however, use C.R.A.P. like partially hydrogenated oil, artificial flavors, colors, and preservatives. Some brands also use perfluorooctanoic acid (PFOA) in their bag liner, which is a compound that doesn't do a body good. Smart SuperSwappers stick with air-popped!

MAKES 2 SERVINGS

1 tablespoon coconut oil or extra-virgin olive oil
1 tablespoon apple cider vinegar
¼ cup organic popcorn kernels
2 tablespoons nutritional yeast
¼ teaspoon sea salt

Put the oil and vinegar into a large bowl. Put the popcorn kernels into an air-popper and pop them directly into the bowl. While the popcorn pops, continually toss it to coat. When all the kernels have popped, immediately sprinkle the popcorn with the nutritional yeast and salt. Toss until the toppings are evenly distributed.

NUTRITION (1 SERVING): 180 calories, 8g total fat, 21g carbs, 5g fiber, 7g protein

OH YEAH, ONE MORE THING . . .

Get your learn on: Read more about apple cider vinegar on page 236 and nutritional yeast on page 235.

Flavorize: Try popcorn tossed with honey and sea salt or drizzle it with warm natural peanut butter or almond butter. Put air-popped popcorn on a parchment paper–lined baking sheet and drizzle away. Serve it on the baking sheet for a great party presentation.

(V) (GF)

SEAWEED SNACK STRIPS

This is a plant-based SuperSwap for anyone who likes jerky. The umami (savory) flavor naturally occurs in seaweed, and sesame seeds provide a small portion of plant protein . . . along with fiber and healthy fat. **MAKES 2 SERVINGS**

2 sheets toasted nori seaweed
I tablespoon honey
I½ teaspoons dark sesame oil
Pinch of cayenne
4 teaspoons sesame seeds
⅛ teaspoon sea salt

1 PREHEAT THE OVEN AND SEASON THE NORI: Preheat the oven to 400°F. Line a baking sheet with parchment paper and lay the nori on the baking sheet. Mix together the honey, sesame oil, and cayenne until smooth. With a pastry brush, spread the honey mixture evenly over the nori sheets. Sprinkle the nori with the sesame seeds and salt.

2 BAKE AND CUT: Bake the nori for 8 minutes, until the honey is bubbling and the seaweed is crisp. Let cool for 3 minutes. With kitchen shears, cut each sheet of nori into 6 strips and then cut each strip in half widthwise for a total of 24 small strips.

NUTRITION (I SERVING): IIO calories, 6g total fat, IIg carbs, Ig fiber, 2g protein

OH YEAH, ONE MORE THING . . .

V+ Swap: Use pure maple syrup instead of honey.

Copper: Sesame seeds contain copper, a mineral that supports healthy blood vessels (bye-bye, dark circles under eyes) and collagen production (hello, tight, youthful skin).

(V) (GF)

SPINACH DIP

Classic spinach dip blends sour cream, mayo, and a spice mix full of C.R.A.P. such as corn syrup, partially hydrogenated oil, MSG, and artificial caramel color. Instead, try a version that's simple and natural. **MAKES 4 SERVINGS**

I tablespoon extra-virgin olive oil
6 cups (6 ounces) baby spinach leaves, finely chopped
I garlic clove, minced (about ½ teaspoon)
¼ teaspoon crushed red pepper flakes
¼ teaspoon sea salt
¼ teaspoon freshly ground black pepper
I cup plain 2% Greek yogurt
¼ cup grated Parmesan cheese
Cut-up veggies and/or Superseed Crackers (page 207), for serving

In a 10-inch skillet, heat the oil over medium heat. Add the spinach, garlic, crushed red pepper, salt, and black pepper and cook for 3 minutes. Put the yogurt in a medium bowl and stir in the spinach mixture and the cheese. Chill in the fridge for at least 15 minutes before serving. Serve with veggies or a few crackers, or both. Store any leftovers in an airtight container in the refrigerator for up to 3 days.

NUTRITION (I SERVING, DIP ONLY): 110 calories, 6g total fat, 6g carbs, 2g fiber, 8g protein

OH YEAH, ONE MORE THING...

Add-ons: Add a few chopped canned artichokes or water chestnuts, or both, to the mix.

Sandwich: This dip also makes a great veggie sandwich spread to use in place of hummus.

Kale lovers: Swap out the spinach for the same amount of kale.

FALL/WINTER
RECEPIES

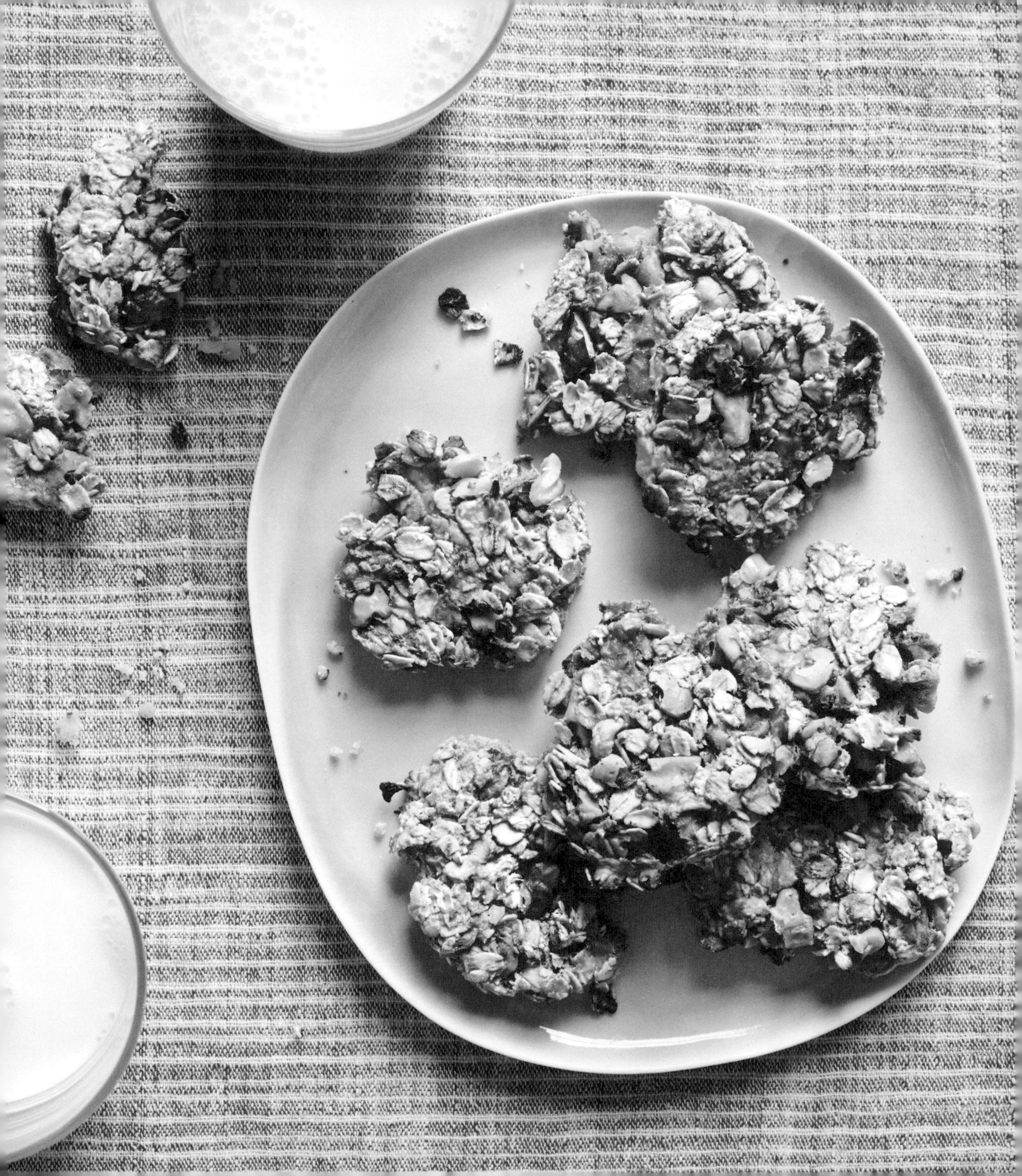

BANANA BREAD COOKIES

Packaged breakfast cookies and granola bars contain C.R.A.P. like high-fructose corn syrup, partially hydrogenated oils, preservatives, and artificial flavors. This simple 4-ingredient SuperSwap takes even less energy to make than it does to toss junk into your shopping cart. **MAKES 2 SERVINGS**

1½ teaspoons coconut oil
2 bananas
I cup rolled oats
¼ cup chopped walnuts

I PREHEAT THE OVEN AND MAKE THE BATTER: Preheat the oven to 375°F. Coat a baking sheet with the coconut oil. In a medium bowl, mash the bananas thoroughly. Stir in the oats and walnuts.

2 FORM INTO COOKIES, BAKE, AND PRESS: Using a scoop, form the banana mixture into 16 cookies and put them on the prepared baking sheet. Bake for 18 to 20 minutes, until firm. Immediately after removing the cookies from the oven, press them flat with the bottom of a small drinking glass.

3 STORE: Let the cookies cool on wire racks and store them in an airtight container for up to 5 days or freeze them for up to 3 months.

NUTRITION (I SERVING): 390 calories, I6g total fat, 56g carbs, 8g fiber, IIg protein **NUTRITION (I COOKIE):** 5O calories, 2g total fat, 7g carbs, Ig fiber, Ig protein

OH YEAH, ONE MORE THING . . .

GF Swap: Use gluten-free oats.

Snack time: The serving size of 8 cookies is for breakfast, but 3 cookies is the right number for a snack.

Cacao nibs: Add I tablespoon cacao nibs to this recipe for a bittersweet chocolate crunch. Read more about cacao nibs on page 238.

CINNAMON OATMEAL MUFFINS

Even healthful-sounding muffins like blueberry, bran, or cinnamon usually come packed with empty calories from refined flour and sugar. When a muffin craving strikes, make yourself baked oatmeal in the shape of muffins instead. Magical oats contain a special fiber called beta-glucan that may improve immune function and lower cholesterol. Not to mention, oats fill you up so you have better appetite control all day.

MAKES 5 SERVINGS (2 MUFFINS EACH)

TOPPING

3 tablespoons coconut oil, melted
½ cup finely chopped pecans
¼ cup coconut sugar
1 tablespoon ground cinnamon
⅛ teaspoon sea salt

MUFFINS

2 cups rolled oats
1 cup unsweetened plant milk, such as almond or hemp milk
2 organic eggs, beaten
2 tablespoons ground flaxseed
1 tablespoon ground cinnamon
1 teaspoon baking powder
1 teaspoon pure vanilla extract, or ½ teaspoon ground vanilla beans
¼ teaspoon sea salt

1 **PREP:** Preheat the oven to 350°F. Line ten cups of a muffin tin with paper liners.

2 **MAKE THE TOPPING:** In a medium bowl, stir together the coconut oil, pecans, coconut sugar, cinnamon, and salt. Set aside.

3 **MAKE THE MUFFINS:** In a medium bowl, stir together the oats, milk, eggs, flaxseed, cinnamon, baking powder, vanilla, and salt. Divide the mixture among the prepared muffin cups. Top each muffin with 1 tablespoon of the topping. Bake for about 30 minutes, until set. Refrigerate any uneaten muffins in an airtight container for up to 5 days.

NUTRITION (2 MUFFINS): 370 calories, 21g total fat, 36g carbs, 6g fiber, 10g protein

OH YEAH, ONE MORE THING . . .

GF Swap: Use gluten-free oats.

Cinnamon roll-ish: These baked muffins taste great with a dollop of Cashew Whip (page 159).

Slow-cooker oats: Learn how to make these on page 234.

BURRITO OMELET CUPS

Frozen packaged egg sandwiches may not be high in calories, but they're loaded with refined white flour and preservatives, and are short on fresh veggies. These mini burritos can be prepped in advance and kept in the fridge or freezer for grab-and-go weekday breakfasts. For a meal, enjoy 4 mini omelets with 1 whole piece of fruit. **MAKES 3 SERVINGS**

3 sprouted organic corn tortillas

6 organic eggs, beaten

½ cup unsweetened plant milk, such as almond or hemp milk

½ tomato, finely chopped and blotted to remove excess liquid (about ½ cup)

½ red onion, finely chopped (about ½ cup)

¼ cup chopped fresh cilantro

I jalapeño, seeded and finely chopped (about 2 tablespoons)

¼ teaspoon sea salt

¼ teaspoon freshly ground black pepper

¾ cup shredded cheddar cheese

I PREHEAT THE OVEN AND LINE THE MUFFIN TIN: Preheat the oven to 350°F. Warm the tortillas in a dry pan over medium heat or in the microwave to make them more pliable. Cut each into 4 triangles and press them into the cups of a 12-cup muffin tin or two 6-cup muffin tins.

2 FILL THE MUFFIN TIN, BAKE, AND STORE: In a medium bowl, stir together the eggs, milk, tomato, onion, cilantro, jalapeño, salt, and pepper. Divide the mixture evenly among the tortilla-lined muffin cups. Sprinkle the cheese evenly on top. Bake for 30 minutes, until the egg is set and the cheese is golden. Store in an airtight container in the fridge for up to 5 days or freeze for up to 3 months.

NUTRITION (I SERVING): 390 calories, 20g total fat, 30g carbs, 6g fiber, 23g protein

OH YEAH, ONE MORE THING . . .

Sprouted tortillas: Sprouting grains helps activate enzymes in the plant that make minerals and protein more absorbable and the food easier to digest.

Spice is nice: The jalapeño in this recipe isn't as spicy as you may think. In fact, jalapeños are pretty low on the Scoville scale, a ranking of how hot and spicy peppers are. If you'd like less kick, swap the jalapeño for the same amount of poblano or bell peppers.

Flavorize: You don't have to make these mini omelets burrito style. Instead you can swap the tomato, onion, cilantro, and jalapeño for a heaping cup of other chopped veggies like broccoli, mushrooms, or spinach.

(V)

ZUCCHINI BREAD FRENCH TOAST

Most often, French toast is made from white bread—and frozen versions come with added C.R.A.P. like artificial dyes. Instead, make SuperSwap French toast that includes a dose of morning veggies. Cinnamon, vanilla, coconut oil, and coconut flakes make this French toast subtly sweet without added sugar. If you like it better with maple syrup, use it! **MAKES 2 SERVINGS**

3 organic eggs, beaten
½ cup unsweetened plant milk, such as almond or hemp milk
2 teaspoons ground cinnamon or pumpkin pie spice
1 teaspoon pure vanilla extract
1 zucchini, grated (about 1 cup)
4 slices sprouted whole-grain bread
2 teaspoons coconut oil
2 tablespoons chopped pecans
4 teaspoons unsweetened coconut flakes
4 teaspoons pure maple syrup (optional)

1 MAKE THE EGG MIXTURE: In a medium bowl, mix together the eggs, milk, cinnamon, and vanilla. Put the zucchini in a medium bowl.

2 ASSEMBLE: Dip each slice of bread in the egg mixture, pressing it so it soaks up the liquid. Press both sides of the bread into the zucchini, using your fingers to pat about ¼ cup onto each slice. Dip the bread back into the egg mixture just to get a little egg on the zucchini.

3 COOK: Brush a 12-inch skillet or a pancake griddle with coconut oil and heat over medium-high heat. Add the bread and cook for about 3 minutes on each side, until the egg is totally set and golden. Top the French toast with chopped pecans and coconut flakes. Serve with pure maple syrup, if desired.

NUTRITION (1 SERVING): 420 calories, 21g total fat, 38g carbs, 10g fiber, 20g protein

OH YEAH, ONE MORE THING . . .

V+ Swap: Swap out the 3 eggs and ½ cup plant milk for 3 tablespoons ground flaxseed, 1 tablespoon natural almond butter, and 1 cup plant milk. In a small bowl, stir together the flax, almond butter, and milk and let the mixture sit for 10 minutes to thicken. Continue with the recipe as written.

Make-ahead: Make this French toast and freeze it in individual airtight containers for up to 3 months. A healthy French toast breakfast is possible even on your busiest days—just heat and eat.

Flavorize: Swap the grated zucchini (zucchini bread style) for 1 cup unsweetened canned pumpkin (pumpkin pie style), grated apples (apple pie style), or grated carrots (carrot cake style).

BLENDER PANCAKES

Love that this recipe is no-fuss. Toss everything in the blender and go for it. Unlike classic pancakes, these have zero white flour or white sugar. Hemp seeds add a dose of plant protein and an awesome nutty flavor. Oh, and the berry syrup beats C.R.A.P. syrup any day. **MAKES 2 SERVINGS**

PANCAKES

½ cup unsweetened plant milk, such as almond or hemp milk
½ cup rolled oats
¼ cup hemp seeds
I organic egg
1½ teaspoons honey
I teaspoon baking powder
⅛ teaspoon sea salt
I tablespoon coconut oil

BERRY SYRUP

I cup fresh or unsweetened frozen berries, such as strawberries, raspberries, blackberries, or blueberries
I tablespoon honey

I MAKE THE PANCAKES: In a blender or food processor, combine the milk, oats, hemp seeds, egg, honey, baking powder, and salt and pulse for 1 minute, until smooth.

2 COOK THE PANCAKES: In a 12-inch skillet, heat the coconut oil over medium heat. Pour the batter into the skillet to form 6 small pancakes and cook for about 2 minutes. You'll know it's time to flip the pancakes when bubbles appear on the surface of the pancakes. Flip them and cook the other side for about 2 minutes more, or until golden.

3 MAKE THE BERRY SYRUP: Once the pancakes are done, in the same skillet, warm the berries and honey over low heat for 2 minutes, mashing the berries with a fork until semismooth. Serve on top of the pancakes.

NUTRITION (I SERVING): 390 calories, 19g total fat, 42g carbs, 4g fiber, 14g protein

OH YEAH, ONE MORE THING . . .

V+ Swap: Swap out the organic egg for a "flax egg." Learn how on page 239. Use pure maple syrup instead of honey.

GF Swap: Use gluten-free oats.

Chia jam: Instead of the berry syrup, try these pancakes topped with Chia Jam (page 137).

PUMPKIN SPICE SMOOTHIE

Typical pumpkin spice lattes use lots of C.R.A.P. such as sugar, artificial flavors and colors, and preservatives. This smoothie is sweetened naturally with prunes and has real pumpkin instead of artificially flavored syrups. **MAKES I SERVING**

1½ cups unsweetened vanilla plant milk, such as almond or hemp milk
½ cup canned pure pumpkin
¼ cup raw cashews
4 pitted prunes
I teaspoon pumpkin pie spice, plus extra for serving
½ cup ice cubes

In a blender, puree the milk, pumpkin, cashews, prunes, and pumpkin pie spice until smooth. Add the ice cubes and blend again until smooth. Top with a pinch of pumpkin pie spice.

NUTRITION (I SERVING): 400 calories, 21g total fat, 50g carbs, 9g fiber, 9g protein

OH YEAH, ONE MORE THING . . .

No added sugar: The prunes naturally sweeten the smoothie. (And don't worry—eating 4 prunes won't cause you to flee to the bathroom!) Prunes support healthy digestion and regularity as well as strong bones.

CASHEW RANCH BOWL

SuperSwap your sandwiches for bowls—they give you far more veggies than you can fit between 2 slices of bread. **MAKES I SERVING, WITH EXTRA DRESSING**

¾ cup cubed sweet potatoes (½-inch cubes)
½ teaspoon extra-virgin olive oil
½ cup canned chickpeas, drained and rinsed
I tablespoon C.R.A.P.-free BBQ sauce (or use the Beet BBQ Sauce on page 222)
3 cups chopped romaine lettuce
½ cup grape tomatoes, halved
3 tablespoons Cashew Ranch Dressing (recipe follows)

I BROIL AND TOSS: Preheat the broiler. Line a baking sheet with aluminum foil. In a medium bowl, toss the potato cubes with the oil and spread them over the lined baking sheet. Broil for about 15 minutes, flipping once halfway through the cooking time, until tender. At the midway point, toss the chickpeas with the BBQ sauce and add them to the baking sheet. Note: Keeping the potatoes small helps them cook more quickly.

2 ASSEMBLE: In a bowl, mix together the lettuce, tomatoes, potatoes, and chickpeas. Drizzle with the dressing. You can eat this warm or at room temperature.

NUTRITION (I SERVING): 420 calories, 16g total fat, 60g carbs, IIg fiber, 15g protein

---

CASHEW RANCH DRESSING

I'm obsessed with "whole food salad dressing," meaning those in which the fat comes from things like nuts, seeds, or similar ingredients rather than from oil (an extracted part of a whole food). **MAKES I CUP**

I cup raw cashews
¾ cup almost-boiling water
Juice of I lemon (about 3 tablespoons)
I garlic clove, minced (about ½ teaspoon)
I teaspoon sea salt
I teaspoon freshly ground black pepper
¼ teaspoon dried oregano
¼ teaspoon dried dill
2 tablespoons finely chopped fresh chives

In a food processor, puree the cashews, water, lemon juice, garlic, salt, pepper, oregano, and dill. Stir in the fresh chives. Store in a lidded airtight container in the refrigerator for up to 7 days.

NUTRITION (I TABLESPOON): 50 calories, 4g total fat, 3g carbs, 0g fiber, 2g protein

OH YEAH, ONE MORE THING . . .

Time savers: Instead of using raw cashews, put ½ cup jarred cashew butter, ¾ cup water, and the remaining ingredients in a lidded jar and shake. Adjust the water amount if necessary to get the right consistency. Or toss your salad with avocado cubes and red wine vinegar until the avocado breaks down a bit to make a creamy dressing. You can do this with feta cheese instead of avocado, too.

C.R.A.P.-free BBQ sauce: When choosing store-bought BBQ sauce, look for brands with tomatoes as the first ingredient and no high-fructose corn syrup.

CHICKPEA NOODLE SOUP

My husband is an amazing soup cook—this soup is inspired by his recipe. The SuperSwap is using chickpeas instead of chicken for hearty doses of plant protein and fiber. Serving the noodles separately allows you to control portions, while topping the soup with parsley offers a dose of blood-building vitamin K and immune-boosting vitamin C. **MAKES 6 SERVINGS (3 CUPS PER SERVING)**

8 ounces uncooked whole-grain quinoa noodles or brown rice noodles

6 teaspoons extra-virgin olive oil

I large onion, diced (about 1½ cups)

4 carrots, halved lengthwise and cut into thin half-moons (about 1½ cups)

4 celery stalks, diced (I heaping cup)

1½ tablespoons Italian seasoning (rosemary, thyme, oregano, basil, and sage)

½ teaspoon sea salt

I teaspoon freshly ground black pepper

I bunch kale, chopped (about 8 cups)

6 garlic cloves, minced (I tablespoon)

10 cups low-sodium vegetable broth

2 bay leaves

Two 15-ounce cans chickpeas, rinsed and drained

½ cup chopped fresh flat-leaf parsley

Shredded Parmesan cheese (optional)

I MAKE THE NOODLES: Bring a pot of water to a boil. Cut the noodles into 1- to 2-inch pieces and cook according to the package directions. Drain and then toss with 2 teaspoons of the oil to prevent sticking.

2 MAKE THE SOUP: In a large pot, heat the remaining 4 teaspoons olive oil over medium heat. Add the onion, carrots, celery, Italian seasoning, salt, and pepper. Cook for 7 minutes. Add the kale and garlic and cook for 5 minutes more. Add the broth and bay leaves and bring to a boil. Turn down the heat to maintain a simmer, add the chickpeas, cover, and cook for about 20 minutes.

3 SERVE: Remove the bay leaves and serve the soup over the noodles, topped with parsley and Parmesan, if desired. Freeze any uneaten soup in an airtight container for up to 3 months.

NUTRITION (I SERVING): 380 calories, 8g total fat, 68g carbs, 13g fiber, 13g protein

RAMEN JAR

Sure, packaged ramen seems like a convenient lunch option—but offers your body nothing but refined white noodles (sometimes even prefried), swimming in a broth made with seasoning full of preservatives, artificial flavors, and MSG. Instead, make this SuperSwap of whole-grain noodles and veggies ahead of time, and when you're ready to eat, just add hot water. **MAKES 2 SERVINGS**

FLAVOR BASE

1½ tablespoons tahini (sesame seed paste)
1½ tablespoons organic white miso paste (shiro miso)
Juice of ½ lime (about 1 tablespoon)
1½ teaspoons organic reduced-sodium gluten-free soy sauce
1 teaspoon grated fresh ginger
¼ teaspoon crushed red pepper flakes

NOODLES AND VEGGIES

4 ounces uncooked brown rice thin spaghetti noodles
2 teaspoons dark sesame oil
1 cup halved and thinly sliced mushrooms
1 cup baby spinach leaves
¼ cup frozen organic shelled edamame, thawed
2 green onions, chopped
2 cups almost-boiling water

1 MAKE THE FLAVOR BASE: In a small bowl, stir together the tahini, miso, lime, soy sauce, ginger, and crushed red pepper. Divide the mixture evenly between two 4-cup lidded glass jars (such as Mason jars).

2 MAKE THE NOODLES AND VEGGIES: Cook the noodles according to the package directions (don't overcook them), drain, and transfer to a medium bowl. Toss with the sesame oil to coat. Divide the cooked noodles, mushrooms, spinach, edamame, and green onions between the jars. Store in the fridge for up to 4 days.

3 ADD HOT WATER AND SERVE: When ready to eat, add 1 cup of the water to each container. Cover and let the noodles sit for 3 minutes, shaking the jar a couple of times. Stir well before eating.

NUTRITION (1 SERVING): 400 calories, 12g total fat, 59g carbs, 5g fiber, 12g protein

OH YEAH, ONE MORE THING...

Miso: Miso is a mixture of fermented soybeans, salt, and a grain such as rice or barley. The fermentation process produces good bacteria to aid immunity and digestion. Find miso in the refrigerated section of the grocery store and choose organic unpasteurized versions to get the most beneficial bacteria. Don't add boiling water to miso; it will kill the good bacteria. If you follow a strict gluten-free diet, read labels to avoid versions of miso with barley. An open container of miso can last over a year in the fridge.

BRUSSELS SPROUT PAD THAI

When you SuperSwap pad thai noodles for Brussels sprouts, you feed your body vegetable nutrients such as fiber and immune-boosting vitamin C—all for a third of the calories. **MAKES 2 SERVINGS**

3 teaspoons dark sesame oil
2 organic eggs, beaten
1 tablespoon natural peanut butter
1 tablespoon organic reduced-sodium gluten-free soy sauce
2 garlic cloves, minced (about 1 teaspoon)
¼ teaspoon crushed red pepper flakes
1 pound Brussels sprouts, very thinly sliced (about 5 cups)
2 carrots, cut into very thin matchsticks (about 1 cup)
2 green onions, thinly sliced (about ½ cup)
¼ cup chopped fresh cilantro
2 tablespoons chopped raw peanuts
Juice of 1 lime (about 2 tablespoons)

1 COOK THE EGG: In a 12-inch skillet, heat 1 teaspoon of the sesame oil over medium heat, tilting the pan so it thinly coats the whole skillet. Add the eggs and tilt pan to make a thin egg pancake that covers the bottom of the skillet. Cook for 1 to 2 minutes, until the eggs are set. Scrape the egg pancake onto a cutting board and cut it into thin strips. Set aside.

2 QUICKLY COOK THE VEGGIES: In the same skillet, heat the remaining 2 teaspoons sesame oil over medium-high heat. Add the peanut butter, soy sauce, garlic, crushed red pepper, Brussels sprouts, and carrots and cook for about 3 minutes, without much stirring (too much stirring makes the veggies soggy). Don't overcook these; they should be crisp-tender.

3 ASSEMBLE: Top the veggies with egg strips, green onions, cilantro, peanuts, and a squeeze of lime.

NUTRITION (1 SERVING): 390 calories, 22g total fat, 30g carbs, 12g fiber, 18g protein

OH YEAH, ONE MORE THING . . .

V+ Swap: Swap out the 2 eggs for ½ cup crumbled organic firm tofu.

Cutting Brussels sprouts: Cut each sprout in half from top to stem. Place the halves cut side down on the cutting board and slice the sprouts crosswise into paper-thin slices.

Time saver: Buy presliced Brussels sprouts or a bag of shredded cabbage or coleslaw.

LENTIL TACOS

Lentils make a great SuperSwap for ground beef. Brown lentils really look like ground beef and provide a healthy dose of plant protein and fiber.

MAKES 2 SERVINGS

2 teaspoons extra-virgin olive oil

2 tablespoons taco seasoning

1 green bell pepper, seeded and finely chopped (about 1 cup)

1 tomato, finely chopped (about 1 cup)

½ red onion, finely chopped (about ½ cup)

1 jalapeño, seeded and diced (about 2 tablespoons)

2 garlic cloves, minced (about 1 teaspoon)

1 cup cooked lentils

6 sprouted organic corn tortillas, warmed

½ avocado, cubed

½ cup thinly sliced radish

½ cup chopped fresh cilantro

2 lime wedges

1 MAKE THE LENTIL "GROUND BEEF": In a 12-inch skillet, heat the oil over medium heat. Add the taco seasoning, bell pepper, tomato, onion, jalapeño, and garlic and cook for 5 minutes. Add the lentils and cook for 5 minutes more, or until the lentils are warm.

2 ASSEMBLE THE TACOS: Put the lentil mix into the warm tortillas and top with the avocado, radish, cilantro, and lime juice.

NUTRITION (1 SERVING): 430 calories, 13g total fat, 70g carbs, 18g fiber, 16g protein

OH YEAH, ONE MORE THING...

Time saver: Use ready-to-eat steamed lentils, found in the produce section. Freeze what you don't use in an airtight container for up to 3 months.

Taco seasoning: Look for brands that contain only spices, without C.R.A.P. like dextrose, hydrolyzed soy protein, caramel color, potato starch, whey, or MSG. You can blend your own by mixing chili powder, cumin, smoked paprika, sea salt, and pepper.

How to warm tortillas: Warm the corn tortillas directly on an electric or gas burner over low heat. Use tongs to flip the tortillas from one side to the other. They get toasty and brown when you warm them this way, but they can easily burn—so watch them!

TORTILLA SOUP

Tortilla soup is really a magic food. The water content makes it more filling than other Mexican-inspired meals. What's the key to making any soup seem decadent? It's all in the toppings, baby! This tortilla soup is blended smooth, but what goes on top makes it a substantial meal. *¡Olé!* **MAKES 4 SERVINGS**

TORTILLA STRIPS

4 sprouted organic corn tortillas
I tablespoon extra-virgin olive oil

SOUP

2 tablespoons extra-virgin olive oil
I onion, chopped (about I cup)
4 garlic cloves, minced (about 2 teaspoons)
I tablespoon ground cumin
I teaspoon smoked paprika
½ bunch Swiss chard, stemmed and leaves chopped
     (about 3 cups)
2 poblano peppers, seeded and chopped (about 2 cups)
4 cups low-sodium vegetable broth
One 28-ounce can no-salt-added diced tomatoes,
     with juice

TOPPINGS

One 15-ounce can black beans, drained and rinsed
     (I½ cups)
I avocado, cut into 8 slices
¼ cup chopped fresh cilantro
I lime, quartered

1 MAKE THE TORTILLA STRIPS: Preheat the oven to 375°F. Line a baking sheet with parchment paper. Brush both sides of the tortillas with the oil and slice them into thin strips. Place the strips on the prepared baking sheet and bake for 12 to 15 minutes, until crisp.

2 MAKE THE SOUP: In a large pot, heat the oil over medium heat. Add the onion, garlic, cumin, and paprika and cook for 2 minutes. Add the chard and poblano peppers and cook for about 8 minutes, until soft. Add the broth and tomatoes with their juices and bring to a boil. Turn down the heat to maintain a simmer and cook for about 15 minutes.

3 PUREE AND SERVE: Use an immersion blender to puree the soup until smooth, taking care not to splash yourself with the hot liquid. When serving, top each bowl evenly with baked tortilla strips, black beans, avocado slices, cilantro, and a squeeze of lime.

NUTRITION (I SERVING): 410 calories, 19g total fat, 52g carbs, 17g fiber, IIg protein

OH YEAH, ONE MORE THING . . .

Immersion blender: Blending soup so that it's 50 to 100% smooth is the key to making it look and taste like more than veggies floating in broth. Use an immersion blender to puree soups right in the pot.

(V)

TOMATO SOUP WITH GRILLED CHEESE CROUTONS

I need grilled cheese with my tomato soup, so here's the SuperSwap version . . . mini grilled cheese croutons swimming on top! **MAKES 4 SERVINGS**

TOMATO SOUP
1 tablespoon extra-virgin olive oil
1 onion, chopped (about 1 cup)
4 cups baby spinach leaves
3 garlic cloves, minced (about 2 teaspoons)
¼ teaspoon crushed red pepper flakes
4 tomatoes, finely chopped (about 4 cups)
One 28-ounce can no-salt added crushed tomatoes
½ cup chopped fresh basil
4 cups low-sodium vegetable broth

GRILLED CHEESE CROUTONS
4 slices sprouted whole-grain bread, toasted (so the croutons are crunchy!)
4 slices cheddar cheese (*not* American or processed cheese)

2 tablespoons balsamic vinegar, for serving

1 MAKE THE SOUP: In a large pot, heat the oil over medium heat. Add the onion, spinach, garlic, and crushed red pepper and cook for 3 minutes. Add the fresh tomatoes, canned tomatoes, and basil (save a few leaves for garnish) and cook for 5 minutes more. Add the broth and bring to a boil. Cover, turn the heat down to maintain a simmer, and cook for about 15 minutes. Use an immersion blender to puree the soup to a semismooth consistency, being careful not to splash yourself with hot soup.

2 MAKE THE CROUTONS: Preheat the broiler. Top each slice of toast with cheese and place them on a baking sheet. Broil for 4 minutes, or until the cheese is bubbling. Cut the toast into crouton-size pieces.

3 ASSEMBLE: Drizzle the soup with the vinegar and top with the croutons and remaining basil.

NUTRITION (1 SERVING): 380 calories, 13g total fat, 48g carbs, 13g fiber, 18g protein

OH YEAH, ONE MORE THING . . .

GF Swap: Use gluten-free bread.

Broth: I like to keep vegan organic bouillon cubes around to make an easy broth anytime. There are no-salt-added versions available, too.

Vinegar: Drizzling tart vinegar on soup wakes up the flavor. I love lime on black bean soup and lemon on lentil soup, since tart citrus brightens flavors, too.

EGGPLANT PARMESAN WITH SPAGHETTI SQUASH NOODLES

When you SuperSwap spaghetti squash for noodles, you consume a third of the calories. You can also use zoodles instead of the spaghetti squash, like in the Pesto Zoodles on page 111.

MAKES 2 SERVINGS

One 2- to 3-pound spaghetti squash
½ cup water
I tablespoon extra-virgin olive oil
2 organic eggs
20 brown rice crackers, crushed into crumbs (about ½ cup)
I tablespoon dried oregano
I eggplant, cut into six ½-inch-thick slices
I¼ cups C.R.A.P.-free marinara sauce (or use the Supersauce Marinara on page 226)
¼ cup shredded Parmesan cheese

I COOK THE SQUASH IN A SLOW COOKER: Clean the outer skin of the spaghetti squash and put it in a slower cooker. Add the water, cover, and cook on high for 2½ hours, until the squash is tender. Cut it in half lengthwise and with a spoon remove and discard the seeds. Run a fork across the flesh to get spaghetti-like strands.

2 BREAD THE EGGPLANT AND BAKE: When the squash is almost done, preheat the oven to 400°F. Line a baking sheet with parchment paper and coat the paper with the oil. In a medium bowl, whisk the eggs. In another bowl, mix the cracker crumbs and oregano. Coat the eggplant slices with egg and then bread them with cracker crumbs. Arrange the eggplant slices on the prepared baking sheet in a single layer. Bake for 15 minutes, flip, and bake for 10 minutes more, until tender.

3 SPOON ON THE SAUCE, SPRINKLE ON THE CHEESE, MELT, AND SERVE: Leave the eggplant on the baking sheet and spoon on half the marinara. Sprinkle the cheese over the eggplant. Return to the oven for 10 minutes more, or until the cheese is melted and golden. Serve the eggplant on the hot squash tossed with the remaining marinara sauce.

NUTRITION (I SERVING): 430 calories, I7g total fat, 56g carbs, I3g fiber, I7g protein

OH YEAH, ONE MORE THING . . .

V+ Swap: Swap out the organic eggs for "flax eggs." Learn how on page 239. Swap in very finely chopped walnuts for the Parmesan.

No slow cooker, no problem: Preheat the oven to 400°F. Cradle the squash in a kitchen towel on the counter so it doesn't move around when you're cutting it. Cut the squash in half lengthwise and clean out the seeds with a spoon. Place the squash cut side down on a rimmed baking sheet, add 6 tablespoons water, and bake for 40 minutes, until tender.

C.R.A.P.-free marinara sauce: Look for marinara with a simple ingredient list and no *added* sugar (it will have some natural sugar from the tomatoes).

SUPERFOOD CHILI

Canned veggie chili is made with soy protein isolate crumbles in a sugary tomato base. This version supplies whole-food protein from beans and sneaks in 4 cups of kale. **MAKES 4 SERVINGS**

1 tablespoon extra-virgin olive oil
¼ cup chili powder
½ teaspoon crushed red pepper flakes
1 onion, chopped (about 1 cup)
1 green bell pepper, seeded and chopped (about 1 cup)
4 cups chopped kale (about ½ bunch)
2 cups cubed sweet potato (1-inch cubes)
One 28-ounce can no-salt-added diced tomatoes, with juice
4 cups low-sodium vegetable broth
One 15-ounce can kidney beans, drained and rinsed
One 15-ounce can black beans, drained and rinsed
Sea salt
4 green onions, chopped
1 avocado, cubed

1 MAKE THE CHILI: In a 3-quart or larger pot, heat the oil, chili powder, and crushed red pepper over medium heat. Add the onion and bell pepper and cook for 3 minutes. Add the kale and sweet potatoes and cook for 10 minutes more. Add the tomatoes and broth and bring to a boil. Turn down the heat to maintain a simmer, add the beans, cover, and cook for 15 minutes.

2 BLEND AND SERVE: With an immersion blender, puree about a quarter of the chili to thicken it. Be careful not to splash yourself with the hot chili. Season with salt. Top each bowl with green onions and avocado.

NUTRITION (1 SERVING): 390 calories, 10g total fat, 66g carbs, 22g fiber, 16g protein

OH YEAH, ONE MORE THING . . .

Better beans: Beans soaked and cooked from scratch are easier to digest and have more absorbable protein and minerals. Learn how to cook your own beans on page 241.

Corn bread: Since I need corn bread with chili, I scale back the portion of chili to account for a corn bread muffin! Check out the corn bread on page 229.

SPINACH ENCHILADA CASSEROLE

This SuperSwap offers less cheese and more veggies than either restaurant or traditional homemade enchiladas. Plus, the enchilada sauce has no added sugar, hydrolyzed soy, corn protein, or added color like many of the commercial versions on the market. **MAKES 4 SERVINGS**

ENCHILADA SAUCE

I tablespoon extra-virgin olive oil
I onion, finely chopped (about I cup)
2 tablespoons chili powder
2 garlic cloves, minced (about I teaspoon)
One 15-ounce can no-salt-added tomato sauce
Juice of I lime (about 2 tablespoons)

ENCHILADAS

One 15-ounce can vegetarian refried beans
6 organic sprouted corn tortillas
One 10-ounce package frozen chopped spinach, thawed
   and squeezed dry
¾ cup shredded cheddar cheese
3 green onions, thinly sliced (about ½ cup)
I tomato, chopped (about I cup)
¼ cup sliced black olives

I   MAKE THE ENCHILADA SAUCE: Preheat the oven to 350°F. In a 12-inch skillet, heat the oil over medium heat. Add the onion, chili powder, and garlic and cook for 2 minutes. Add the tomato sauce and bring to a boil. Turn down the heat to maintain a simmer and cook, uncovered, for about 5 minutes. Remove from the heat and stir in the lime juice.

2   MAKE THE ENCHILADAS: Spread the beans evenly on the tortillas and cut each in half. Pour a third of the enchilada sauce over the bottom of an 8-inch square baking dish. Arrange 4 of the bean-topped tortilla halves on top of the sauce. Top with a third of the spinach and a third of the cheese. Repeat the layers, ending with the cheese. Cover the dish with aluminum foil and bake for 30 minutes. Serve with the green onions, tomatoes, and olives on top.

NUTRITION (I SERVING): 390 calories, 16g total fat, 49g carbs, 14g fiber, 19g protein

OH YEAH, ONE MORE THING . . .

Slow cooker: Instead of making this in the oven, make it in a slow cooker. Layer the ingredients in the slow cooker and cook on high for 2 hours or on low for 4 hours.

LENTIL MEATBALLS AND PASTA

To SuperSwap spaghetti and meatballs, start with the ratios—use way more veggies than noodles. Then, replace white noodles with whole-grain. The lentil meatballs add plant protein, missing from most vegan pasta dishes. **MAKES 2 SERVINGS**

I cup cooked quinoa pasta or your favorite whole-grain pasta
3 cups chopped steamed broccoli florets
I cup C.R.A.P.-free marinara sauce (or use the Supersauce Marinara on page 226)
8 Lentil Meatballs (page 196)

Top the pasta with the broccoli, marinara, and meatballs.

NUTRITION (I SERVING): 4IO calories, 8g total fat, 7Og carbs, 19g fiber, 19g protein

OH YEAH, ONE MORE THING...

C.R.A.P.-free marinara sauce: Look for marinara with a simple ingredient list and no *added* sugar (it will have some natural sugar from the tomatoes).

LENTIL MEATBALLS

You can use any color lentils, but I usually use brown because they imitate the look of ground beef, so the meatballs look like meatballs. You don't need a food processor to make them, so cleanup is a breeze. **MAKES 12 MEATBALLS**

2 tablespoons ground flaxseed
2 tablespoons warm water
1½ cups cooked lentils
½ onion, very finely chopped (about ½ cup)
2 garlic cloves, minced (about 1 teaspoon)
6 brown rice crackers, crushed into crumbs (about 2 tablespoons)
¼ cup chopped fresh flat-leaf parsley
¼ teaspoon Italian seasoning
¼ teaspoon cayenne
¼ teaspoon sea salt
¼ teaspoon freshly ground black pepper

1 PREP: Preheat the oven to 350°F. Line a baking sheet with parchment paper. Mix the flaxseed and water and let sit for 5 minutes, or until the mixture has the gooey texture of an egg.

2 MIX: In a medium bowl, using a fork, mash the flax mixture with the lentils, onion, garlic, crackers, parsley, Italian seasoning, cayenne, salt, and pepper until it holds together.

3 FORM AND BAKE THE MEATBALLS: Using a 1-tablespoon cookie scoop, make 12 balls from the lentil mixture and put them on the prepared baking sheet. Do not use a dish with sides, or the meatballs will be soggy. Bake for about 30 minutes and eat immediately. Freeze extra cooked meatballs in an airtight container for up to 3 months.

NUTRITION (1 MEATBALL): 45 calories, 0g total fat, 7g carbs, 3g fiber, 3g protein

OH YEAH, ONE MORE THING . . .

Time saver: Use ready-to-eat steamed lentils, found in the produce section. Freeze what you don't use in an airtight container for up to 3 months.

FISH AND CHIPS

With classic fish and chips, the fish is breaded with refined white flour before it's fried, and served with french fries. SuperSwap style means the fish is breaded with healthful nuts and seeds. Then it's baked and served with parsnip fries, fresh from the oven. **MAKES 2 SERVINGS**

PARSNIP FRIES

2 large parsnips, peeled, trimmed, and cut into fry shapes (about 2 cups)
2 teaspoons extra-virgin olive oil
⅛ teaspoon sea salt
⅛ teaspoon freshly ground black pepper

FISH

1 tablespoon ground flaxseeds
3 tablespoons water
6 tablespoons almond flour (or pulse your own almonds into flour using a food processor)
1½ teaspoons paprika
Two 5-ounce white fish fillets, such as trout or mackerel

3 cups mixed salad greens
2 lemon wedges

1 MAKE THE PARSNIP FRIES: Preheat the oven to 400°F. Line a baking sheet with parchment paper. In a medium bowl, toss the parsnips, oil, salt, and pepper. Spread them over the prepared baking sheet and bake for 35 to 40 minutes, flipping once halfway through the cooking time, until crunchy and golden.

2 MAKE THE FISH: While the parsnip fries are baking, in a small bowl, stir together the flaxseed and water and set aside for 5 minutes until thickened. On a plate, stir together the almond flour and paprika. Dip the fish in the flax mixture and then into the almond mixture. Put the fish on a parchment paper–lined baking sheet and pop it in the oven with the parsnip fries for the last 8 minutes of baking. Before serving, broil the fish about 4 inches away from heat for about 3 minutes longer for extra crunch, until the fish is opaque and registers 145°F on an instant-read thermometer.

3 ASSEMBLE: Serve the fish on a bed of greens with fries and a lemon wedge.

NUTRITION (1 SERVING): 420 calories, 17g total fat, 34g carbs, 12g fiber, 36g protein

OH YEAH, ONE MORE THING...

Pickles, please: The sourness of pickles tastes great as a side to this meal. Check out the 15-Minute Pickles on page 153 and Pickles Plus on page 228.

Fish tip: General rule of thumb: Cook fish for 8 to 10 minutes per inch of thickness, whether you are baking, broiling, or grilling.

C.R.A.P.-free ketchup: You can serve parsnip fries with ketchup. Buy brands with tomatoes as the first ingredient and no high-fructose corn syrup. Give your ketchup a healthy boost by adding curry powder, which contains turmeric, a superfood spice. You can also try making your own Beet Ketchup (page 222).

BUTTERNUT SQUASH LASAGNA

In this lasagna, butternut squash and zucchini slices are the SuperSwap for noodles. There's a significant amount of cheese in this recipe, but there are even more veggies. To me, this is the perfect vice-virtue balance. **MAKES 4 SERVINGS**

LASAGNA

One 2- to 3-pound butternut squash, with a long neck
2 medium zucchini
One 15-ounce container organic part-skim ricotta cheese
1 organic egg, beaten
1 teaspoon dried oregano
1 garlic clove, minced (about ½ teaspoon)
One 24-ounce jar C.R.A.P.-free marinara sauce (or use the Supersauce Marinara on page 226)
1 cup shredded Parmesan cheese

BASIC SIDE SALAD

4 cups mixed salad greens
1 cup grape tomatoes, halved
¼ red onion, thinly sliced (about ¼ cup)
2 tablespoons red wine vinegar
Sea salt and freshly ground black pepper

1 MAKE THE LASAGNA: Preheat the oven to 375°F. Peel the butternut squash. Cut off the round end and reserve for another use. Discard the seeds. Using a mandoline or your own amazing knife skills, slice the squash neck and the zucchini lengthwise into thin slices about ⅛ inch thick. The slices should look like lasagna noodles.

2 STIR TOGETHER THE CHEESE AND ASSEMBLE: In a medium bowl, stir together the ricotta, egg, oregano, and garlic. Pour a quarter of the sauce into an 8-by-8-inch dish. Layer a third of the butternut squash, a third of the ricotta mixture, a third of the zucchini, and a quarter of the sauce. Continue the layers, ending with the sauce. Sprinkle with the Parmesan cheese.

3 BAKE: Cover the baking dish with aluminum foil and bake for 40 minutes. Remove from the oven and turn on the broiler. Remove the foil and broil the lasagna for about 5 minutes, until the cheese is golden.

4 MEANWHILE, MAKE THE SALAD: In a medium bowl, toss the greens, tomatoes, onion, and vinegar. Season with salt and pepper. Serve the lasagna with the salad on the side.

NUTRITION (1 SERVING): 420 calories, 17g total fat, 44g carbs, 8g fiber, 27g protein

OH YEAH, ONE MORE THING...

Slow cooker: Instead of making this in the oven, make it in a slow cooker. Layer the ingredients in the slow cooker and cook on high for 2 hours or on low for 4 hours.

C.R.A.P.-free marinara sauce: Look for marinara sauce with a simple ingredient list and no *added* sugar (it will have some natural sugar from the tomatoes).

CHIA CHOCOLATE CHUNK COOKIES

OMG. These hit the spot, and your body loves you for the oats, almond butter, and chia seed nutrition. No cell-depleting white sugar or white flour in these. Now that's a treat! **MAKES 18 COOKIES**

½ cup rolled oats or oat flour

¼ teaspoon baking soda

⅛ teaspoon sea salt

½ cup natural almond butter

¼ cup coconut sugar

I tablespoon chia seeds

3 tablespoons water

I teaspoon pure vanilla extract, or ½ teaspoon ground vanilla beans

¾ ounce dark chocolate, chopped (about 3 tablespoons)

I PREHEAT THE OVEN AND MAKE THE DOUGH: Preheat the oven to 350°F. Line a baking sheet with parchment paper. In a blender, pulse the oats until they have a fine, flourlike texture (or use oat flour). Add the baking soda and salt and pulse to mix. In a medium bowl, mix together the almond butter, coconut sugar, chia seeds, water, and vanilla. Stir the oat mixture into the almond butter mixture (it will be thick). Stir in the chocolate.

2 BAKE: Drop tablespoon-size portions of the dough (I use a small cookie scoop) on the prepared baking sheet. Bake for 8 to 10 minutes, until the tops and bottoms are golden. As soon as you take them from the oven, use a small glass to press down gently on each mound. Let the cookies cool for 5 minutes on the pan and then transfer to wire racks to cool completely. Store in an airtight container at room temperature for up to 7 days.

NUTRITION (2 COOKIES): 140 calories, 10g total fat, 11g carbs, 3g fiber, 4g protein

OH YEAH, ONE MORE THING . . .

GF Swap: Use gluten-free oats.

Portion tricks: For less temptation, make only a half batch of cookies: Use I mini dark chocolate square (about 0.35 ounce) for the half batch instead of buying a whole candy bar.

CHOCOLATE PECAN CANDY CLUSTERS

Chocolate caramel candies typically contain sugar, pecans, glucose, modified milk ingredients, cocoa butter, cocoa mass, modified palm oil, lactose, salt, soya lecithin, and artificial and natural flavors. This sweet, satisfying SuperSwap has just 6 simple ingredients. **MAKES 2 SERVINGS (2 CANDIES PER SERVING)**

4 pecan halves
2 Medjool dates, pitted and halved
1 tablespoon coconut oil, melted
1 tablespoon unsweetened cocoa powder
   (avoid Dutched versions)
1½ teaspoons pure maple syrup
Sea salt

1 STUFF: On a parchment paper–lined baking sheet or plate, press the pecan halves onto the sticky side of the date halves.

2 WARM, STIR, AND SPOON: In a small bowl, stir together the coconut oil, cocoa powder, and maple syrup. Spoon the chocolate mixture evenly over each pecan-topped date.

3 SPRINKLE AND SET: Sprinkle the candies with the salt and refrigerate for about 10 minutes, until the chocolate sets. Store in an airtight container in the fridge for up to 2 weeks.

NUTRITION (1 SERVING): 160 calories, 9g total fat, 21g carbs, 2g fiber, 1g protein

OH YEAH, ONE MORE THING . . .

Dates: Dates are a naturally supersweet fruit. The types you'll most likely find in the store are Deglet Noor and Medjool. I buy Medjool dates because they are more tender and taste more like caramel. Each Medjool date has 1½ grams of filling fiber, which means this sticky, delish treat has more staying power than your typical candy bar.

Time saver: Melt pieces of a dark chocolate bar or dark chocolate chips instead of using the coconut oil, cocoa powder, and maple syrup.

Get your learn on: Read more about cocoa powder and cacao powder on page 237.

GINGERSNAP COOKIES

Make this SuperSwap cookie in a flash with just 5 superfood ingredients. No butter, added sugar, or flour here, and it's a perfect after-meal treat since ginger helps digestion—a real smart cookie.

MAKES 30 MINI COOKIES

¾ cup unsweetened coconut flakes
½ cup raw sesame seeds
8 Medjool dates, pitted
2 teaspoons grated fresh ginger
⅛ teaspoon sea salt

1 PREHEAT THE OVEN AND MAKE THE DOUGH: Preheat the oven to 300°F. Line a baking sheet with parchment paper. In a food processor, combine the coconut, sesame seeds, dates, ginger, and salt and process for about 5 minutes, scraping down the sides of the bowl a couple of times. At first, the mixture may not seem like it will come together, but with enough processing, it will form a nice, sticky dough.

2 MAKE TEASPOON-SIZE ROUNDS, BAKE, AND PRESS: Use a 1-teaspoon measuring spoon to make tiny balls. Place them on the prepared baking sheet and bake for 15 minutes, until golden on the bottom. As soon as you take the cookies from the oven, gently press them flat with the bottom of a small drinking glass.

3 STORE: Let the cookies cool on the pan for a few minutes and then transfer to wire racks to cool completely. Store them in an airtight container at room temperature for up to 5 days or freeze for up to 3 months.

NUTRITION (3 COOKIES): 130 calories, 8g total fat, 16g carbs, 3g fiber, 2g protein

OH YEAH, ONE MORE THING . . .

Lemon Cookies: Swap out the ginger for 1 teaspoon finely grated lemon zest and 3 tablespoons fresh lemon juice (from 1 lemon).

Carrot Cake Cookies: Swap out the ginger for ¼ cup finely grated carrot (1 carrot) and ¼ teaspoon freshly grated nutmeg. I also top each with a little grated carrot before baking—so pretty.

VANILLA "SUGAR" COOKIES

I whipped these up when I was time-crunched and nailed it. They are fast and flavorful with no white sugar or flour. For chocolate cookies, stir in 1½ tablespoons unsweetened cocoa powder (avoid Dutched versions). **MAKES 16 COOKIES**

1½ cups almond meal
½ teaspoon baking soda
¼ teaspoon sea salt
2 tablespoons pure maple syrup
2 tablespoons coconut oil, melted
1 organic egg, beaten
½ teaspoon pure vanilla extract, or ¼ teaspoon ground vanilla beans

1 PREHEAT THE OVEN AND MAKE THE DOUGH: Preheat the oven to 350°F. Line a baking sheet with parchment paper. In a bowl, mix together the almond meal, baking soda, and salt. In a separate bowl, stir together the maple syrup, coconut oil, egg, and vanilla. Mix the wet ingredients into the dry.

2 BAKE: Drop tablespoon-size portions of the dough (I use a small cookie scoop) onto the prepared baking sheet. Bake for 15 minutes, until the bottoms are golden. As soon as you take them from the oven, use a small glass to press down gently on each cookie. Let the cookies cool for 5 minutes on the pan and then transfer them to wire racks to cool completely. Store in an airtight container at room temperature for up to 7 days.

Nutrition (2 cookies): 170 calories, 14g total fat, 8g carbs, 2g fiber, 5g protein

NATURAL CARAMEL APPLES

Packaged caramel apples are made with perfectly healthy apples coated with corn syrup, artificial flavors, and other food additives. This SuperSwap is sweet and gooey from the natural sugars in fruit (dates). The almond butter and chopped almonds balance the natural sugars with healthy fat and protein. I like the sourness of green Granny Smith apples best with this sweet sauce. **MAKES 4 SERVINGS (2 TABLESPOONS SAUCE EACH)**

6 Medjool dates, pitted
½ cup almost-boiling water
1 tablespoon natural almond butter
¼ teaspoon sea salt
1 green apple, quartered and cored
4 tablespoons chopped almonds

1 BLEND THE INGREDIENTS: In a food processor, combine the dates, hot water, almond butter, and salt and process until totally smooth.

2 SERVE: For each serving, plate 2 tablespoons of the caramel, a quarter of the apple, and 1 tablespoon of the chopped almonds.

NUTRITION (1 SERVING): 170 calories, 6g total fat, 31g carbs, 4g fiber, 3g protein

OH YEAH, ONE MORE THING . . .

Apple a day: Apples are linked to all sorts of benefits like heart and lung health and blood sugar control. New research even suggests that apples may help promote the growth of healthy digestive bacteria linked to weight control.

(V) (GF)

FRENCH ONION DIP

Dip into this SuperSwap instead of the packaged version and you'll scoop up only simple ingredients loaded with nutrition—so much better than C.R.A.P. such as caramel color, partially hydrogenated soybean oil, MSG, corn syrup, and preservatives. **MAKES 4 SERVINGS**

2 tablespoons extra-virgin olive oil
1 onion, finely chopped (about 1 cup)
2 teaspoons organic reduced-sodium gluten-free soy sauce
1 garlic clove, minced (about ½ teaspoon)
½ teaspoon freshly ground black pepper
½ teaspoon dried thyme
¼ teaspoon sea salt
1 tablespoon balsamic vinegar
1 cup plain 2% Greek yogurt
Cut-up veggies, for serving

1 COOK AND COOL: In a 10-inch skillet, heat the oil over medium heat. Add the onion, soy sauce, garlic, pepper, thyme, and salt and cook, stirring a couple of times, for 8 minutes. Add the vinegar and cook for 2 minutes more, until the onions are super-soft.

2 STIR AND STORE: In a small bowl, stir the onions into the yogurt, cover, and refrigerate for at least 30 minutes before serving. Refrigerate any extra dip in an airtight container for up to 3 days. Serve with veggies like carrots and cucumbers cut into chip shapes.

NUTRITION (1 SERVING): 120 calories, 8g total fat, 6g carbs, 1g fiber, 5g protein

OH YEAH, ONE MORE THING...

Root Veggie Chips: If you love this dip with chips, make homemade beet, parsnip, or sweet potato chips: Using a mandoline, cut the veggies into paper-thin slices (1/16 inch), toss with a little extra-virgin olive oil, and bake in a preheated 350°F oven for about 30 minutes, turning once. The chips will be golden and crisp when you take them out of the oven, and they will get even crisper as they cool.

BROWN RICE CRISPY TREATS

The typical treat uses refined-white-rice cereal and marshmallows made from gelatin, corn syrup, sugar, artificial flavor, and artificial blue #1. This SuperSwap has whole-grain brown rice cereal and brown rice syrup to hold it together. Plus, the added dose of almond butter adds protein and healthy fat. **MAKES 4 SERVINGS**

¼ cup brown rice syrup
2 tablespoons natural almond butter
1½ cups puffed brown rice cereal
Sea salt

In a small pot, stir together the brown rice syrup and almond butter. Bring the mixture to a boil over low heat. In a medium bowl, pour the hot mixture over the cereal and stir. Press the mixture into an 8½-by-4½-inch loaf pan and refrigerate for at least 30 minutes, until set. Cut into 4 bars.

NUTRITION (1 SERVING): 160 calories, 4.5g total fat, 29g carbs, 1g fiber, 3g protein

OH YEAH, ONE MORE THING . . .

Cuckoo for cocoa: Add 2 teaspoons unsweetened cocoa powder (avoid Dutched versions) to the brown rice syrup and almond butter mixture to make these chocolaty. Read more about cocoa powder and cacao powder on page 237.

Extra brown rice cereal: Check out the recipe for the Cereal Puff Bowl on page 92, or crush it up and use it as a breading for baked fish or chicken.

WASABI CHICKPEAS

Surprisingly, typical wasabi peas contain C.R.A.P. like starch, glutinous rice flour (aka white flour), wheat flour (aka white flour), white sugar, and artificial color (yellow #5 and blue #1). Here's the SuperSwap. **MAKES 4 SERVINGS (ABOUT ⅓ CUP PER SERVING)**

One 15-ounce can chickpeas, drained and rinsed
1 tablespoon extra-virgin olive oil
1 tablespoon wasabi powder (add more if you like extra kick)
¼ teaspoon sea salt

1 PREHEAT THE OVEN AND PREP THE CHICKPEAS: Preheat the oven to 400°F. Line a baking sheet with parchment paper. Pat the chickpeas with a towel until very dry. In a medium bowl, toss the chickpeas with the oil, wasabi powder, and salt. Pour them onto the prepared baking sheet.

2 BAKE AND TOSS: Bake for 40 minutes, shaking the pan every 10 minutes, until the chickpeas are golden and firm. Serve hot out of the oven or let them cool and store in an airtight container for up to 1 week.

NUTRITION (1 SERVING): 120 calories, 5g total fat, 15g carbs, 4g fiber, 4g protein

OH YEAH, ONE MORE THING . . .

Better beans: Beans soaked and cooked from scratch are easier to digest and have more absorbable protein and minerals. Learn how to cook your own beans on page 241.

Flavorize: Swap wasabi powder for flavor pairings such as rosemary and garlic, curry powder and lime, allspice and cumin, or vanilla and cinnamon.

SUPERSEED CRACKERS

A crunchy snack cracker that is totally packed with protein, fiber, and healthy fat: yes, please! Once you make these no-grain crackers a couple of times, you'll have the recipe memorized so you'll be able to whip up a batch in no time.

MAKES 40 CRACKERS

I cup water
½ cup chia seeds
½ cup unsalted sunflower seeds (raw, if you can find them)
½ cup sesame seeds
½ teaspoon sea salt

I PREP: Preheat the oven to 350°F. Line a 10-by-14-inch baking sheet with parchment paper.

2 STIR AND SPREAD: In a medium bowl, stir together the water, chia seeds, sunflower seeds, sesame seeds, and salt. Spread the seed mixture over the prepared baking sheet. There will be enough to cover most of the baking sheet.

3 BAKE, CUT, AND STORE: Bake the crackers for 20 minutes. Using a pizza cutter, cut the rectangle into 40 crackers or cut them into rounds with a cookie cutter and bake for 20 minutes longer, or until crisp. Store in a covered container at room temperature for up to 2 weeks.

NUTRITION (5 CRACKERS): I50 calories, I0g total fat, I0g carbs, 5g fiber, 5g protein

OH YEAH, ONE MORE THING . . .

Seed superstars: Chia is rich in selenium, which supports a healthy thyroid and may reduce the risk of cancer; sunflower seeds are loaded with vitamin E, which is an antioxidant that may protect skin against sun damage; sesame seeds are packed with calcium for strong bones.

DRINKS, CONDIMENTS
& SIDES

DRINKS

MORNING
Green Bull Energy Drink 210

Matcha Jolt 212

Coconut Coffee 212

Super Latte 213

REFRESHING
Super Soda 213

Real Ginger Ale 214

Coconut Lemonade 214

Mojito Water 215

NIGHT
Natural Hot Chocolate 215

Golden Milk 216

PARTY
Kombucha Margarita 216

Hibiscus Sangria 219

Sparkling Bitters 220

WELLNESS
Wellness Shot 220

Natural Sports Drink 221

CONDIMENTS
Beet Ketchup 222

Beet BBQ Sauce 222

Cashew Mayo 224

Olive Oil Hummus 224

Potato Croutons 225

Mushroom Bacon Bits 225

Supersauce Marinara 226

SIDES
Buffalo Cauliflower Poppers 226

Carrot and Green Bean Fries 227

Zucchini Wedges 227

Pickles Plus 228

SuperSwap Corn Bread 229

GREEN BULL ENERGY DRINK

The energy boost comes from healthy compounds in the greens that increase blood flow to the brain and muscles. Since this drink is a slim 80 calories, it isn't meant to be a meal on its own—use it to accompany a meal or as a snack for an added boost. **MAKES 1 SERVING**

¾ cup water
1 kale leaf, stemmed and chopped (about 1 cup)
½ green apple, cored and chopped (about ½ cup)
Juice of ½ lemon (about 1½ tablespoons)
Pinch of cayenne (optional)

In a blender, combine the water, kale, apple, and lemon juice and blend until smooth. Add a pinch of cayenne for an extra eye opener. Drink immediately or store in an airtight container (such as a lidded jar) in the fridge for up to 24 hours. Shake before drinking.

NUTRITION (1 SERVING): 50 calories, 0g total fat, 13g carbs, 2g fiber, 1g protein

OH YEAH, ONE MORE THING . . .

Time-saver: Prep and portion out kale, apples, and lemon juice into a few small lidded glass containers, such as Mason jars, and store them in the fridge. When you want a freshly blended green juice, toss the preportioned amounts into the blender with ¾ cup water.

Make it a snack: Pair a 10-ounce serving of Green Bull with 10 almonds.

Extra lemon half: Starting the day with hot lemon water—¼ lemon squeezed into a mug of hot water (before my coffee!)—gives me the feeling that I've already done something good for my body. It puts me mentally on track for a healthy day and snaps me out of less-than-healthy eating funks, too. Magic.

MATCHA JOLT

No interest in using and cleaning a blender, but still want a green jolt of energy? Try this easy way to get healthfully caffeinated. Swap the plain water for coconut water if you want the drink naturally sweeter. Be sure to buy coconut water with no added sugar. **MAKES I SERVING**

1 cup hot or cold water or unsweetened coconut water
1 tablespoon fresh lemon juice
½ teaspoon matcha green tea powder
Pinch of cayenne (optional)

In a lidded jar, shake the water, lemon juice, and matcha. Add the cayenne for an extra kick, if desired.

NUTRITION (I SERVING): 5 calories, 0g total fat, 1g carbs, 0g fiber, 0g protein

OH YEAH, ONE MORE THING . . .

Matcha 101: Matcha is powdered green tea. It is made from ground tea leaves, so you get its benefits directly. Put ½ teaspoon in any morning smoothie for steady, time-released caffeine.

COCONUT COFFEE

Coffee can be part of a SuperSwap life. Keep daily portions sensible and stop drinking it at least 8 hours before bedtime so it won't keep you awake. The best way to drink it is black . . . but adding a little fat and flavor from coconut milk is so much better than adding tons of cream, sugar, or artificial sweeteners. **MAKES I SERVING**

1 cup brewed black coffee
2 tablespoons canned full-fat coconut milk

Stir together in a mug and enjoy.

NUTRITION (I SERVING): 60 calories, 6g total fat, 1g carbs, 0g fiber, 1g protein

OH YEAH, ONE MORE THING . . .

Good and good for you: Coffee in the right amount and at the right time actually has health benefits—it increases mental and physical performance and may decrease the risk of diseases such as diabetes and some types of cancer. It's also the number-one source of beneficial antioxidants in the standard American diet!

Coconut cubes: Freeze leftover coconut milk in an ice cube tray. Pop out the cubes and store them in a container in the freezer to make easy coconut rice, coconut oatmeal, or coconut coffee! Make sure you are using full-fat coconut milk since low-fat versions separate.

Herbal coffee: I love instant herbal coffee made with dandelion root, found online or at health food stores. Ingredients are usually a blend of roasted barley, rye, chicory, and dandelion root. Add a teaspoon to hot water, stir, and you will drink something very similar to coffee but without the caffeine. Plus, dandelion root may help both digestive and skin health.

(V+) (GF)

SUPER LATTE

Yerba mate (*yer-bah mah-tay*) is a naturally caffeinated dried tree leaf from South America that can be brewed just like regular tea. It has about the same amount of caffeine as black tea. Try this drink for energy, focus, and improved mood. **MAKES I SERVING**

I yerba mate tea bag
I cup almost-boiling water
½ cup unsweetened plant milk, such as almond or hemp milk
I tablespoon natural almond butter

In a lidded jar, steep the tea bag in the water for 5 minutes. Add the milk and almond butter. Close the jar and shake vigorously before drinking.

NUTRITION (I SERVING): 120 calories, 10g total fat, 5g carbs, 2g fiber, 4g protein

OH YEAH, ONE MORE THING . . .

Turn up your burn: New research suggests that if you drink yerba mate before a moderate workout, you'll increase your calorie burn by 24%. Now, *that's* a skinny latte!

No mate, no problem: Use black, white, or green tea for this latte instead. Tea is nature's own 5-Hour Energy. It naturally contains caffeine for energy and theanine for focus.

(V+) (GF)

SUPER SODA

Many of my clients want to cut out diet or regular soft drinks—a change I wholeheartedly approve. To help them "detox," I suggest healthy replacements for the 3 things soft drinks offer: carbonation, sugar, and caffeine. This SuperSwap provides the bubbles and a splash of natural sugar from 100% fruit juice. As for caffeine, I recommend sticking with natural sources like tea or coffee. **MAKES I SERVING**

¾ cup club soda or sparkling water
I shot glass of 100% fruit juice (3 tablespoons)
A few ice cubes

In a glass, mix the club soda, juice, and ice and drink.

NUTRITION (I SERVING): 25 calories, 0g total fat, 6g carbs, 0g fiber, 0g protein

OH YEAH, ONE MORE THING . . .

Flavorize: Use any 100% fruit juice, such as tart cherry, grape, orange, or, my sweet-tart favorite, pomegranate and pineapple

REAL GINGER ALE

Lots of moms offer their kids ginger ale to help settle their stomachs, and many nauseated travelers order it on planes. Ginger definitely soothes stomachaches, but most canned ginger ale doesn't actually contain any! Read the ingredients and you'll find only carbonated water, high-fructose corn syrup, caramel color, and flavoring. Here's how to make the real deal. **MAKES 1 SERVING**

1 tablespoon hot water
2 teaspoons honey
1 teaspoon grated fresh ginger
1 cup club soda or sparking water
A few ice cubes

In a small bowl, mix the hot water, honey, and ginger. Stir into the club soda until all the honey dissolves. Add the ice and serve.

NUTRITION (1 SERVING): 45 calories, 0g total fat, 12g carbs, 0g fiber, 0g protein

OH YEAH, ONE MORE THING . . .

V+ Swap: You can use pure maple syrup instead of honey, but I really prefer the honey since it has potential immune-boosting and throat-soothing properties.

COCONUT LEMONADE

Most lemonade either comes from a C.R.A.P.-filled powder or contains only water, lots of white sugar, and lemon juice. This version has zero added sugar—the sweetness comes from natural sugars in coconut water. Multiply this for a party and serve it in a big glass pitcher with lemon slices. Hello, gorgeous crowd-pleasing thirst-quencher! **MAKES 2 SERVINGS (1 CUP EACH)**

2 cups unsweetened coconut water
Juice of 1 lemon (about 3 tablespoons)
A few ice cubes

COULDN'T BE EASIER: Just mix the coconut water with the lemon juice. Add ice and drink.

NUTRITION (1 SERVING): 50 calories, 0g total fat, 13g carbs, 0g fiber, 1g protein

OH YEAH, ONE MORE THING . . .

Coconut water: Purchase brands with no added sugars or colors.

Spicy lemonade: Add a sprinkle of cayenne for extra kick.

Watermelon Lemonade: Instead of coconut water, puree 3 cups watermelon cubes (which makes about 2 cups liquid) and add the juice of 1 lemon. Cheers!

MOJITO WATER

"You aren't sick. You're just dehydrated." It's true: Every bodily function needs water. If you do anything for your health, start with drinking enough of this essential. The good news is that there are a million healthy fruits, vegetables, herbs, and spice combos that can punch up the flavor—and so many cute water pitchers. **MAKES I PITCHER**

Pitcher of water
Lime slices
Fresh mint

Let the lime slices and mint float in the water to infuse it with natural flavor. Start drinking.

NUTRITION (I PITCHER): 0 calories, 0g total fat, 0g carbs, 0g fiber, 0g protein, 100% goodness

OH YEAH, ONE MORE THING . . .

Be creative: We drink more when we like the flavor of our beverage! Try all sorts of combos such as jalapeño and lime, cinnamon stick and clementine, raspberry and lemon, cucumber and lavender, peach and coconut, and strawberry and basil.

(V+) (GF)

NATURAL HOT CHOCOLATE

Store-bought packets of hot cocoa have C.R.A.P. like white sugar, corn syrup solids, partially hydrogenated vegetable oil, and artificial flavors and colors. That leaves me feeling cold, not cozy. Try this SuperSwap instead, which has no added sugar but plenty of flavonoid-rich cocoa powder.

MAKES 2 SERVINGS (¾ CUP PER SERVING)

1½ cups unsweetened plant milk, such as almond or hemp milk
4 Medjool dates, pitted
1½ tablespoons unsweetened cocoa powder (avoid Dutched versions)
¼ teaspoon ground cinnamon
Pinch of cayenne
Pinch of sea salt

In a blender, combine all the ingredients and puree until smooth. Heat the mixture in a small pot on the stovetop or in a mug in the microwave until almost boiling. Serve hot.

NUTRITION (I SERVING): 150 calories, 3g total fat, 35g carbs, 5g fiber, 3g protein

OH YEAH, ONE MORE THING . . .

Get your learn on: Read more about cocoa powder and cacao powder on page 237.

GOLDEN MILK

Quality sleep is the foundation of good health. There are many elements to good sleep, but the most important is a peaceful pre-bed routine. Drink this warm milk to help you get your calm on, and turn off anything that emits stimulating blue light, including computers, TVs, tablets, and smartphones. The milk doesn't need sweetener since the fat in almond butter and naturally sweet taste of cinnamon make this taste great, but you can add honey, if you like. **MAKES 1 SERVING**

1 cup unsweetened plant milk, such as almond or hemp milk, warmed
1 tablespoon natural almond butter
½ teaspoon ground cinnamon
½ teaspoon ground turmeric
1 teaspoon honey (optional)

Put the milk, almond butter, cinnamon, and turmeric in a lidded jar, close tightly, and shake until the almond butter has dissolved. Add honey for sweetness, if you like.

NUTRITION (1 SERVING): 140 calories, 12g total fat, 7g carbs, 4g fiber, 5g protein

KOMBUCHA MARGARITA

Forget premade margarita mixes with high-fructose corn syrup, artificial flavors, and dyes. Instead, make this SuperSwap version with just 4 simple ingredients. The kombucha gives you a dose of probiotics for digestion and immunity. What's the lesson here? Kombucha makes a great cocktail mixer. **MAKES 2 SERVINGS (¾ CUP PER SERVING)**

Juice of 2 limes (about ¼ cup)
Sea salt
1 cup original or citrus-flavor kombucha
¼ cup tequila
A few ice cubes

Run one of the squeezed lime halves around the edge of a glass, then dip in the sea salt. Mix all the ingredients. Serve over ice in the salt-rimmed glass.

NUTRITION (1 SERVING): 90 calories, 0g total fat, 7g carbs, 0g fiber, 0g protein

OH YEAH, ONE MORE THING . . .

Kombucha: Kombucha is brewed tea that has been fermented by a combo of bacteria and yeast known as a SCOBY (symbiotic colony of bacteria and yeast). It's lightly fizzy and tangy. I love pouring it straight into fancy champagne glasses to celebrate.

Kombucha Margarita

HIBISCUS SANGRIA

SuperSwap sangria gets its flavor from fresh brewed tea and fresh fruit—there's no added sugar, brandy, or other liqueur. **MAKES 10 SERVINGS (5 OUNCES PER SERVING)**

SUMMER HIBISCUS SANGRIA

6 hibiscus tea bags
3 cups almost-boiling water
One 750 ml bottle red, white, or rosé wine
2 plums, pitted and sliced
I orange, with peel, sliced

WINTER CHAI SANGRIA

6 chai tea bags
3 cups almost-boiling water
One 750 ml bottle red, white, or rosé wine
I pear, cored and sliced
2 clementines, with peel, sliced

1 STEEP AND ICE: In a cup or container, steep the tea bags in the hot water for 8 minutes. Discard the tea bags.

2 MIX AND CHILL: In a pitcher, combine the tea, wine, and fruit. Refrigerate for at least 3 hours or overnight before serving.

NUTRITION (1 SERVING SUMMER): 70 calories, 0g total fat, 6g carbs, 0g fiber, 0g protein **NUTRITION (1 SERVING SUMMER, WITHOUT FRUIT):** 60 calories, 0g total fat, 3g carbs, 0g fiber, 0g protein **NUTRITION (1 SERVING WINTER):** 80 calories, 0g total fat, 7g carbs, Ig fiber, 0g protein **NUTRITION (1 SERVING WINTER, WITHOUT FRUIT):** 60 calories, 0g total fat, 3g carbs, 0g fiber, 0g protein

OH YEAH, ONE MORE THING . . .

Flavorize: You can use any type of tea bags you'd like—try berry or peach for the summer and orange spice or cran-apple for winter.

Some like it hot: Make the Winter Chai Sangria in a pot over low heat and serve it warm.

(V+) (GF)

SPARKLING BITTERS

Bitters soothe the stomach and make for a fun nonalcoholic drink. I make this SuperSwap at home when I feel like having a cocktail but want to stay clear-minded and energized without alcohol. I also order this at bars when I hang out with friends without drinking—it feels festive. It's also a great choice to have between alcoholic drinks to stay hydrated. **MAKES I SERVING**

¾ cup club soda or sparkling water
5 or 6 drops bitters
A few ice cubes

Mix the club soda, bitters, and ice. Cheers!

NUTRITION (I SERVING): 5 calories, 0g total fat, 2g carbs, 0g fiber, 0g protein

OH YEAH, ONE MORE THING . . .

The 411 on bitters: Originally, bitters were developed as medicine to help with digestion. They contain botanical ingredients such as aromatic herbs, bark, roots, and sometimes fruit. Bitters contain about 50% alcohol, but since you only drink 5 or 6 drops at a time, the finished product counts as a nonalcoholic drink.

You can find bitters in all sorts of inspired flavors. Read the ingredients and look for brands without added sugar or colors. When I write, I sip organic lavender bitters in sparkling water—an idea given to me by my friend Cindy Kuzma, the super-talented writer who helped me with this book.

Tonic: Don't confuse tonic water and club soda. Club soda is great since it has no calories, while tonic is bad news, with 130 calories in each cup. Tonic also has C.R.A.P. ingredients such as high-fructose corn syrup, added flavors, and preservatives.

(V+) (GF)

WELLNESS SHOT

Feeling run down from work and travel, I went to a juice bar for a natural boost. This shot with an orange-wedge chaser (like a lime wedge after a shot of tequila) gave me an instant pick-up. Definitely a SuperSwap that beats any over-the-counter remedy that only masks symptoms. **MAKES I SERVING**

Juice of I lemon (about 3 tablespoons)
I teaspoon grated fresh ginger
Pinch of cayenne
Pinch of sea salt
I orange wedge (optional)

Mix the lemon juice, ginger, cayenne, and salt in a shot glass. Drink and then follow it up by biting into the orange wedge, if desired.

NUTRITION (I SERVING): 15 calories, 0g total fat, 4g carbs, 0g fiber, 0g protein

OH YEAH, ONE MORE THING . . .

Magic explained: The juice from I lemon contains about one-third of your daily immune-boosting vitamin C. The ginger helps kill off the bacteria and viruses conspiring to make you sick. Cayenne stimulates circulation and warms up the body. Sea salt draws moisture out of swollen tissues in the throat and cleans away bacteria. The orange wedge provides a refreshing jolt and adds to the vitamin C dose.

(V+) (GF)

NATURAL SPORTS DRINK

There are 3 things your body needs to keep muscles going strong during a workout: hydration, carbohydrates, and sodium. Water keeps the whole body working efficiently, and without enough of it, we are more likely to get injured and feel fatigued. Carbs are the main fuel source that muscles burn, and sodium is the key electrolyte lost in sweat, so it's important to replace it. This SuperSwap has natural sugar from oranges and none of the added sugars and artificial colors commonly found in sports drinks.

MAKES 1 SERVING

½ cup water
½ cup 100% orange juice
1/16 teaspoon sea salt

In a sports bottle, mix the water, juice, and salt.

NUTRITION (1 SERVING): 60 calories, 0g total fat, 13g carbs, 0g fiber, 150mg sodium, 0g protein

OH YEAH, ONE MORE THING . . .

Hangover helper: Most of the symptoms of a hangover relate to dehydration, so this natural sports drink will help on the occasions when you have overcelebrated. You can also add ½ teaspoon matcha tea powder—the caffeine can help with headaches and low energy.

Coconut water plus: Eleven ounces coconut water mixed with 1/16 teaspoon sea salt is also a smart, natural sports drink option. Look for brands of coconut water without added sugar. Some brands have 90mg sodium per 11 ounces, and in that case, it's not totally necessary to add the sea salt. However, if your brand is low in sodium, add the salt.

Fresh OJ lovers: If you squeeze your own, it will take 1 to 2 oranges to get ½ cup fresh juice.

(V) (GF)

BEET KETCHUP

In most store-bought ketchup, tomatoes are listed as the *last* ingredient, and various types of refined white sugars come first. This SuperSwap relies on energizing beets instead of tomatoes, and just a drizzle of honey for sweetness. **MAKES I CUP**

2 teaspoons coconut oil
I beet, peeled and chopped into ½-inch cubes (about I cup)
½ onion, chopped (about ½ cup)
I garlic clove, minced (about ½ teaspoon)
Water, if needed
2 tablespoons apple cider vinegar
I tablespoon honey
¼ teaspoon sea salt

In a 10-inch skillet, heat the oil over medium heat. Add the beets, onion, and garlic and cook, stirring occasionally, for 10 to 15 minutes, until the beets are tender. Add a few tablespoons of water if the beets stick to the bottom of the pan. Remove from the heat and stir in the vinegar, honey, and salt. Transfer the mixture to a blender or food processor and puree until smooth. Store in an airtight container in the refrigerator for up to 7 days.

NUTRITION (I TABLESPOON): I5 calories, 0.5g total fat, 2g carbs, 0g fiber, 0g protein

OH YEAH, ONE MORE THING...

V+ Swap: Use pure maple syrup instead of honey.

Ketchup with a kick: Stir curry powder into your favorite ketchup. Not only is the flavor awesome, but curry contains turmeric, a spice with anti-cancer and anti-inflammatory health benefits.

(V) (GF)

BEET BBQ SAUCE

BBQ sauce is one of my favorite condiments, but store-bought brands come loaded with C.R.A.P. ingredients like high-fructose corn syrup, artificial flavor, caramel color, and artificial colors like yellow #6, red #40, and blue #1. This SuperSwap gets its smoky flavor from real food and healthful spices. **MAKES I CUP**

I cup Beet Ketchup (at left)
½ teaspoon blackstrap molasses
½ teaspoon chili powder
½ teaspoon smoked paprika
½ teaspoon dry mustard powder
⅛ teaspoon cayenne

Stir together the ketchup, molasses, chili powder, paprika, mustard powder, and cayenne. Store in an airtight container in the refrigerator for up to 7 days.

NUTRITION (I TABLESPOON): I5 calories, 0.5g total fat, 2g carbs, 0g fiber, 0g protein

OH YEAH, ONE MORE THING...

V+ Swap: Use pure maple syrup instead of honey in the ketchup recipe.

Blackstrap molasses: This super-thick and sticky superfood syrup flavors gingerbread and baked beans. It's loaded with minerals our body needs such as iron, calcium, magnesium, copper, selenium, and potassium.

CLOCKWISE FROM LEFT: Beet BBQ Sauce,
Beet Ketchup, Cashew Mayo (page 224),
Olive Oil Hummus (page 224)

CASHEW MAYO

Classic mayo doesn't have much in the way of nutrition, but this version has healthy fat, protein, and fiber from cashews. **MAKES 1 CUP**

1 cup raw cashews
½ cup almost-boiling water
Juice of ½ lemon (about 1½ tablespoons)
¼ teaspoon sea salt
4 teaspoons distilled white vinegar

In a food processor, puree the cashews, water, lemon juice, salt, and vinegar until smooth. Store in an airtight container in the refrigerator for up to 7 days.

NUTRITION (1 TABLESPOON): 40 calories, 3g total fat, 2g carbs, 0g fiber, 1g protein

OH YEAH, ONE MORE THING . . .

Flavorize: Stir seasonings such as dried chipotle pepper or roasted garlic into the mayo.

OLIVE OIL HUMMUS

Homemade hummus has just about the same basic nutrition stats as premade tubs, but this version uses high-quality extra-virgin olive oil, which is a healthier fat than the soybean oil found in most store-bought versions. Some brands even sneak in high-fructose corn syrup or preservatives—yuck. **MAKES 3 CUPS**

2 cans (15 ounces each) garbanzo beans, rinsed and drained (3 cups)
¼ cup tahini (sesame seed paste)
2 lemons, juiced (6 tablespoons)
¼ cup water
2 tablespoons extra-virgin olive oil, plus more for drizzling
1 garlic clove, minced
½ teaspoon sea salt (1 teaspoon if using homemade beans)
Dried dill or oregano for sprinkling

1 BLEND SMOOTH: In a food processor or blender, puree all the ingredients except the dill.

2 STORE: Refrigerate in a covered container for up to 5 days. Drizzle with a little olive oil and sprinkle with dried dill or oregano before serving.

NUTRITION (¼ CUP): 110 calories, 6g total fat, 11g carbs, 3g fiber, 4g protein

OH YEAH, ONE MORE THING . . .

Better beans: Beans soaked and cooked from scratch are easier to digest and have more absorbable protein and minerals. See how to cook your own beans on page 241.

POTATO CROUTONS

Warning: Fun crouton SuperSwap here. Cubes of potassium-rich roasted potatoes do your body good and make a salad much more filling than if you just tossed on a few toasted white bread croutons. **MAKES 2 CUPS**

2 white or sweet potatoes, unpeeled, scrubbed and cut into ¾-inch cubes (about 2 cups)
1 tablespoon extra-virgin olive oil
¼ teaspoon sea salt
¼ teaspoon freshly ground black pepper

1 **BAKE:** Preheat the oven to 400°F. Line a baking sheet with parchment paper. In a medium bowl, toss the potato cubes with the oil, salt, and pepper. Spread the potatoes in a single layer over the prepared baking sheet and bake for about 40 minutes, flipping once, until golden.

2 **BROIL:** After baking, turn the oven to broil and place the croutons under the broiler for a few minutes for extra browning and crispiness.

NUTRITION (½ CUP): 100 calories, 3.5g total fat, 17g carbs, 3g fiber, 2g protein

OH YEAH, ONE MORE THING . . .

Potato 101: Hey! Stop demonizing white potatoes. Ditch white bread, white rice, and white pasta, but potatoes are naturally white coming straight from the ground and loaded with nutrition such as fiber, vitamin C, and potassium. Plus, they contain a compound called resistant starch, which helps us feel full and keeps our gut healthy.

Stock up and storage: Make a big batch of these and keep them in the fridge for quick meals and to top salads during the week. They lose their crispness in the refrigerator, but still taste great. If you like crisp leftovers, put the potatoes in a hot pan or under the broiler for a few minutes.

MUSHROOM BACON BITS

Processed meats such as bacon, sausage, hot dogs, and deli meat are linked to increased risk of diabetes and heart disease, particularly because of their high levels of sodium and nitrates, a chemical preservative. Since mushrooms naturally have an "umami," or meaty, flavor and have natural immune-boosting properties, they make the perfect bacon SuperSwap. **MAKES 1½ CUPS**

16 ounces white mushrooms, thinly sliced (about 6 cups)
1 tablespoon extra-virgin olive oil
1 teaspoon smoked paprika
1 teaspoon ground cumin
½ teaspoon sea salt
⅛ teaspoon cayenne (optional)

1 **PREHEAT THE OVEN AND TOSS:** Preheat the oven to 350°F. Line two baking sheets with parchment paper. In a large bowl, toss the mushrooms with the oil, paprika, cumin, salt, and cayenne (if using). Spread the mushrooms in a single layer over the prepared baking sheets.

2 **BAKE AND STORE:** Bake for 45 minutes, flipping every 10 to 15 minutes, until golden and crisp. Store any leftovers in an airtight container in the fridge for up to 3 days. They will lose their crispness after the first day, but you can pop them under the broiler for a few minutes to crisp them back up.

NUTRITION (1 TABLESPOON): 10 calories, 0.5g total fat, 1g carbs, 0g fiber, 1g protein

(V+) (GF)

SUPERSAUCE MARINARA

Although you can buy great C.R.A.P.-free marinara sauce, making your own lets you pump up the types of veggies you use. Note: Cut the vegetables to roughly the same size so they cook at about the same rate. **MAKES 3 CUPS**

I tablespoon extra-virgin olive oil
½ onion, chopped (about I cup)
4 garlic cloves, minced (about 2 teaspoons)
4 tomatoes, quartered (about 4 cups)
I cup chopped broccoli
4 cups baby spinach leaves
I cup chopped carrot
I cup chopped zucchini
I tablespoon dried oregano
½ teaspoon sea salt
½ teaspoon freshly ground black pepper
Water, if needed
I tablespoon balsamic vinegar

1 ROAST THE VEGETABLES: Preheat the oven to 425°F. Line two baking sheets with parchment paper. In a large bowl, toss the oil with all the veggies to coat. Add the oregano, salt, and pepper and toss again. Spread the veggies over the prepared baking sheets. Roast for 30 minutes, flipping halfway through the cooking time, until the vegetables are tender and golden.

2 BLEND SMOOTH: Puree the roasted vegetables until they are the consistency of marinara sauce. Add water if the sauce is too thick. Stir in the vinegar. Store in an airtight container in the fridge for 3 to 4 days or freeze for up to 3 months.

NUTRITION (½ CUP): 80 calories, 2.5g total fat, 12g carbs, 4g fiber, 3g protein

(V+) (GF)

BUFFALO CAULIFLOWER POPPERS

Standard chicken wings are bad news, because each one is coated with C.R.A.P. batter, deep-fried, and contains more than 100 calories. Instead, go for this SuperSwap version made from whole grains (brown rice) and veggies (cauliflower) . . . at 12 calories per popper. The batter has only 3 ingredients! Easy. **MAKES 3 CUPS**

I teaspoon extra-virgin olive oil
½ cup brown rice flour
½ cup hot sauce (I recommend Frank's RedHot Original sauce)
¼ cup water
3 cups cauliflower florets, cut into I½-inch pieces

1 PREP: Preheat the oven to 450°F. Line a baking sheet with parchment paper and brush the paper with the oil.

2 MAKE THE BATTER AND DIP THE CAULI-FLOWER: In a medium bowl, stir together the flour, ¼ cup of the hot sauce, and the water. Dip the cauliflower pieces into the batter and place them on the prepared baking sheet as you go.

3 COOK: Bake for 15 minutes, remove from the oven, flip, and brush with the remaining ¼ cup hot sauce. Then bake for 10 minutes more.

NUTRITION (I CUP): 140 calories, 2.5g total fat, 26g carbs, 3g fiber, 4g protein

OH YEAH, ONE MORE THING . . .

Classic side: Serve these buffalo poppers with a quick blue cheese dip and veggies. Here's how: Stir together ½ cup plain 2% Greek yogurt and 3 tablespoons crumbled blue cheese. Serve with carrot and celery sticks.

CARROT AND GREEN BEAN FRIES

Green beans and carrots . . . good. Green bean and carrot fries . . . OMG good. This is so much more than a recipe to me. These fries are an attitude, a philosophy: Healthy living should be fun. They have 5 times fewer calories than regular fries (70 calories per cup versus 350 calories for regular fries). **MAKES 4 CUPS**

2 cups carrots, cut into fry shapes similar to the green beans in size
2 cups whole green beans
1½ teaspoons extra-virgin olive oil
¼ teaspoon sea salt
¼ teaspoon freshly ground black pepper

1 TURN ON THE BROILER AND TOSS THE VEGETABLES: Preheat the broiler. Line a baking sheet with aluminum foil. In a large bowl, toss the carrots, green beans, oil, salt, and pepper.

2 FILL THE BAKING SHEET: Spread the carrots and green beans in a single layer on the prepared baking sheet. I often put the carrots and green beans on separate baking sheets and cook them separately, since the green beans cook a little faster (6 minutes) than the carrots (8 minutes), but mixing them together works, too.

3 BROIL: Broil for about 7 minutes, turning once halfway through the cooking time. These are best right out of the oven.

NUTRITION (1 CUP): 45 calories, 2g total fat, 6g carbs, 2g fiber, 1g protein

ZUCCHINI WEDGES

This is a quick side vegetable for burgers, grilled chicken, fish, or pasta. The SuperSwap goal is for veggies to make up half of most meals! This is a great way to meet that quota. **MAKES 8 PIECES**

¼ cup shredded Parmesan cheese
1 teaspoon Italian seasoning
Sea salt and freshly ground black pepper
2 zucchini, quartered lengthwise
2 teaspoons extra-virgin olive oil

Preheat the broiler. Line a baking sheet with aluminum foil. In a small bowl, stir together the cheese, Italian seasoning, salt, and pepper. In a large bowl, toss the zucchini with the oil and place on the prepared baking sheet. Sprinkle with the cheese mixture and broil for about 8 minutes, until tender and golden.

NUTRITION (1 PIECE): 30 calories, 2g total fat, 2g carbs, 0g fiber, 2g protein

OH YEAH, ONE MORE THING . . .

V+ Swap: Use 2 tablespoons nutritional yeast or very finely chopped walnuts (the consistency of a chunky flour) instead of the Parmesan. Make your own vegan Parm blend by pulsing walnuts with nutritional yeast in a food processor. Refrigerate in a cheese shaker for up to 1 month.

Tomatoes, too: You can make this same recipe using tomatoes instead of zucchini. Parmesan tomatoes make an awesome side to eggs and sprouted whole-grain toast in the morning.

(V+) (GF)

PICKLES PLUS

These veggies are left at room temperature in salted water for 3 to 7 days to ferment and create good bacteria, also known as probiotics. I call these Pickles Plus since the probiotics are great for a healthy digestive tract and for boosting immunity. Enjoy them as a snack right out of the jar, or chop them for salads, sandwiches, or bowls.

MAKES I CUP EACH

1¼ cups water
1 teaspoon sea salt

CUCUMBER PICKLES

1 garlic clove
1 cup cucumber sticks

GREEN BEAN PICKLES

½ teaspoon crushed pepper flakes
1 cup whole green beans (do not snap off the ends)

CARROT PICKLES

½ teaspoon ground turmeric
1 cup thin carrot sticks

1 kale leaf

1 MAKE THE PICKLING LIQUID: Put the water and the sea salt in a 16-ounce lidded jar. Cover tightly and shake until the salt has dissolved. Add the seasoning for the pickle of your choice at this point.

2 ADD THE VEGGIES: Pack the vegetables into the jar so they are submerged in the brine. Top with the kale leaf to help keep the vegetables submerged and to prevent mold.

3 WAIT: Screw on the lid and set aside at room temperature for 3 to 7 days: Cucumbers need 3 days; green beans need 5 days; carrots need 7 days. You may want to "burp" the jar every 24 hours to let air escape. To do so, carefully open the jar and close it again.

4 STORE: Open the jar, throw away the kale leaf, close the jar, and refrigerate the pickles, submerged in the liquid, for up to 2 weeks.

NUTRITION (¼ CUP): 10 calories, 0g total fat, 3g carbs, 0g fiber, 1g protein

OH YEAH, ONE MORE THING . . .

Make more: I make three or more jars at a time.

White layer: If you see a flat white layer on the vegetables, skim it off. This is called kahm yeast, and it is harmless. However, fuzzy colorful spots are mold. If they appear, discard the whole batch—and to prevent this in the future, try using a jar with a tighter air-lock lid.

(V) (GF)

SUPERSWAP CORN BREAD

Boxed corn bread mixes usually have C.R.A.P. ingredients like white flour, degermed cornmeal (which means part of the whole grain has been removed), partially hydrogenated oil, and preservatives. This super-quick SuperSwap version uses whole-grain cornmeal and apple cider vinegar to imbue the muffins with great flavor. I put enough honey and coconut oil in the batter so these muffins won't need a pat of butter; they are decadent straight out of the wrapper. **MAKES 8 MUFFINS**

1 cup organic whole-grain cornmeal (fine grind)
1 teaspoon baking soda
½ teaspoon sea salt
1 organic egg
1 cup unsweetened plant milk, such as almond or
    hemp milk
2 tablespoons apple cider vinegar
2 tablespoons honey
2 tablespoons coconut oil, melted

Preheat the oven to 425°F. Line eight cups of a muffin tin with paper liners. In a medium bowl, mix together the cornmeal, baking soda, and salt. In another bowl, beat the egg until fluffy. Stir in the milk, vinegar, honey, and oil. Stir the dry ingredients into the bowl with the wet ingredients. Divide the batter among the prepared muffin cups. Bake for about 20 minutes, until golden.

NUTRITION (1 MUFFIN): 120 calories, 5g total fat, 17g carbs, 3g fiber, 2g protein

OH YEAH, ONE MORE THING . . .

V+ Swap: Swap out the organic egg for a "flax egg." Learn how on page 239. And use pure maple syrup instead of honey.

Flavorize: Add up to ½ cup of goodies to the corn bread batter, such as fresh sliced jalapeños, corn kernels, and/or cheddar cheese. Don't limit yourself to savory additions. Add ½ cup blueberries to the batter before baking for a berry good version!

MEAL-PLANNING
WORKSHEET

	MONDAY	TUESDAY	WEDNESDAY	THURSDAY
BREAKFAST				
LUNCH				
DINNER				
SNACKS & TREATS				

	FRIDAY	SATURDAY	SUNDAY
BREAKFAST			
LUNCH			
DINNER			
SNACKS & TREATS			

HACKS

1 **Practice Delicious Monotony.** Do not put a different recipe into each box. Choose only 1 breakfast, 2 lunch, 3 dinner, and a few snack/treat recipes to **repeat** for the week. Repetition = Success. You can pick all new stuff next week, so there's no threat of being bored.

2 **Make a List.** After you plan which meals you are making this week, write out the ingredients you need on a piece of paper, in a computer file, or on your phone notes app. Eating well starts with a good list and a smart trip to the grocery store.

3 **Enjoy 3 Meals Each Day.** Use recipes from the book and/or eat your favorite foods using **SuperSwap Ratios**: a little grain + a little protein + lots of produce topped with your favorite fat.

4 **Add 0 to 2 Snacks (or Treats) Daily,** if/when you feel hungriest. Snacks are a filling and nutritious combo of **produce + protein** (see page 126). Treats (even when made C.R.A.P.-free) are less filling so should be eaten only occasionally.

5 **Make Extra.** Don't be afraid to make extra servings of recipes: Leftovers are great for lunch or quick dinners. Having food prepared and ready to grab is a true success hack.

SUPERFOOD
GLOSSARY
& SCIENTIFIC TRUTHS

GRAINS

I gravitate toward quick-cooking, gluten-free, wet (cooked in water) whole grains such as brown rice, oats, and quinoa. Researchers have found that when food has water cooked into it, it's more filling. Whole-grain bread, cold cereal, and crackers don't satisfy as well as a bowl of "wet" oatmeal, brown rice, quinoa, or pasta. When available, choose sprouted grains; they contain more absorbable minerals and protein.

OATS

Oats contain no natural gluten but are often cross-contaminated with wheat during processing. To avoid gluten, purchase oats marked "gluten-free" (GF). My oat recipes aren't labeled "gluten-free," but you can easily swap in gluten-free oats or quinoa flakes to make those recipes GF.

I love old-fashioned rolled oats for making granola, soaked oats, and oat flour. I make hot oatmeal with rolled oats most days, but steel-cut oats from the slow cooker are one of my favorites because they have an awesome chewy texture.

Mix 4 cups water, 1 cup steel-cut oats, and a pinch of sea salt in a slow cooker and cook on low for 7 hours while you sleep (or cook on high for 3 hours). Top with a splash of unsweetened coconut milk, a sprinkling of ground cinnamon, chopped fruit, and nuts. Keep extras in the fridge for up to 5 days or freeze in single-serving containers, which can be heated and eaten on your busiest mornings. The oatmeal keeps in the freezer for up to 3 months.

QUINOA

This protein-rich grain cooks extremely quickly and absorbs flavors easily. Use it in any meal that would normally contain rice or couscous. Whole-grain pasta made with quinoa is one of my favorite types of pasta.

CORN

We often think of it as a summer vegetable, but corn is actually a whole grain. I always choose organic versions of corn tortillas, popcorn, and cornmeal. Corn is often genetically modified, so purchasing organic means steering clear of these versions (more on GMOs on page 48). Avoid corn products with "degermed" on the label; much like refining, degerming removes one of the three parts of the whole corn grain, along with the important nutrients it contains.

POTATOES

Yes, potatoes are technically a vegetable, but I list them under grains because I'd like you to think of them as a healthy, starchy carb. In the past, they've had a bad rap, but potatoes (sweet *and* white) are loaded with vitamin C and potassium. They also contain a healthy compound called resistant starch, which stabilizes blood sugar and improves weight loss and digestive health.

FLOURS

I usually avoid purchasing flours, since processing a food into flour tends to have the unfortunate effect of creating a higher-calorie, less-filling food. In the few instances where I use flour in this book or at home, I like these:

OAT FLOUR: I don't bother buying this but instead make my own by putting rolled oats into the food processor and pulsing until they reach a flourlike consistency. If you follow a gluten-free diet, use GF oats.

ORGANIC SPROUTED WHOLE-GRAIN FLOUR: Sprouting makes grains easier to digest and improves nutrient absorption. If you can't find it at your grocery store, request it or buy it online from sites like amazon.com.

FERMENTED FOODS

Fermented foods such as yogurt, kefir, tempeh, miso, kombucha, sauerkraut, and kimchi have big benefits for our bellies.

Fermentation occurs thanks to good-for-you bacteria (probiotics) or yeast in these foods. The hungry bugs nosh on carbohydrates (starches or sugars) and convert them into alcohols or acids. For example, some strains of yeast convert sugar into alcohol to produce wine or beer from grapes and grains. Certain bacteria convert carbohydrates into the lactic acids that give yogurt, kombucha, and sauerkraut their tang.

Once upon a time, fermented foods made up a much larger part of the human diet because fermentation was used to preserve food and keep it safe longer. But now that we have more "advanced processes" like heat-intensive pasteurization to preserve food, we've stopped relying on fermentation and unfortunately eliminated many important sources of probiotics.

As modern research increasingly supports the benefits of probiotics, old-fashioned fermentation has staged a comeback. Beneficial bacteria make foods easier to digest, increase the body's ability to absorb some nutrients, and support a healthy bacterial balance throughout the digestive tract. One thing to keep in mind is that the high heat in pasteurization destroys most bacteria, so if a food has the word "pasteurized" on the label, it probably doesn't contain probiotics unless they're specifically listed as an ingredient.

SEASONINGS

Herbs, spices, and similar seasonings offer a burst of flavor for little or no calories or fat, and many have their own superfood powers. Choose organic when possible to limit exposure to pesticides and added chemicals.

NUTRITIONAL YEAST

Meet *S. cerevisiae*—yeast grown on sugarcane or beets and then deactivated, heated, washed, and packaged as bright-yellow flakes. Some call it the vegan Parmesan, but even meat-eaters can get behind its nutty, cheesy flavor and the fiber and protein it contains. Use it anywhere you'd normally reach for the Parm—in fact, I keep mine in a glass shaker in the fridge and use it for making vegan cheese sauces and dressings, as well as seasoning popcorn (delish). I buy it in the bulk section of the health food store so I get just the amount I want, and I look for brands fortified with B_{12}.

TAMARI AND SOY SAUCE

Tamari is a type of soy sauce that is slightly darker, richer, and a little less aggressive than products labeled just soy sauce. Typical soy sauce is usually made with wheat, whereas tamari is usually made without wheat, so read the labels carefully if you eat a gluten-free diet. I try to buy organic tamari and other soy-based foods to reduce my dependence on GMOs (genetically modified organisms). Since both tamari and soy sauce are high in sodium, I get reduced-sodium versions.

TRUFFLE SALT

Truffles, fungi that grow underneath the ground, qualify as a specialty ingredient (aka expensive). To get the taste of truffles at a reasonable price, buy truffle salt, which contains flecks of this flavorful fungus. Just a pinch on top of plant-based dishes can add a deep umami (meaty) flavor. Beware of truffle oil, since most are made with synthetic truffle flavor. Read the ingredients before buying truffle oil.

SEAWEED

Seaweed brings a unique nutrition profile to the table. All types of seaweed—red seaweed (nori and dulse), brown seaweed (kombu), and green seaweed (chlorella and spirulina)—contain all the essential amino acids and some healthy fat and fiber. Seaweed is also particularly rich in minerals, especially iodine, which supports a healthy thyroid. If you are new to seaweed, start with nori in recipes like Sea Cakes (page 146), Seaweed Snack Strips (page 165), or the Sushi Bowl (page 141). Or you can add a little spirulina to recipes such as the No-Bake Peanut Butter Cookies (page 121), Brownie Bites (page 159), or the Belly Love Smoothie (page 96). Or just buy ground dried dulse in a shaker bottle and sprinkle it on anything you would normally season with salt. It's flavorful and low in sodium.

GROUND VANILLA BEANS

The deep, subtly sweet flavor of ground vanilla beans helps you attain decadent sweetness with less sugar; they're also great in coffee and tea. Check that the ingredients are nothing more than ground vanilla beans (some companies sell vanilla powder with additives—*not* what you want). Use ground vanilla beans in any recipe calling for vanilla extract, but use half as much ground vanilla beans as extract. If you can't find it at your grocery store, request it, and until it's stocked by the store, buy it online from sites like amazon.com. You can substitute pure vanilla extract for ground beans in anything you cook and bake since the heat helps

evaporate the alcohol flavor. When using vanilla in foods you don't heat, definitely choose ground vanilla beans or use the seeds from an actual vanilla bean.

VINEGARS

Research suggests this superfood condiment keeps food in your stomach longer, so you'll naturally feel more satisfied. Using vinegar can help you cut 200 calories per day without thinking about it. Aim for 1 to 2 tablespoons daily. As a bonus, vinegar is practically calorie-free, brightens the flavor of your food, and reduces your need for salt.

APPLE CIDER VINEGAR

A strong vinegar made by crushing apples, fermenting them by adding bacteria and yeast (which turns the sugars into alcohol), and then fermenting the mixture one more time with bacteria to turn the alcohol into vinegar. Apple cider vinegar is sometimes sold with the "mother"—harmless fiberlike strands produced by the vinegar bacteria—in the bottle. I like seeing the mother; it reminds me that healthy bacteria played a role in the vinegar-making process.

BALSAMIC VINEGAR

Sweet, tangy balsamic tastes great on pasta or drizzled on top of tomato soup. Adding vinegar to pasta dishes pays off—it may help slow carb digestion, keeping your post-meal blood sugar levels steadier.

BROWN RICE VINEGAR

This is a mild vinegar that I use in Asian-inspired slaws and salads.

SUGARS

Swapping sweeteners matters. Making the switch from refined white sugar to healthier alternatives can increase your daily antioxidant intake by 2.6mmol a day—about the same amount found in a single serving of nuts or berries. Still, aim to keep all added sugars to a minimum; they lack the nutrition of whole foods. Here's my go-to list of sweeteners to use in moderation.

BROWN RICE SYRUP

You probably don't think of brown rice as sugary. Manufacturers use enzymes to break down the starches and then collect and concentrate the liquid that remains to form this sticky sweetener. Less sweet than sugar, brown rice syrup also has more calories per tablespoon than most other sweeteners. I use it only when I need a superthick texture, such as in Brown Rice Crispy Treats (page 206) or 5-Minute Chocolate (page 117). Some brands use barley enzymes, which contain gluten, so check labels closely if you're gluten-free.

COCONUT SUGAR

Coconut sugar is made from the sap of flower buds on coconut palm trees. The result is ever so slightly less sweet than refined white sugar, but it can make a near-perfect swap in your sugar bowl and baking recipes.

DATE SUGAR

Grinding dried dates harnesses their sweetness and provides an option that's 100% fruit—amazing. That said, it's usually quite pricy.

HONEY

Busy bees gather the nectar of flowers and store it in honeycombs, where water evaporates and concentrates the sugars. I'm a huge honey fan.

Outside the kitchen, I use it as an antibacterial ointment, rubbing it directly on wounds and blemishes—and as a cough suppressant and throat soother (swallow 2 teaspoons, or stir it into hot water).

PURE MAPLE SYRUP

We are not talking processed pancake syrup here. Maple syrup comes from the clear sap of maple trees, boiled to form a concentrate. I use it to add a buttery, caramel-like flavor to any number of dishes.

CHOCOLATE

DARK CHOCOLATE

When choosing chocolate, purchase bars or chips with a high percentage of cacao. The higher the number, the more cacao bean flavor and the less sugar, preservatives, and other C.R.A.P. in the chocolate. Also avoid milk fat or milk solids in the ingredients—unnecessary additions that do not contribute to the flavor. Dark chocolate is also labeled "semisweet" and "bittersweet" in the baking aisle.

CACAO POWDER VS COCOA POWDER

Some experts will tell you anything labeled "cacao powder" is healthy and anything labeled "cocoa powder" isn't, but that's not true—they both have health benefits. Neither has sugar, and they're both loaded with antioxidants and fiber.

I usually purchase unsweetened "raw cacao powder." I find it in health food stores in the raw food aisle, or I buy it online from amazon.com or other retailers. Though there's no legal definition—or even a clear industry standard—for the term "raw," if a brand is attempting to use less heat during processing, more of the cacao's healthy compounds are likely to stay intact.

That said, don't feel bad about buying the more common unsweetened cocoa powder. I do so when I can't get my hands on raw cacao powder. Just be sure to avoid Dutched versions. Dutching involves adding an alkali to the powder, which mellows its flavor but also destroys some of the healthful flavonols.

Whether you choose cacao powder or cocoa powder, rest assured that you have all the chocolate you need. I may have one or two recipes using a chocolate bar or chips, but I highly recommend avoiding them as often as possible because they beg for mindlessly binging. Instead, put in the loving effort and concoct your own chocolate when you need a fix. Check out the 5-Minute Chocolate recipe on page 117 for details.

CACAO NIBS

"Nature's chocolate chips" are the roasted center of a cacao bean broken into small pieces—nothing more, nothing less. They are chocolaty but bitter, since they have no added sugars or fats to round out their flavor. Still, their earthy depth has its own appeal. Eat them right out of the bag or use them anywhere you would chocolate chips—sprinkled on yogurt, tossed with trail mix, or baked into cookie recipes.

FATS

Add fat to every meal—use whole foods like nuts, seeds, and avocado more often than oils. When you do use oil, choose these.

EXTRA-VIRGIN OLIVE OIL (EVOO)

There's a rumor that you can't heat extra-virgin olive oil and that you should limit its use to salads. Not true! You can safely and healthfully cook with extra-virgin olive oil up to about 410°F. In fact, thanks to its antioxidants, and compounds called stable oleic acids that protect it from degrading, olive oil holds up better under hot temperatures than other oils. Consider this the green light to use EVOO for sautéing, baking, and panfrying (which is typically done at 365°F).

AVOCADO OIL

For very high heat cooking, such as grilling, I gravitate toward avocado oil, which provides a heaping dose of healthy and stable monounsaturated fats. Other healthy oils for high-heat cooking include organic canola, high-oleic sunflower, and high-oleic safflower oils.

COCONUT OIL

I use virgin coconut oil to add light coconut flavor. It's best for moderate heats up to 350°F. Solid at room temperature, refined coconut oil can be heated up to 400°F and has a subtle flavor. I like to make coconut cubes for easy use and measuring (see page 212).

GRASS-FED BUTTER

I like knowing my butter comes from the milk of happy cows roaming outside, eating leafy green grass. The finished product has a superior fat and antioxidant profile compared to butter from the milk of grain-fed cows. Butter should only be heated up to 350°F, so it's better for low- to moderate-heat cooking or as a spread.

NUTS AND SEEDS

RAW ALMONDS, CASHEWS, WALNUTS, SUNFLOWER SEEDS, AND MORE

Buying nuts and seeds in their most unprocessed form means they taste great—but not so addictive that you can't stop eating them. Consider it natural portion control. Plus, you'll skip added C.R.A.P. like excess salt, sugar, and preservatives.

GROUND FLAXSEED

Flaxseeds are packed with 2 grams of fiber per tablespoon, anticancer compounds called lignans, and the healthy omega-3 fat alpha-linolenic acid (ALA). Grinding flaxseeds makes it easier for our bodies to absorb these healthy fats. You can buy whole flaxseeds (which last about 1 year at room temperature) and grind them yourself in a blender, food processor, or coffee grinder as you need them. Or you can save time by buying them preground—I do this—but you have to take extra care when storing them. Once you open the vacuum-sealed package, transfer the flaxseeds to an opaque airtight container and store them in the fridge or freezer. Be sure to label the container with the date you opened them—toss any you haven't used after about 90 days.

I used to worry that cooking ground flaxseed destroyed its oils. Exhaustive research reveals that both whole and ground flaxseeds can safely take the heat with their oils intact.

>> **Flax eggs:** When I want to make a totally plant-based or vegan recipe, I use "flax eggs" instead of chicken eggs to bind ingredients together. To make 1 flax egg (equal to 1 chicken egg), mix 3 tablespoons warm water with 1 tablespoon ground flaxseed. Let sit for 5 minutes, until it's thick, stirring occasionally.

NUT AND SEED BUTTERS

Nut and seed butters are a creamy way to get plant protein, healthy fat, and a variety of vitamins and minerals. Read ingredient labels to get natural butters made with only nuts or seeds, without added sugar or fat. I tend to use almond butter in many Superfood Swap recipes because it's easy to find, not super expensive, and packed with skin-protective vitamin E.

EGGS

The egg yolk is a powerhouse of nutrients: choline for brain health, along with vitamins A, E, D, and K. And contrary to popular beliefs, eating 1 or 2 whole eggs per day won't wreak havoc on your blood cholesterol levels. Eat the yolk! A recent study in the *American Journal of Clinical Nutrition* confirms that. Here's some egg-cellent cooking help:

HARD-BOILED: I like to keep hard-boiled eggs around for a quick breakfast with a piece of fruit or to chop up on a salad. Here's how: Put 1 or more eggs in a pot large enough to hold them in a single layer. Add cold water to cover the egg(s) by 1 inch. Bring the water to a boil, immediately turn off the heat, cover the pot, and let sit for 10 minutes. Drain the egg(s), cool under cold running water, and refrigerate for up to 1 week.

POACHED: Typical poaching by cracking eggs into swirling water is a little complicated for me. I prefer cheating by using silicone poaching pods, which you can buy in any kitchen store.

7-MINUTE EGG: I like these medium-boiled eggs even better than poached. How-to: Bring a saucepan of water to a boil. Use a slotted spoon to gently lower 1 or more eggs into the boiling water. Cook, uncovered, for exactly 7 minutes (set a timer!), then plunge them into a bowl filled with ice and water for about 1 minute. The white will be set and the yolk will be custardy.

DAIRY

Choose organic when possible. Eat plain 2% kefir and yogurt. These dairy foods have a powerful function, providing good bacteria for immunity and digestion. Don't go fat-free, because dairy fat contains CLA (conjugated linoleic acid), which boosts immunity and, paradoxically, increases fat burning. Eat flavorful cheese as a vegetable and salad condiment, rather than for straight snacking. My philosophy: There's no need to be against cheese if it's helping you get more veggies into your diet.

PLANT MILK

When buying nondairy (plant) milk, there are a couple of things to consider: first, the vitamins and minerals, and second, the sugar. Sadly, most plant milks (made from beans, nuts, seeds, and grains) don't have much in the way of protein, so you're really choosing these milks for their vitamins and minerals. Read labels to make sure the brand you've chosen has calcium and vitamin D. Also read labels to choose unsweetened versions—no need to drink sugary milk. The final ingredient to check for on plant milk labels is carrageenan, a thickener made from seaweed. Carrageenan may cause inflammation in the gut for some people, so if you consume a lot of plant milk, it's worth finding brands without this additive. If you don't drink much plant milk and are a splash-in-your-coffee kind of person, this isn't really a big deal.

LENTILS AND BEANS

LENTILS

Lentils are a convenient way to get plant protein. You can soak them overnight like beans, which makes them slightly easier to digest and faster to cook, but soaking isn't as essential as it is with beans. I use green and brown lentils for things like veggie meatballs and a ground beef swap because they keep their shape more than the red, orange, or yellow varieties. The key to cooking lentils is to *be gentle*. Put 1 cup lentils and 2 to 3 cups water in a pot (it's no big deal if you use more water because you can drain off any extra liquid when they are done cooking). Bring the water to a boil, then immediately turn the heat down to maintain a low, gentle simmer and cook for about 20 minutes, or until the lentils are tender but not mushy. Drain any extra water. I also love the healthy convenience of buying precooked lentils in the produce section of many grocery stores.

TEMPEH

Fermented soybeans are pressed into a rectangular patty to form tempeh. It's high in vegan-friendly protein and has a satisfying, meaty texture. Find it in the produce section of many grocery stores—choose organic so it's made with non-GMO soybeans. You can use it as a chicken substitute on a BBQ sandwich or cut it into strips for a lunch wrap. You can also crumble it and use it as a ground beef substitute in chili, pasta, and tacos.

CANNED BEANS

These guys are the definition of a healthy convenience food—wholesome, cooked, and ready to go. Keep your house stocked with cans of beans for occasions when you don't have time to make dried beans from scratch. Choose cans labeled BPA-free, since this endocrine-disrupting chemical is often used in can linings. Soaking and cooking dried beans, though, is even better for you.

SLOW-COOKER BEANS

I recently started making beans in a slow cooker, and let me tell you, it's totally worth the effort. Slow-cooked soaked beans taste awesome; plus, they are easier to digest (I definitely notice a difference in the side effects, if you know what I mean) and beans that you cook yourself are a better source of protein and minerals than canned. The magical difference is the *soaking* step—it reduces compounds called phytates, which block your body from absorbing some of the healthy nutrition beans have to offer and can be difficult to digest.

Use slow-cooker beans to make veggie burgers, mash for tacos, puree for hummus, or chop into veggie-friendly sandwich fillings. More beans in your life means more plant protein and fiber. One note: When you SuperSwap homemade beans for canned beans in recipes, you will probably have to add additional sea salt, since canned beans bring along their own salty flavor. Some bean math for you: one 15-ounce can beans = 1½ cups home-cooked bean beauties.

TRY IT: SLOW-COOKER BEANS

I typically cook chickpeas and black beans because they are so versatile, but you can cook any beans you'd like.

1 **Soak and drain.** In a large bowl, cover 1 pound dried beans with 8 cups water. Cover the bowl with a kitchen towel. Leave at room temperature overnight or for at least 8 hours. This is where the magic happens—do not omit this step. Drain.

2 **Cook and drain.** Rinse the beans and pick out any rocks or debris (you're not likely to find many of these). Put the beans in a slow cooker and add enough fresh water to cover by 2 inches. Cook on low for about 8 hours or on high for 4 hours, until tender. The beans are ready when you can easily smash them between your fingers. Drain.

3 **Measure and store.** This process makes 6 cups beans (equivalent to four 15-ounce cans). Measure 1½-cup portions of the cooked beans (equivalent to 1 can) and put them into containers with lids. Keep some in the fridge for up to 1 week and freeze the rest for up to 6 months.

COMPLETE
» NUTRITION «
ANALYSES

Every recipe has basic nutrition information;
here, you'll find more details.

EXPRESS RECIPES

BREAKFAST

AVOCADO TOAST

NUTRITION INFO (PER SERVING): 390 calories, 21g total fat, 2g saturated fat, 0g trans fat, 0mg cholesterol, 450mg sodium, 42g carbohydrate, 13g fiber, 2g sugar, 0g added sugar, 14g protein, vitamin A 715 IU (15%), vitamin C 15mg (25%), vitamin D 0mcg (0%), calcium 29mg (2%), iron 2.96mg (15%), potassium 608mg (10%)

BETTERTELLA BREAKFAST

NUTRITION INFO (PER SERVING): 380 calories, 19g total fat, 2.5g saturated fat, 0g trans fat, 0mg cholesterol, 150mg sodium, 49g carbohydrate, 12g fiber, 19g sugar, 0g added sugar, 12g protein, vitamin A 45 IU (0%), vitamin C 8mg (15%), vitamin D 0mcg (0%), calcium 127mg (15%), iron 2.28mg (15%), potassium 446mg (15%)

CEREAL PUFF BOWL

NUTRITION INFO (PER SERVING): 390 calories, 11g total fat, 3.5g saturated fat, 0g trans fat, 15mg cholesterol, 260mg sodium, 51g carbohydrate, 10g fiber, 16g sugar, 0g added sugar, 25g protein, vitamin A 140 IU (2%), vitamin C 33mg (60%), vitamin D 0mcg (0%), calcium 232mg (25%), iron 1.64mg (10%), potassium 270mg (6%)

PEANUT BUTTER OATMEAL

NUTRITION INFO (PER SERVING): 380 calories, 18g total fat, 2g saturated fat, 0g trans fat, 0mg cholesterol, 270mg sodium, 47g carbohydrate, 9g fiber, 21g sugar, 0g added sugar, 11g protein, vitamin A 102 IU (2%), vitamin C 8mg (15%), vitamin D 0mcg (0%), calcium 38mg (4%), iron 1.59mg (8%), potassium 200mg (4%)

SUPERFOOD SCRAMBLE BOWL

NUTRITION INFO (PER SERVING): 410 calories, 23g total fat, 5g saturated fat, 0g trans fat, 370mg cholesterol, 530mg sodium, 31g carbohydrate, 9g fiber, 2g sugar, 0g added sugar, 21g protein, vitamin A 8,097 IU (160%), vitamin C 48mg (80%), vitamin D 2.0mcg (15%), calcium 198mg (20%), iron 7.27mg (40%), potassium 597mg (112%)

GREEN OMELET

NUTRITION INFO (PER SERVING): 380 calories, 27g total fat, 6g saturated fat, 0g trans fat, 370mg cholesterol, 450mg sodium, 23g carbohydrate, 7g fiber, 2g sugar, 0g added sugar, 16g protein, vitamin A 4,528 IU (90%), vitamin C 94mg (160%), vitamin D 2.0mcg (10%), calcium 134mg (15%), iron 2.86mg (15%), potassium 842mg (18%)

BELLY LOVE SMOOTHIE

NUTRITION INFO (PER SERVING): 390 calories, 12g total fat, 2.5g saturated fat, 0g trans fat, 10mg cholesterol, 210mg sodium, 57g carbohydrate, 17g fiber, 26g sugar, 0g added sugar, 20g protein, vitamin A 7,902 IU (160%), vitamin C 45mg (80%), vitamin D 0mcg (0%), calcium 609mg (60%), iron 6.45mg (35%), potassium 556mg (10%)

LUNCH

HUMMUS BOWL

NUTRITION INFO (PER SERVING): 390 calories, 15g total fat, 3.5g saturated fat, 0g trans fat, 20mg cholesterol, 560mg sodium, 52g carbohydrate, 7g fiber, 6g sugar, 0g added sugar, 17g protein, vitamin A 6,282 IU (130%), vitamin C 47mg (80%), vitamin D 0mcg (0%), calcium 255mg (25%), iron 6.46mg (35%), potassium 387mg (8%)

MEXICAN BURRITO BOWL

NUTRITION INFO (PER SERVING): 420 calories, 13g total fat, 1.5g saturated fat, 0g trans fat, 0mg cholesterol, 500mg sodium, 66g carbohydrate, 20g fiber, 14g sugar, 0g added sugar, 15g protein, vitamin A 7,220 IU (140%), vitamin C 220mg (370%), vitamin D 0mcg (0%), calcium 135mg (15%), iron 5.31mg (30%), potassium 1,348mg (30%)

SUNFLOWER CAESAR SALAD

NUTRITION INFO (PER SERVING): 420 calories, 9g total fat, 1g saturated fat, 0g trans fat, 0mg cholesterol, 490mg sodium, 65g carbohydrate, 16g fiber, 11g sugar, 0g added sugar, 21g protein, vitamin A 4,634 IU (90%), vitamin C 59mg (100%), vitamin D 0mcg (0%), calcium 113mg (10%), iron 4.97mg (30%), potassium 469mg (10%)

SUNFLOWER CAESAR DRESSING

NUTRITION INFO (1 TABLESPOON): 25 calories, 1.5g total fat, 2g carbs, 1g fiber, 1g protein

AVOCADO TUNA SANDWICH

NUTRITION INFO (PER SERVING): 390 calories, 14g total fat, 2g saturated fat, 0g trans fat, 45mg cholesterol, 880mg sodium, 37g carbohydrate, 10g fiber, 7g sugar, 0g added sugar, 33g protein, vitamin A 5,933 IU (120%), vitamin C 21mg (35%), vitamin D 1.51mcg (10%), calcium 113mg (10%), iron 4.00mg (20%), potassium 950mg (20%)

ASIAN PEANUT BOWL

NUTRITION INFO (PER SERVING): 410 calories, 16g total fat, 1.5g saturated fat, 0g trans fat, 0mg cholesterol, 210mg sodium, 48g carbohydrate, 11g fiber, 8g sugar, 0g added sugar, 18g protein, vitamin A 748 IU (15%), vitamin C 66mg (110%), vitamin D 0mcg (0%), calcium 132mg (15%), iron 3.37mg (20%), potassium 382mg (8%)

LOX LUNCH PLATE

NUTRITION INFO (PER SERVING): 400 calories, 18g total fat, 3g saturated fat, 0g trans fat, 15mg cholesterol, 560mg sodium, 48g carbohydrate, 15g fiber, 4g sugar, 0g added sugar, 17g protein, vitamin A 797 IU (15%), vitamin C 27mg (45%), vitamin D 9.7mcg (65%), calcium 57mg (6%), iron 2.59mg (15%), potassium 980mg (20%)

COLLARD GREEN BURRITOS

NUTRITION INFO (2 BURRITOS): 420 calories, 16g total fat, 2.5g saturated fat, 0g trans fat, 0mg cholesterol, 500mg sodium, 63g carbohydrate, 20g fiber, 6g sugar, 0g added sugar, 13g protein, vitamin A 3,961 IU (80%), vitamin C 38mg (60%), vitamin D 0mcg (0%), calcium 249mg (25%), iron 3.21mg (20%), potassium 1,248mg (25%)

DINNER

QUICK KALE PIZZA

NUTRITION INFO (PER SERVING): 380 calories, 21g total fat, 6g saturated fat, 0g trans fat, 15mg cholesterol, 770mg sodium, 34g carbohydrate, 8g fiber, 4g sugar, 0g added sugar, 16g protein, vitamin A 3,807 IU (80%), vitamin C 41mg (70%), vitamin D 0.1mcg (0%), calcium 365mg (35%), iron 2.89mg (15%), potassium 198mg (4%)

GUAC AND GREENS TACOS

NUTRITION INFO (PER SERVING): 430 calories, 16g total fat, 2g saturated fat, 0g trans fat, 0mg cholesterol, 400mg sodium, 65g carbohydrate, 19g fiber, 1g sugar, 0g added sugar, 13g protein, vitamin A 5,631 IU (110%), vitamin C 33mg (50%), vitamin D 0mcg (0%), calcium 153mg (15%), iron 4.95mg (30%), potassium 891mg (20%)

BBQ SALMON AND CAULIFLOWER MASH

NUTRITION INFO (PER SERVING): 390 calories, 14g total fat, 3g saturated fat, 0g trans fat, 90mg cholesterol, 660mg sodium, 24g carbohydrate, 7g fiber, 11g sugar, 0g added sugar, 44g protein, vitamin A 3,627 IU (70%), vitamin C 185mg (310%), vitamin D 18.7mcg (125%), calcium 131mg (15%), iron 2.62mg (15%), potassium 612mg (15%)

PESTO ZOODLES WITH GARLIC BREAD

NUTRITION INFO (PER SERVING): 410 calories, 14g total fat, 1.5g saturated fat, 0g trans fat, 0mg cholesterol, 770mg sodium, 58g carbohydrate, 15g fiber, 11g sugar, 0g added sugar, 18g protein, vitamin A 2,752 IU (60%), vitamin C 64mg (110%), vitamin D 0mcg (0%), calcium 146mg (15%), iron 5.16mg (30%), potassium 1,321mg (30%)

COCONUT CURRY AND SUPER RICE

NUTRITION INFO (PER SERVING): 400 calories, 20g total fat, 13g saturated fat, 0g trans fat, 0mg cholesterol, 210mg sodium, 47g carbohydrate, 8g fiber, 12g sugar, 0g added sugar, 10g protein, vitamin A 2,349 IU (45%), vitamin C 95mg (160%), vitamin D 0mcg (0%), calcium 108mg (10%), iron 3.97mg (20%), potassium 567mg (10%)

OLIVE OIL PASTA

NUTRITION INFO (PER SERVING): 380 calories, 23g total fat, 2.5g saturated fat, 0g trans fat, 0mg cholesterol, 170mg sodium, 43g carbohydrate, 6g fiber, 3g sugar, 0g added sugar, 8g protein, vitamin A 6,490 IU (130%), vitamin C 78mg (130%), vitamin D 0mcg (0%), calcium 113mg (10%), iron 2.55mg (15%), potassium 381mg (8%)

CHEDDAR GRITS WITH BEANS AND GREENS

NUTRITION INFO (PER SERVING): 380 calories, 17g total fat, 6g saturated fat, 0g trans fat, 30mg cholesterol, 1100mg sodium, 44g carbohydrate, 12g fiber, 1g sugar, 0g added sugar, 16g protein, vitamin A 2,991 IU (60%), vitamin C 20mg (35%), vitamin D 0.17mcg (1%), calcium 388mg (40%), iron 3.06mg (15%), potassium 448mg (10%)

TREATS

5-MINUTE CHOCOLATE

NUTRITION INFO (1 PIECE): 110 calories, 10g total fat, 9g saturated fat, 0g trans fat, 0mg cholesterol, 10mg sodium, 8g carbohydrate, 1g fiber, 4g sugar, 4g added sugar, 1g protein, vitamin A 0 IU (0%), vitamin C 0mg (0%), vitamin D 0mcg (0%), calcium 2mg (0%), iron 0.25mg (2%), potassium 17mg (0%)

5-MINUTE CHOCOLATE WITH BERRIES

NUTRITION INFO (1 PIECE + 5 BERRIES): 130 calories, 10g total fat, 9g

saturated fat, 0g trans fat, 0mg cholesterol, 10mg sodium, 12g carbohydrate, 2g fiber, 7g sugar, 4g added sugar, 1g protein, vitamin A 7 IU (0%), vitamin C 35mg (60%), vitamin D 0mcg (0%), calcium 11mg (2%), iron 0.50mg (2%), potassium 108mg (2%)

ALMOND JOY SNACK MIX

NUTRITION INFO (PER SERVING): 200 calories, 17g total fat, 7g saturated fat, 0g trans fat, 0mg cholesterol, 0mg sodium, 10g carbohydrate, 4g fiber, 4g sugar, 3g added sugar, 5g protein, vitamin A 0 IU (0%), vitamin C 0mg (0%), vitamin D 0mcg (0%), calcium 53mg (6%), iron 1.14mg (6%), potassium 131mg (2%)

FREEZER FUDGE

NUTRITION INFO (PER SERVING): 130 calories, 11g total fat, 4.5g saturated fat, 0g trans fat, 0mg cholesterol, 130mg sodium, 4g carbohydrate, 1g fiber, 1g sugar, 0g added sugar, 4g protein, vitamin A 0 IU (0%), vitamin C 0mg (0%), vitamin D 0mcg (0%), calcium 0mg (0%), iron 0.22mg (2%), potassium 0mg (0%)

BANANA SKINNIES

NUTRITION INFO (PER SERVING): 150 calories, 9g total fat, 1g saturated fat, 0g trans fat, 0mg cholesterol, 35mg sodium, 17g carbohydrate, 3g fiber, 8g sugar, 0g added sugar, 4g protein, vitamin A 38 IU (0%), vitamin C 5mg (8%), vitamin D 0mcg (0%), calcium 58mg (6%), iron 0.77mg (4%), potassium 331mg (8%)

CHOCOLATE YOGURT MOUSSE

NUTRITION INFO (PER SERVING): 110 calories, 2g total fat, 1g saturated fat, 0g trans fat, 5mg cholesterol, 30mg sodium, 17g carbohydrate, 3g fiber, 13g sugar, 9g added sugar, 8g protein, vitamin A 48 IU (0%), vitamin C 8mg (15%), vitamin D 0mcg (0%), calcium 65mg (6%), iron 1.16mg (6%), potassium 52mg (1%)

NO-BAKE PEANUT BUTTER COOKIES

NUTRITION INFO (PER SERVING): 140 calories, 10g total fat, 1.5g saturated fat, 0g trans fat, 0mg cholesterol, 0mg sodium, 9g carbohydrate, 3g fiber, 1g sugar, 0g added sugar, 6g protein, vitamin A 3 IU (0%), vitamin C 0mg (0%), vitamin D 0mcg (0%), calcium 19mg (2%), iron 0.88mg (4%), potassium 0mg (0%)

SPINACH CHIPS

NUTRITION INFO (PER SERVING): 120 calories, 8g total fat, 1g saturated fat, 0g trans fat, 0mg cholesterol, 240mg sodium, 7g carbohydrate, 3g fiber, 0g sugar, 0g added sugar, 5g protein, vitamin A 7,343 IU (150%), vitamin C 33mg (50%), vitamin D 0mcg (0%), calcium 128mg (15%), iron 4.26mg (25%), potassium 69mg (2%)

SESAME SEAWEED POPCORN

NUTRITION INFO (PER SERVING): 180 calories, 12g total fat, 1.5g saturated fat, 0g trans fat, 0mg cholesterol, 50mg sodium, 16g carbohydrate, 4g fiber, 0g sugar, 0g added sugar, 5g protein, vitamin A 2,532 IU (50%), vitamin C 5mg (8%), vitamin D 0mcg (0%), calcium 109mg (10%), iron 2.18mg (10%), potassium 95mg (2%)

SUPERFOOD PARTY MIX

NUTRITION INFO (PER SERVING): 170 calories, 11g total fat, 1.5g saturated fat, 0g trans fat, 0mg cholesterol, 170mg sodium, 13g carbohydrate, 2g fiber, 2g sugar, 0g added sugar, 5g protein, vitamin A 122 IU (2%), vitamin C 2mg (4%), vitamin D 0mcg (0%), calcium 21mg (2%), iron 1.29mg (8%), potassium 93mg (2%)

SPRING/SUMMER RECIPES

BREAKFAST

LEAFY OMELET ROLL-UP

NUTRITION INFO (PER SERVING): 390 calories, 22g total fat, 7g saturated fat, 0g trans fat, 390mg cholesterol, 390mg sodium, 27g carbohydrate, 6g fiber, 3g sugar, 0g added sugar, 21g protein, vitamin A 7,212 IU (140%), vitamin C 17mg (30%), vitamin D 2.0mcg (8%), calcium 138mg (15%), iron 4.12mg (25%), potassium 314mg (6%)

GOLDEN SMOOTHIE BOWL

NUTRITION INFO (PER SERVING): 390 calories, 19g total fat, 9g saturated fat, 0g trans fat, 10mg cholesterol, 125mg sodium, 44g carbohydrate, 6g fiber, 27g sugar, 0g added sugar, 15g protein, vitamin A 553 IU (10%), vitamin C 13mg (20%), vitamin D 0mcg (0%), calcium 312mg (30%), iron 0.63mg (10%), potassium 513mg (10%)

CHOCOLATE BEETBERRY SMOOTHIE

NUTRITION INFO (PER SERVING): 380 calories, 22g total fat, 3.5g saturated fat, 0g trans fat, 0mg cholesterol, 180mg sodium, 41g carbohydrate, 8g fiber, 18g sugar, 0g added sugar, 11g protein, vitamin A 442 IU (8%), vitamin C 57mg (90%), vitamin D 1.87mcg (12%), calcium 204mg (20%), iron 4.09mg (25%), potassium 646mg (14%)

CARROT CAKE OATS

NUTRITION INFO (PER SERVING): 380 calories, 19g total fat, 1.5g saturated fat, 0g trans fat, 0mg cholesterol, 180mg sodium, 45g carbohydrate, 8g fiber, 19g sugar, 0g added sugar, 9g protein, vitamin A 9,575 IU (190%), vitamin C 3mg (6%), vitamin D 1.87mcg (12%), calcium 208mg (20%), iron 2.85mg (15%), potassium 558mg (12%)

ALMOND BUTTER AND CHIA JAM SANDWICH

NUTRITION INFO (PER SERVING): 380 calories, 20g total fat, 2g saturated fat, 0g trans fat, 0mg cholesterol, 220mg sodium, 40g carbohydrate, 11g fiber, 4g sugar, 0g added sugar, 15g protein, vitamin A 6 IU (0%), vitamin C 22mg (35%), vitamin D 0mcg (0%), calcium 134mg (15%), iron 2.91mg (15%), potassium 308mg (6%)

CHIA JAM

NUTRITION INFO (1 TABLESPOON): 10 calories, 0g total fat, 0.5g saturated fat, 0g trans fat, 0mg cholesterol, 0mg sodium, 2g carbohydrate, 1g fiber, 1g sugar, 0g added sugar, 0g protein, vitamin A 3 IU (0%), vitamin C 11mg (20%), vitamin D 0mcg (0%), calcium 11mg (2%), iron 0.18mg (0%), potassium 35mg (1%)

NO-SUGAR GRANOLA PARFAIT

NUTRITION INFO (1 SERVING): 390 calories, 16g total fat, 9g saturated fat, 0g trans fat, 10mg cholesterol, 105mg sodium, 41g carbohydrate, 6g fiber, 23g sugar, 0g added sugar, 22g protein, vitamin A 156 IU (4%), vitamin C 15mg (25%), vitamin D 0mcg (0%), calcium 140mg (15%), iron 2.65mg (15%), potassium 116mg (5%)

NO-SUGAR GRANOLA

NUTRITION INFO (1/4 CUP): 150 calories, 10g total fat, 5g saturated fat, 0g trans fat, 0mg cholesterol, 40mg sodium, 10g carbohydrate, 2g fiber, 1g sugar, 0g added sugar, 5g protein, vitamin A 1 IU (0%), vitamin C 0mg (0%), vitamin D 0mcg (0%), calcium 15mg (2%), iron 1.80mg (10%), potassium 1mg (0%)

LUNCH

SUSHI BOWL

NUTRITION INFO (1 BOWL): 390 calories, 14g total fat, 1.5g saturated fat, 0g trans fat, 0mg cholesterol, 330mg sodium, 53g carbohydrate, 13g fiber, 9g sugar, 0g added sugar, 16g protein, vitamin A 13,435 IU (270%), vitamin C 39mg (60%), vitamin D 0mcg (0%), calcium 149mg (15%), iron 3.79mg (20%), potassium 820mg (18%)

BBQ SANDWICH AND COLLARD CHIPS

NUTRITION INFO (1 SANDWICH): 410 calories, 14g total fat, 1.5g saturated fat, 0g trans fat, 0mg cholesterol, 570mg sodium, 56g carbohydrate, 17g fiber, 14g sugar, 0g added sugar, 21g protein, vitamin A 7,086 IU (140%), vitamin C 57mg (90%), vitamin D 0mcg (0%), calcium 441mg (45%), iron 4.82mg (25%), potassium 606mg (12%)

CASHEW BUTTER CLUB

NUTRITION INFO (PER SERVING): 380 calories, 18g total fat, 3.5g saturated fat, 0g trans fat, 0mg cholesterol, 340mg sodium, 45g carbohydrate, 8g fiber, 6g sugar, 0g added sugar, 13g protein, vitamin A 1,085 IU (20%), vitamin C 17mg (30%), vitamin D 0mcg (0%), calcium 67mg (6%), iron 3.14mg (15%), potassium 304mg (6%)

FAST FALAFEL BOWL

NUTRITION INFO (PER SERVING): 420 calories, 24g total fat, 2.5g saturated fat, 0g trans fat, 0mg cholesterol, 720mg sodium, 41g carbohydrate, 15g fiber, 9g sugar, 0g added sugar, 16g protein, vitamin A 3,996 IU (80%), vitamin C 48mg (80%), vitamin D 0mcg (0%), calcium 177mg (20%), iron 5.55mg (30%), potassium 282mg (6%)

SEA CAKES AND SALAD

NUTRITION INFO (PER SERVING): 410 calories, 14g total fat, 2g saturated fat, 0g trans fat, 5mg cholesterol, 600mg sodium, 58g carbohydrate, 14g fiber, 11g sugar, 0g added sugar, 14g protein, vitamin A 9,729 IU (190%), vitamin C 57mg (100%), vitamin D 0mcg (0%), calcium 166mg (15%), iron 3.36mg (20%), potassium 452mg (10%)

DINNER

BLACK BEAN BURGERS

NUTRITION INFO (PER SERVING): 420 calories, 13g total fat, 2g saturated fat, 0g trans fat, 0mg cholesterol, 710mg sodium, 67g carbohydrate, 17g fiber, 3g sugar, 0g added sugar, 15g protein, vitamin A 5,699 IU (110%), vitamin C 17mg (30%), vitamin D 0mcg (0%), calcium 212mg (20%), iron 4.77mg (25%), potassium 983mg (20%)

CAULIFLOWER FRIED RICE BOWL

NUTRITION INFO (PER SERVING): 410 calories, 25g total fat, 5g saturated fat, 0g trans fat, 185mg cholesterol, 400mg sodium, 31g carbohydrate, 9g fiber, 10g sugar, 0g added sugar, 20g protein, vitamin A 1,162 IU (25%), vitamin C 155mg (260%), vitamin D 1mcg (6%), calcium 140mg (15%), iron 4.80mg (25%), potassium 1,095 mg (24%)

CAULIFLOWER MAC AND CHEESE

NUTRITION INFO (PER SERVING): 370 calories, 13g total fat, 5g saturated fat, 0g trans fat, 25mg cholesterol, 840mg sodium, 47g carbohydrate, 7g fiber, 8g sugar, 0g added sugar, 22g protein, vitamin A 1,228 IU (25%), vitamin C 36mg (60%), vitamin D 0.2mcg (1%), calcium 655mg (70%), iron 3.51mg (20%), potassium 373mg (8%)

FISH TACOS WITH CRUNCHY CABBAGE SLAW

NUTRITION INFO (PER SERVING): 410 calories, 10g total fat, 2g saturated fat, 0g trans fat, 55mg cholesterol, 830mg sodium, 54g carbohydrate, 14g fiber, 3g sugar, 0g added sugar, 31g protein, vitamin A 1,652 IU (35%), vitamin C 115mg (190%), vitamin D 3.52mcg (25%), calcium 205mg (20%), iron 3.80mg (20%), potassium 1,371mg (30%)

BEET BURGERS AND 15-MINUTE PICKLES

NUTRITION INFO (PER SERVING): 380 calories, 6g total fat, 0g saturated fat, 0g trans fat, 0mg cholesterol, 980mg sodium, 68g carbohydrate, 19g fiber, 9g sugar, 0g added sugar, 19g protein, vitamin A 2,158 IU (45%), vitamin C 13mg (20%), vitamin D 0mcg (0%), calcium 188mg (20%), iron 5.51mg (30%), potassium 996mg (20%)

KALE BURGERS AND VEGGIE DIPPERS

NUTRITION INFO (PER SERVING): 400 calories, 15g total fat, 2g saturated fat, 0g trans fat, 0mg cholesterol, 530mg sodium, 54g carbohydrate, 13g fiber, 9g sugar, 0g added sugar, 16g protein, vitamin A 4,871 IU (100%), vitamin C 83mg (140%), vitamin D 0mcg (0%), calcium 173mg (15%), iron 4.18mg (25%), potassium 803mg (18%)

SPROUTED PIZZA

NUTRITION INFO (2 SLICES): 380 calories, 15g total fat, 5g saturated fat, 0g trans fat, 20mg cholesterol, 720mg sodium, 50g carbohydrate, 7g fiber, 7g sugar, 4g added sugar, 14g protein, vitamin A 1,960 IU (40%), vitamin C 71mg (120%), vitamin D 0mcg (0%), calcium 149mg (15%), iron 0.36mg (2%), potassium 152mg (4%)

CASHEW ALFREDO

NUTRITION INFO (PER SERVING): 410 calories, 12g total fat, 1.5g saturated fat, 0g trans fat, 0mg cholesterol, 340mg sodium, 64g carbohydrate, 11g fiber, 6g sugar, 0g added sugar, 16g protein, vitamin A 1,929 IU (40%), vitamin C 19mg (30%), vitamin D 0mcg (0%), calcium 61mg (6%), iron 6.43mg (35%), potassium 517mg (11%)

TREATS

BROWNIE BITES

NUTRITION INFO (PER SERVING): 150 calories, 6g total fat, 1g saturated fat, 0g trans fat, 0mg cholesterol, 55mg sodium, 27g carbohydrate, 5g fiber, 20g sugar, 0g added sugar, 3g protein, vitamin A 101 IU (2%), vitamin C 0mg (0%), vitamin D 0mcg (0%), calcium 41mg (4%), iron 0.86mg (4%), potassium 170mg (4%)

CASHEW WHIP AND BERRIES

NUTRITION INFO (PER SERVING): 190 calories, 12g total fat, 2g saturated fat, 0g trans fat, 0mg cholesterol, 10mg sodium, 16g carbohydrate, 3g fiber, 8g sugar, 2g added sugar, 6g protein, vitamin A 14 IU (0%), vitamin C 45mg (70%), vitamin D 0mcg (0%), calcium 38mg (4%), iron 2.13mg (10%), potassium 127mg (2%)

CASHEW WHIP

NUTRITION INFO (1 TABLESPOON): 30 calories, 2g total fat, 0g saturated fat, 0g trans fat, 0mg cholesterol, 0mg sodium, 2g carbohydrate, 0g fiber, 1g sugar, 0g added sugar, 1g protein, vitamin A 0 IU (0%), vitamin C 0mg (0%), vitamin D 0mcg (0%), calcium 4mg (0%), iron 0.30mg (2%), potassium 1mg (0%)

DARK CHOCOLATE CHERRY MILK SHAKE

NUTRITION INFO (PER SERVING): 140 calories, 6g total fat, 1.5g saturated fat, 0g trans fat, 0mg cholesterol, 180mg sodium, 24g carbohydrate, 7g fiber, 14g sugar, 0g added sugar, 4g protein, vitamin A 1,849 IU (35%), vitamin C 2.63mg (4%), vitamin D 2.5mcg (16%), calcium 220mg (20%), iron 1.90mg (10%), potassium 382mg (8%)

GREEN SMOOTHIE ICE POPS

NUTRITION INFO (PER SERVING): 130 calories, 6g total fat, 0.5g saturated fat, 0g trans fat, 0mg cholesterol, 110mg sodium, 17g carbohydrate, 3g fiber, 8g sugar, 0g added sugar, 3g protein, vitamin A 1,087 IU (20%), vitamin C 15mg (25%), vitamin D 1.25mcg (8%), calcium 143mg (15%), iron 0.73mg (4%), potassium 405mg (8%)

MINI YOGURT CHEESECAKE

NUTRITION INFO (PER SERVING): 90 calories, 4.5g total fat, 2g saturated fat, 0g trans fat, 50mg cholesterol, 40mg sodium, 9g carbohydrate, 2g fiber, 7g sugar, 6g added sugar, 5g protein, vitamin A 80 IU (2%), vitamin C 2mg (4%), vitamin D 0.25mcg (2%), calcium 35mg (4%), iron 0.50mg (2%), potassium 51mg (1%)

NICE CREAM

NUTRITION INFO (1/2 CUP): 160 calories, 5g total fat, 0.5g saturated fat, 0g trans fat, 0mg cholesterol, 15mg sodium, 28g carbohydrate, 4g fiber, 15g sugar, 0g added sugar, 2g protein, vitamin A 107 IU (2%), vitamin C 10mg (15%), vitamin D 0mcg (0%), calcium 25mg (2%), iron 0.54mg (4%), potassium 434mg (10%)

CHEEZY POPCORN

NUTRITION INFO (PER SERVING): 180 calories, 8g total fat, 7g saturated fat, 0g trans fat, 0mg cholesterol, 290mg sodium, 21g carbohydrate, 5g fiber, 0g sugar, 0g added sugar, 7g protein, vitamin A 0 IU (0%), vitamin C 0mg (0%), vitamin D 0mcg (0%), calcium 1.15mg (0%), iron 1.06mg (6%), potassium 223mg (5%)

SEAWEED SNACK STRIPS

NUTRITION INFO (PER SERVING): 110 calories, 6g total fat, 1g saturated fat, 0g trans fat, 0mg cholesterol, 200mg sodium, 11g carbohydrate, 1g fiber, 9g sugar, 8g added sugar, 2g protein, vitamin A 2,524 IU (50%), vitamin C 4.9mg (8%), vitamin D 0mcg (0%), calcium 79mg (8%), iron 1.28mg (8%), potassium 35mg (0%)

SPINACH DIP

NUTRITION INFO (PER SERVING, DIP ONLY): 110 calories, 6g total fat, 2g saturated fat, 0g trans fat, 10mg cholesterol, 320mg sodium, 6g carbohydrate, 2g fiber, 2g sugar, 0g added sugar, 8g protein, vitamin A 5,621 IU (110%), vitamin C 24mg (40%), vitamin D 0mcg (0%), calcium 162mg (15%), iron 2.78mg (15%), potassium 16mg (0%)

FALL/WINTER RECIPES

BREAKFAST

BANANA BREAD COOKIES

NUTRITION INFO (PER SERVING): 390 calories, 16g total fat, 4.5g saturated fat, 0g trans fat, 0mg cholesterol, 0mg sodium, 56g carbohydrate, 8g fiber, 16g sugar, 0g added sugar, 11g protein, vitamin A 76 IU (2%), vitamin C 10mg (15%), vitamin D 0mcg (0%), calcium 40mg (4%), iron 2.53mg (15%), potassium 422mg (10%)
NUTRITION INFO (PER 1 COOKIE): 50 calories, 2g total fat, 7g carbs, 1g fiber, 1g protein

CINNAMON OATMEAL MUFFINS

NUTRITION INFO (PER SERVING): 370 calories, 21g total fat, 9g saturated fat, 0g trans fat, 75mg cholesterol, 340mg sodium, 36g carbohydrate, 6g fiber, 11g sugar, 10g added sugar, 10g protein, vitamin A 224 IU (4%), vitamin C 3mg (6%), vitamin D 0.90mcg (6%), calcium 166mg (15%), iron 2.47mg (15%), potassium 175mg (4%)

BURRITO OMELET CUPS

NUTRITION INFO (PER SERVING): 390 calories, 20g total fat, 9g saturated fat, 0g trans fat, 400mg cholesterol, 550mg sodium, 30g carbohydrate, 6g fiber, 14g sugar, 0g added sugar, 23g protein, vitamin A 1,430 IU (30%), vitamin C 79mg (130%), vitamin D 2.59mcg (17%), calcium 360mg (35%), iron 2.41mg (15%), potassium 563mg (12%)

ZUCCHINI BREAD FRENCH TOAST

NUTRITION INFO (PER SERVING): 420 calories, 21g total fat, 9g saturated fat, 0g trans fat, 280mg cholesterol, 310mg sodium, 36g carbohydrate, 10g fiber, 3g sugar, 0g added sugar, 20g protein, vitamin A 737 IU (15%), vitamin C 18mg (30%), vitamin D 2.12mcg (15%), calcium 139mg (15%), iron 3.68mg (20%), potassium 449mg (10%)

BLENDER PANCAKES

NUTRITION INFO (PER SERVING): 390 calories, 19g total fat, 7g saturated fat, 0g trans fat, 95mg cholesterol, 450mg sodium, 42g carbohydrate, 4g fiber, 22g sugar, 13g added sugar, 14g protein, vitamin A 300 IU (6%), vitamin C 8mg (15%), vitamin D 1.12mcg (8%), calcium 257mg (25%), iron 4.10mg (25%), potassium 147mg (4%)

PUMPKIN SPICE SMOOTHIE

NUTRITION INFO (PER SERVING): 400 calories, 21g total fat, 3.5g saturated fat, 0g trans fat, 0mg cholesterol, 290mg sodium, 50g carbohydrate, 9g fiber, 20g sugar, 0g added sugar, 9g protein, vitamin A 20,116 IU (400%), vitamin C 6mg (10%), vitamin D 3.75mcg (25%), calcium 377mg (40%), iron 4.99mg (10%), potassium 1,021mg (20%)

LUNCH

CASHEW RANCH BOWL

NUTRITION INFO (PER SERVING): 420 calories, 16g total fat, 2.5g saturated fat, 0g trans fat, 0mg cholesterol, 820mg sodium, 60g carbohydrate, 11g fiber, 18g sugar, 0g added sugar, 15g protein, vitamin A 18,319 IU (370%), vitamin C 49mg (80%), vitamin D 0mcg (0%), calcium 147mg (15%), iron 5.26mg (30%), potassium 794mg (16%)

CASHEW RANCH DRESSING

NUTRITION INFO (1 TABLESPOON): 50 calories, 4g total fat, 0.5g saturated fat, 0g trans fat, 0mg cholesterol, 150mg sodium, 3g carbohydrate, 0g fiber, 1g sugar, 0g added sugar, 2g protein, vitamin A 18 IU (0%), vitamin C 1mg (2%), vitamin D 0mcg (0%), calcium 6mg (0%), iron 0.63mg (4%), potassium 66mg (2%)

CHICKPEA NOODLE SOUP

NUTRITION INFO (PER SERVING): 380 calories, 8g total fat, 1g saturated fat, 0g trans fat, 0mg cholesterol, 690mg sodium, 68g carbohydrate, 13g fiber, 12g sugar, 0g added sugar, 13g protein, vitamin A 10,794 IU (220%), vitamin C 39mg (60%), vitamin D 0mcg (0%), calcium 120mg (10%), iron 2.94mg (15%), potassium 534mg (20%)

RAMEN JAR

NUTRITION INFO (PER SERVING): 400 calories, 12g total fat, 1.5g saturated fat, 0g trans fat, 0mg cholesterol, 570mg sodium, 59g carbohydrate, 5g fiber, 3g sugar, 0g added sugar, 12g protein, vitamin A 2,208 IU (45%), vitamin C 17mg (30%), vitamin D 0.03mcg (0%), calcium 85mg (8%), iron 6.46mg (35%), potassium 380mg (8%)

BRUSSELS SPROUT PAD THAI

NUTRITION INFO (PER SERVING): 390 calories, 22g total fat, 3.5g saturated fat, 0g trans fat, 185mg cholesterol, 500mg sodium, 30g carbohydrate, 12g fiber, 10g sugar, 0g added sugar, 18g protein, vitamin A 11,809 IU (240%), vitamin C 209mg (350%), vitamin D 1.00mcg (6%), calcium 133mg (15%), iron 1.99mg (10%), potassium 441mg (10%)

LENTIL TACOS

NUTRITION INFO (PER SERVING): 430 calories, 13g total fat, 2g saturated fat, 0g trans fat, 0mg cholesterol, 270mg sodium, 70g carbohydrate, 18g fiber, 9g sugar, 0g added sugar, 16g protein, vitamin A 1,168 IU (25%), vitamin C 91mg (150%), vitamin D 0mcg (0%), calcium 120mg (10%), iron 5.23mg (30%), potassium 1,112mg (25%)

TORTILLA SOUP

NUTRITION INFO (PER SERVING): 410 calories, 19g total fat, 2.5g saturated fat, 0g trans fat, 0mg cholesterol, 380mg sodium, 52g carbohydrate, 17g fiber, 12g sugar, 0g added sugar, 11g protein, vitamin A 3,393 IU (70%), vitamin C 99mg (160%), vitamin D 0mcg (0%), calcium 166mg (15%), iron 4.86mg (25%), potassium 957mg (20%)

DINNER

TOMATO SOUP WITH GRILLED CHEESE CROUTONS

UTRITION INFO (PER SERVING): 380 calories, 13g total fat, 6g saturated fat, 0g trans fat, 30mg cholesterol, 520mg sodium, 48g carbohydrate, 13g fiber, 14g sugar, 0g added sugar, 18g protein, vitamin A 5,794 IU (120%), vitamin C 44mg (70%), vitamin D 0mcg (0%), calcium 313mg (30%), iron 3.70mg (20%), potassium 503mg (10%)

EGGPLANT PARMESAN WITH SPAGHETTI SQUASH NOODLES

NUTRITION INFO (PER SERVING): 430 calories, 17g total fat, 4.5g saturated fat, 0g trans fat, 195mg cholesterol, 470mg sodium, 56g carbohydrate, 13g fiber, 21g sugar, 0g added sugar, 17g protein, vitamin A 951 IU (20%), vitamin C 20mg (35%), vitamin D 1.05mcg (7%), calcium 276mg (30%), iron 4.95mg (25%), potassium 997mg (20%)

SUPERFOOD CHILI

NUTRITION INFO (PER SERVING): 390 calories, 10g total fat, 1.5g saturated fat, 0g trans fat, 0mg cholesterol, 580mg sodium, 66g carbohydrate, 22g fiber, 15g sugar, 0g added sugar, 16g protein, vitamin A 11,437 IU (230%), vitamin C 53mg (90%), vitamin D 0mcg (0%), calcium 148mg (15%), iron 3.5mg (20%), potassium 1,159mg (25%)

SPINACH ENCHILADA CASSEROLE

NUTRITION INFO (PER SERVING): 390 calories, 16g total fat, 5g saturated fat, 0g trans fat, 20mg cholesterol, 890mg sodium, 49g carbohydrate, 14g fiber, 8g sugar, 0g added sugar, 19g protein, vitamin A 10,797 IU (220%), vitamin C 21mg (35%), vitamin D 0.13mcg (0%), calcium 369mg (35%), iron 5.82mg (30%), potassium 1,237mg (25%)

LENTIL MEATBALLS AND PASTA

NUTRITION INFO (4 MEATBALLS + PASTA): 410 calories, 8g total fat, 1.5g saturated fat, 0g trans fat, 0mg cholesterol, 1,040mg sodium, 70g carbohydrate, 19g fiber, 13g sugar, 0g added sugar, 19g protein, vitamin A 1,813 IU (35%), vitamin C 131mg (220%), vitamin D 0mcg (0%), calcium 147mg (15%), iron 6.81mg (40%), potassium 501mg (10%)

LENTIL MEATBALLS

NUTRITION INFO (1 MEATBALL): 45 calories, 0g total fat, 0g saturated fat, 0g trans fat, 0mg cholesterol, 110mg sodium, 7g carbohydrate, 3g fiber, 1g sugar, 0g added sugar, 3g protein, vitamin A 123 IU (2%), vitamin C 3mg (4%), vitamin D 0mcg (0%), calcium 11mg (2%), iron 1.08mg (6%), potassium 21mg (0%)

FISH AND CHIPS

NUTRITION INFO (PER SERVING): 420 calories, 17g total fat, 2g saturated fat, 0g trans fat, 70mg cholesterol, 260mg sodium, 34g carbohydrate, 12g fiber, 8g sugar, 0g added sugar, 36g protein, vitamin A 5,851 IU (120%), vitamin C 37mg (60%), vitamin D 4.39mcg (30%), calcium 150mg (15%), iron 3.56mg (20%), potassium 974mg (20%)

BUTTERNUT SQUASH LASAGNA

NUTRITION INFO (PER SERVING): 420 calories, 17g total fat, 9g saturated fat, 0g trans fat, 95mg cholesterol, 670mg sodium, 44g carbohydrate, 8g fiber, 15g sugar, 0g added sugar, 27g protein, vitamin A 22,846 IU (460%), vitamin C 73mg (120%), vitamin D 0.46mcg (3%), calcium 709mg (70%), iron 5.11mg (30%), potassium 1,132mg (25%)

TREATS

CHIA CHOCOLATE CHUNK COOKIES

NUTRITION INFO (2 COOKIES): 140 calories, 10g total fat, 1.5g saturated fat, 0g trans fat, 0mg cholesterol, 95mg sodium, 11g carbohydrate, 3g fiber, 5g sugar, 3g added sugar, 4g protein, vitamin A 2 IU (0%), vitamin C 2mg (0%), vitamin D 0mcg (0%), calcium 17mg (2%), iron 1.06mg (6%), potassium 154mg (3%)

CHOCOLATE PECAN CANDY CLUSTERS

NUTRITION INFO (PER SERVING): 160 calories, 9g total fat, 7g saturated fat, 0g trans fat, 0mg cholesterol, 80mg sodium, 21g carbohydrate, 2g fiber, 17g sugar, 17g added sugar, 1g protein, vitamin A 2 IU (0%), vitamin C 0mg (0%), vitamin D 0mcg (0%), calcium 17mg (2%), iron 1.16mg (6%), potassium 118mg (2%)

GINGERSNAP COOKIES

NUTRITION INFO (3 COOKIES): 130 calories, 8g total fat, 4.5g saturated fat, 0g trans fat, 0mg cholesterol, 35mg sodium, 16g carbohydrate, 3g fiber, 11g sugar, 0g added sugar, 2g protein, vitamin A 0 IU (0%), vitamin C 0mg (0%), vitamin D 0mcg (0%), calcium 78mg (8%), iron 1.34mg (8%), potassium 111mg (0%)

VANILLA "SUGAR" COOKIES

NUTRITION INFO (PER SERVING): 170 calories, 14g total fat, 4.5g saturated fat, 0g trans fat, 25mg cholesterol, 170mg sodium, 8g carbohydrate, 2g fiber, 4g sugar, 3g added sugar, 5g protein, vitamin A 34 IU (0%), vitamin C 0mg (0%), vitamin D 0.12mcg (1%), calcium 54mg (6%), iron 0.93mg (6%), potassium 20mg (0%)

NATURAL CARAMEL APPLES

NUTRITION INFO (PER SERVING): 170 calories, 6g total fat, 0.5g saturated fat, 0g trans fat, 0mg cholesterol, 160mg sodium, 31g carbohydrate, 4g fiber, 25g sugar, 0g added sugar, 3g protein, vitamin A 20 IU (0%), vitamin C 2mg (2%), vitamin D 0mcg (0%), calcium 50mg (6%), iron 0.70mg (4%), potassium 262mg (6%)

FRENCH ONION DIP

NUTRITION INFO (PER SERVING): 120 calories, 8g total fat, 2g saturated fat, 0g trans fat, 5mg cholesterol, 260mg sodium, 6g carbohydrate, 1g fiber, 4g sugar, 0g added sugar, 5g protein, vitamin A 32 IU (0%), vitamin C 2mg (4%), vitamin D 0mcg (0%), calcium 51mg (6%), iron 0.32mg (2%), potassium 62mg (1%)

BROWN RICE CRISPY TREATS

NUTRITION INFO (PER SERVING): 160 calories, 4.5g total fat, 0.5g saturated fat, 0g trans fat, 0mg cholesterol, 160mg sodium, 29g carbohydrate, 1g fiber, 12g sugar, 11g added sugar, 3g protein, vitamin A 0 IU (0%), vitamin C 0mg (0%), vitamin D 0mcg (0%), calcium 41mg (4%), iron 0.45mg (2%), potassium 111mg (2%)

WASABI CHICKPEAS

NUTRITION INFO (PER SERVING): 120 calories, 5g total fat, 0.5g saturated fat, 0g trans fat, 0mg cholesterol, 280mg sodium, 15g carbohydrate, 4g fiber, 3g sugar, 0g added sugar, 4g protein, vitamin A 14 IU (0%), vitamin C 0mg (0%), vitamin D 0mcg (0%), calcium 27mg (2%), iron 0.64mg (4%), potassium 69mg (4%)

SUPERSEED CRACKERS

NUTRITION INFO (1 CRACKER): 30 calories, 2g total fat, 0g saturated fat, 0g trans fat, 0mg cholesterol, 30mg sodium, 2g carbohydrate, 1g fiber, 0g sugar, 0g added sugar, 1g protein, vitamin A 0 IU (0%), vitamin C 0mg (0%), vitamin D 0mcg (0%), calcium 32mg (4%), iron 0.5mg (2%), potassium 17mg (0%)

DRINKS, CONDIMENTS & SIDES

DRINKS

GREEN BULL ENERGY DRINK

NUTRITION INFO (PER SERVING): 50 calories, 0g total fat, 0g saturated fat, 0g trans fat, 0mg cholesterol, 15mg sodium, 13g carbohydrate, 2g fiber, 9g sugar, 0g added sugar, 1g protein, vitamin A 1,640 IU (35%), vitamin C 32mg (50%), vitamin D 0mcg (0%), calcium 35mg (4%), iron 0.34mg (2%), potassium 183mg (4%)

GREEN BULL AND ALMONDS

NUTRITION INFO (PER SERVING): 120 calories, 6g total fat, 0.5g saturated fat, 0g trans fat, 0mg cholesterol, 15mg sodium, 16g carbohydrate, 4g fiber, 9g sugar, 0g added sugar, 4g protein, vitamin A 1,640 IU (35%), vitamin C 32mg (50%), vitamin D 0mcg (0%), calcium 68mg (6%), iron 0.79mg (4%), potassium 271mg (6%)

MATCHA JOLT

NUTRITION INFO (PER SERVING): 5 calories, 0g total fat, 0g saturated fat, 0g trans fat, 0mg cholesterol, 10mg sodium, 1g carbohydrate, 0g fiber, 0g sugar, 0g added sugar, 0g protein, vitamin A 1 IU (0%), vitamin C 6mg (10%), vitamin D 0mcg (0%), calcium 8mg (0%), iron 0.01mg (0%), potassium 16mg (0%)

COCONUT COFFEE

NUTRITION INFO (PER SERVING): 60 calories, 6g total fat, 5g saturated fat, 0g trans fat, 0mg cholesterol, 10mg sodium, 1g carbohydrate, 0g fiber, 0g sugar, 0g added sugar, 1g protein, vitamin A 0 IU (0%), vitamin C 0mg (0%), vitamin D 0mcg (0%), calcium 10mg (0%), iron 0.96mg (6%), potassium 178mg (4%)

SUPER LATTE

NUTRITION INFO (PER SERVING): 120 calories, 10g total fat, 1g saturated fat, 0g trans fat, 0mg cholesterol, 135mg sodium, 5g carbohydrate, 2g fiber, 1g sugar, 0g added sugar, 4g protein, vitamin A 250 IU (6%), vitamin C 0mg (0%), vitamin D 1.25mcg (8%), calcium 163mg (15%), iron 0.74mg (4%), potassium 215mg (4%)

SUPER SODA

NUTRITION INFO (PER SERVING): 25 calories, 0g total fat, 0g saturated fat, 0g trans fat, 0mg cholesterol, 45mg sodium, 6g carbohydrate, 0g fiber, 5g sugar, 0g added sugar, 0g protein, vitamin A 0 IU (0%), vitamin C 0mg (0%), vitamin D 0mcg (0%), calcium 16mg (2%), iron 0.29mg (2%), potassium 81mg (2%)

REAL GINGER ALE

NUTRITION INFO (PER SERVING): 45 calories, 0g total fat, 0g saturated fat, 0g trans fat, 0mg cholesterol, 50mg sodium, 12g carbohydrate, 0g fiber, 12g sugar, 12g added sugar, 0g protein, vitamin A 0 IU (0%), vitamin C 0mg (0%), vitamin D 0mcg (0%), calcium 13mg (2%), iron 0.09mg (0%), potassium 20mg (0%)

COCONUT LEMONADE

NUTRITION INFO (PER SERVING): 50 calories, 0g total fat, 0g saturated fat, 0g trans fat, 0mg cholesterol, 45mg sodium, 13g carbohydrate, 0g fiber, 11g sugar, 0g added sugar, 1g protein, vitamin A 2 IU (0%), vitamin C 9mg (15%), vitamin D 0mcg (0%), calcium 32mg (4%), iron 0.02mg (0%), potassium 512mg (10%)

MOJITO WATER

NUTRITION INFO (PER SERVING): 0 calories, 0g total fat, 0g saturated fat, 0g trans fat, 0mg cholesterol, 10mg sodium, 0g carbohydrate, 0g fiber, 0g sugar, 0g added sugar, 0g protein, vitamin A 13 IU (0%), vitamin C 1mg (2%), vitamin D 0mcg (0%), calcium 8mg (%), iron 0.04mg (0%), potassium 4mg (0%)

NATURAL HOT CHOCOLATE

NUTRITION INFO (PER SERVING): 150 calories, 3g total fat, 0.5g saturated fat, 0g trans fat, 0mg cholesterol, 220mg sodium, 35g carbohydrate, 5g fiber, 27g sugar, 0g added sugar, 3g protein, vitamin A 399 IU (8%), vitamin C 0mg (0%), vitamin D 1.87mcg (12%), calcium 173mg (15%), iron 0.93mg (6%), potassium 335mg (7%)

GOLDEN MILK

NUTRITION INFO (PER SERVING): 140 calories, 12g total fat, 1g saturated fat, 0g trans fat, 0mg cholesterol, 220mg sodium, 7g carbohydrate, 4g fiber, 1g sugar, 0g added sugar, 5g protein, vitamin A 504 IU (10%), vitamin C 0mg (0%), vitamin D 2.5mcg (16%), calcium 270mg (25%), iron 1.63mg (10%), potassium 338mg (7%)

KOMBUCHA MARGARITA

NUTRITION INFO (PER SERVING): 90 calories, 0g total fat, 0g saturated fat, 0g trans fat, 0mg cholesterol, 10mg sodium, 7g carbohydrate, 0g fiber, 2g sugar, 0g added sugar, 0g protein, vitamin A 22 IU (0%), vitamin C 13mg (20%), vitamin D 0mcg (0%), calcium 8mg (0%), iron 0.05mg (0%), potassium 53mg (0%)

HIBISCUS SANGRIA, WITH FRUIT

NUTRITION INFO (PER SERVING): 70 calories, 0g total fat, 0g saturated fat, 0g trans fat, 0mg cholesterol, 0mg sodium, 6g carbohydrate, 0g fiber, 3g sugar, 0g added sugar, 0g protein, vitamin A 75 IU (2%), vitamin C 8mg (15%), vitamin D 0mcg (0%), calcium 8mg (0%), iron 0.04mg (0%), potassium 44mg (1%)

HIBISCUS SANGRIA, WITHOUT FRUIT

NUTRITION INFO (PER SERVING): 60 calories, 0g total fat, 0g saturated fat, 0g trans fat, 0mg cholesterol, 0mg sodium, 3g carbohydrate, 0g fiber, 0g sugar, 0g added sugar, 0g protein, vitamin A 0 IU (0%), vitamin C 0mg (0%), vitamin D 0mcg (0%), calcium 8mg (0%), iron 0mg (0%), potassium 0mg (0%)

WINTER CHAI SANGRIA, WITH FRUIT

NUTRITION INFO (PER SERVING): 80 calories, 0g total fat, 0g saturated fat, 0g trans fat, 0mg cholesterol, 0mg sodium, 7g carbohydrate, 1g fiber, 3g sugar, 0g added sugar, 0g protein, vitamin A 4 IU (0%), vitamin C 8mg (15%), vitamin D 0mcg (0%), calcium 8mg (0%), iron 0.05mg (0%), potassium 59mg (1%)

WINTER CHAI SANGRIA, WITHOUT FRUIT

NUTRITION INFO (PER SERVING): 60 calories, 0g total fat, 0g saturated fat, 0g trans fat, 0mg cholesterol, 0mg sodium, 3g carbohydrate, 0g fiber, 0g sugar, 0g added sugar, 0g protein, vitamin A 0 IU (0%), vitamin C 0mg (0%), vitamin D 0mcg (0%), calcium 2mg (0%), iron 0mg (0%), potassium 12mg (0%)

SPARKLING BITTERS

NUTRITION INFO (PER SERVING): 5 calories, 0g total fat, 0g saturated fat, 0g trans fat, 0mg cholesterol, 40mg sodium, 2g carbohydrate, 0g fiber, 2g sugar, 0g added sugar, 0g protein, vitamin A 0 IU (0%), vitamin C 0mg (0%), vitamin D 0mcg (0%), calcium 12mg (2%), iron 0.02mg (0%), potassium 5mg (0%)

WELLNESS SHOT

NUTRITION INFO (PER SERVING): 15 calories, 0g total fat, 0g saturated fat, 0g trans fat, 0mg cholesterol, 150mg sodium, 4g carbohydrate, 0g fiber, 1g sugar, 0g added sugar, 0g protein, vitamin A 50 IU (0%), vitamin C 19mg (30%), vitamin D 0mcg (0%), calcium 3mg (0%), iron 0.06mg (0%), potassium 60mg (1%)

NATURAL SPORTS DRINK

NUTRITION INFO (PER SERVING): 60 calories, 0g total fat, 0g saturated fat, 0g trans fat, 0mg cholesterol, 150mg sodium, 13g carbohydrate, 0g fiber, 10g sugar, 0g added sugar, 1g protein, vitamin A 248 IU (4%), vitamin C 62mg (100%), vitamin D 0mcg (0%), calcium 17mg (2%), iron 0.25mg (2%), potassium 248mg (5%)

CONDIMENTS

BEET KETCHUP

NUTRITION INFO (1 TABLESPOON): 15 calories, 0.5g total fat, 0.5g saturated fat, 0g trans fat, 0mg cholesterol, 40mg sodium, 2g carbohydrate, 0g fiber, 2g sugar, 1g added sugar, 0g protein, vitamin A 2 IU (0%), vitamin C 1mg (0%), vitamin D 0mcg (0%), calcium 2mg (0%), iron 0.06mg (0%), potassium 23mg (0%)

BEET BBQ SAUCE

NUTRITION INFO (1 TABLESPOON): 15 calories, 0.5g total fat, 0.5g saturated fat, 0g trans fat, 0mg cholesterol, 45mg sodium, 2g carbohydrate, 0g fiber, 2g sugar, 1g added sugar, 0g protein, vitamin A 43 IU (0%), vitamin C 1mg (0%), vitamin D 0mcg (0%), calcium 3mg (0%), iron 0.09mg (0%), potassium 28mg (0%)

CASHEW MAYO

NUTRITION INFO (1 TABLESPOON): 40 calories, 3g total fat, 0.5g saturated fat, 0g trans fat, 0mg cholesterol, 40mg sodium, 2g carbohydrate, 0g fiber, 1g sugar, 0g added sugar, 1g protein, vitamin A 0 IU (0%), vitamin C 1mg (0%), vitamin D 0mcg (0%), calcium 5mg (0%), iron 0.45mg (2%), potassium 2mg (0%)

OLIVE OIL HUMMUS

NUTRITION INFO (PER SERVING): 110 calories, 6g total fat, 1g saturated fat, 0g trans fat, 0mg cholesterol, 190mg sodium, 11g carbohydrate, 3g fiber, 2g sugar, 0g added sugar, 4g protein, vitamin A 13 IU (0%), vitamin C 3mg (6%), vitamin D 0mcg (0%), calcium 26mg (2%), iron 0.65mg (4%), potassium 78mg (2%)

POTATO CROUTONS

NUTRITION INFO (PER SERVING): 100 calories, 3.5g total fat, 0g saturated fat, 0g trans fat, 0mg cholesterol, 160mg sodium, 17g carbohydrate, 3g fiber, 1g sugar, 0g added sugar, 2g protein, vitamin A 9 IU (0%), vitamin C 10mg (15%), vitamin D 0mcg (0%), calcium 10mg (2%), iron 0.59mg (4%), potassium 435mg (10%)

MUSHROOM BACON BITS

NUTRITION INFO (PER SERVING): 10 calories, 0.5g total fat, 0g saturated fat, 0g trans fat, 0mg cholesterol, 50mg sodium, 1g carbohydrate, 0g fiber, 1g sugar, 0g added sugar, 1g protein, vitamin A 51 IU (2%), vitamin C 0mg (0%), vitamin D 0mcg (0%), calcium 2mg (0%), iron 0.11mg (0%), potassium 80mg (2%)

SUPERSAUCE MARINARA

NUTRITION INFO (PER SERVING): 80 calories, 2.5g total fat, 0g saturated fat, 0g trans fat, 0mg cholesterol, 250mg sodium, 12g carbohydrate, 4g fiber, 5g sugar, 0g added sugar, 3g protein, vitamin A 6,834 IU (140%), vitamin C 43mg (70%), vitamin D 0mcg (0%), calcium 80mg (8%), iron 1.99mg (10%), potassium 421mg (9%)

SIDES

BUFFALO CAULIFLOWER POPPERS

NUTRITION INFO (PER SERVING): 140 calories, 2.5g total fat, 0.5g saturated fat, 0g trans fat, 0mg cholesterol, 780mg sodium, 26g carbohydrate, 3g fiber, 3g sugar, 0g added sugar, 4g protein, vitamin A 46 IU (0%), vitamin C 73mg (120%), vitamin D 0mcg (0%), calcium 29mg (2%), iron 1.11mg (6%), potassium 437mg (10%)

CARROT AND GREEN BEAN FRIES

NUTRITION INFO (PER SERVING): 45 calories, 2g total fat, 0g saturated fat, 0g trans fat, 0mg cholesterol, 170mg sodium, 6g carbohydrate, 2g fiber, 3g sugar, 0g added sugar, 1g protein, vitamin A 5,441 IU (110%), vitamin C 8mg (15%), vitamin D 0mcg (0%), calcium 29mg (2%), iron 0.63mg (4%), potassium 6mg (0%)

ZUCCHINI WEDGES

NUTRITION INFO (PER SERVING): 30 calories, 2g total fat, 0.5g saturated fat, 0g trans fat, 0mg cholesterol, 65mg sodium, 2g carbohydrate, 0g fiber, 1g sugar, 0g added sugar, 2g protein, vitamin A 120 IU (2%), vitamin C 9mg (15%), vitamin D 0mcg (0%), calcium 39mg (4%), iron 0.21mg (2%), potassium 131mg (2%)

PICKLES PLUS

NUTRITION INFO (PER SERVING): 10 calories, 0g total fat, 0.5g saturated fat, 0g trans fat, 0mg cholesterol, 75mg sodium, 3g carbohydrate, 0g fiber, 1g sugar, 0g added sugar, 1g protein, vitamin A 79 IU (2%), vitamin C 2mg (4%), vitamin D 0mcg (0%), calcium 12mg (2%), iron 0.21mg (2%), potassium 111mg (2%)

SUPERSWAP CORN BREAD

NUTRITION INFO (PER SERVING): 120 calories, 5g total fat, 3.5g saturated fat, 0g trans fat, 25mg cholesterol, 240mg sodium, 17g carbohydrate, 3g fiber, 4g sugar, 4g added sugar, 2g protein, vitamin A 96 IU (2%), vitamin C 0mg (0%), vitamin D 0.44mcg (3%), calcium 75mg (8%), iron 0.72mg (4%), potassium 35mg (0%)

» SOURCES «

INTRODUCTION

Craving healthy food: "Pilot randomized trial demonstrating reversal of obesity-related abnormalities in reward system responsivity to food cues with a behavioral intervention." T. Deckersbach et al. *Nutrition & Diabetes.* 2014, vol. 4, pp. 1–7.

Greens and cravings: "Body weight loss, reduced urge for palatable food and increased release of GLP-1 through daily supplementation with green-plant membranes for three months in overweight women." C. Montelius et al. *Appetite.* 2014, vol. 8, pp. 295–304.

Mindful eating: "The effect of a mindful restaurant eating intervention on weight management in women." A. Brown and G. M. Timmerman. *Journal of Nutrition and Education Behavior.* Jan.–Feb. 2012, vol. 44, no. 1, pp. 22–8.

Prep your own food: "Greater effort boosts the affective taste properties of food." Alexander W. Jöyson et al. *Proceedings of the Royal Society B.* May 22, 2011, vol. 278, no. 1711, pp. 1450-6.

Sleep and cravings: "The effects of extended bedtimes on sleep duration and food desire in overweight young adults: A home-based intervention." E. Tasali et al. *Appetite.* 2014, vol. 80, pp. 220–224.

Weigh-ins and weight loss: "Long-term weight loss maintenance." R. R. Wing and S. Phelan. *American Journal of Clinical Nutrition.* July 2005, vol. 82, pp. 222S–225S.

WEEK 1

Almonds and blood vessels: "An almond-enriched diet increases plasma α-tocopherol and improves vascular function but does not affect oxidative stress markers or lipid levels." K. Choudhury et al. *Free Radical Research,* May 2014, vol. 48, no. 5, pp. 599–606.

Almonds and cholesterol: "Effects of Almond Dietary Supplementation on Coronary Heart Disease Lipid Risk Factors and Serum Lipid Oxidation Parameters in Men with Mild Hyperlipidemia." B. Jalali-Khanabadi et al. *Journal of Alternative and Complementary Medicine.* 2010, vol. 16, no. 12, pp. 1279–1283.

Almonds and cholesterol: "Effects of almond consumption on the reduction of LDL-cholesterol: a discussion of potential mechanisms and future research directions." C. E. Berryman et al. *Nutrition Reviews.* 2011, vol. 69, no. 4, pp. 171–185.

Almonds and gut bacteria: "Prebiotic effects of almonds and almond skins on intestinal microbiota in healthy adult humans." Z. Liu et al. *Anaerobe.* 2014, vol. 26, pp. 1–6.

Almonds and second meal effect: "Acute and second-meal effects of almond form in impaired glucose tolerant adults: a randomized crossover trial." A. M. Mori et al. *Nutrition & Metabolism.* 2011, vol. 8, no. 6, pp. 1–8.

Almonds and weight loss: "A randomized trial of the effects of an almond-enriched, hypocaloric diet in the treatment of obesity." G. D. Foster et al. *American Journal of Clinical Nutrition.* 2012, vol. 96, pp. 249–54.

Almonds, body weight, glucose regulation, oxidative stress, and inflammation: "Health benefits of almonds beyond cholesterol reduction." A. Kamil et al. *Journal of Agricultural Food Chemistry.* 2012, vol. 60, pp. 6694–6702.

Almonds fill you up: "Appetitive, dietary and health effects of almonds consumed with meals or as snacks: a randomized, controlled trial." S. Y. Tan et al. *European Journal of Clinical Nutrition.* 2013, vol. 67, pp. 1205–1214.

Almonds for athletes: "The effect of almond consumption on elements of endurance exercise performance in trained athletes." M. Yi et al. *Journal of the International Society of Sports Nutrition.* 2014, vol. 11, no. 18, pp. 1–8.

Almonds for diabetes: "Almond consumption improved glycemic control and lipid profiles in patients with type 2 diabetes mellitus." S. Li et al. *Metabolism Clinical and Experimental.* 2011, vol. 60, pp. 474–479.

Almonds for diabetes: "Almond ingestion at mealtime reduces postprandial glycemia and chronic ingestion reduces hemoglobin A1c in individuals with well-controlled type 2 diabetes mellitus." A. E. Cohen et al. *Metabolism Clinical and Experimental.* 2011, vol. 60, pp. 1312–1317.

Almonds, pistachios, and gut bacteria: "Effects of almond and pistachio consumption on gut microbiota composition in a randomised cross-over human feeding study." M. Ukhanova et al. *British Journal of Nutrition.* 2014, vol. 111, no. 12, pp. 2146–52.

Almonds, walnuts, and PCOS: "Differential effects of walnuts vs. almonds on improving metabolic and endocrine parameters in PCOS." S. Kalgaonkar et al. *European Journal of Clinical Nutrition.* 2011, vol. 65, pp. 386–393.

Antioxidants background: "Inflammation and Diet." Academy of Nutrition and Dietetics, September 1, 2014. www.eatright.org/resource/health/wellness /preventing-illness/inflammation-and-diet

Antioxidants and optimism: "The association between optimism and serum antioxidants in the midlife in the United States study." J. K. Boehm et al. *Psychosomatic Medicine.* January 2013, vol. 75, no. 1, pp. 2–10.

Apples and mortality: "A statin a day keeps the doctor away: comparative proverb assessment modelling study." A. D. M. Briggs et al. *BMJ.* November 27, 2013.

Avocados and satiety: "A randomized 3x3 crossover study to evaluate the effect of Hass avocado intake on post-ingestive satiety, glucose and insulin levels, and subsequent energy intake in overweight adults." M. Wien et al. *Nutrition Journal.* 2013, vol. 12. no. 55, pp. 1–9.

Bananas during exercise: "Bananas as an energy source during exercise: A metabolomics approach." D. C. Nieman et al. *PLOS ONE.* May 2012, vol. 7, no. 5, pp. 1–7.

Beans, lentils, and weight control: "Dietary pulses, satiety and food intake: A systematic review and meta-analysis of acute feeding trials." S. S. Li et al. *Obesity.* 2014, vol. 22, 1773–1780.

Beans, brown rice, and polyps: "Foods and food groups associated with the incidence of colorectal polyps: The Adventist Health Study." Y. M. Tantamango et al. *Nutrition and Cancer.* 2001, vol. 63, no. 4, pp. 565–572.

Beans, lentils, and the second-meal effect: "First and second meal effects of pulses on blood glucose, appetite, and food intake at a later meal." R. C. Mollard et al. *Applied Psychology, Nutrition, and Metabolism.* October 2011, vol. 36, no. 5, pp. 634–42.

Brown rice and insulin: "Effect of brown rice, white rice, and brown rice with legumes on blood glucose and insulin responses in overweight Asian Indians: a randomized controlled trial." V. Mohan et al. *Diabetes Technology and Therapeutics.* 2014, vol. 16, no. 5, pp. 317–325.

Brown rice—obesity and endothelial function: "Effects of the brown rice diet on visceral obesity and endothelial function: the BRAVO study." M. Shimabukuro et al. *British Journal of Nutrition.* January 2014, vol. 111, no. 2, pp. 310–320.

Brown rice, inflammation, and cardiovascular risk: "Effect of brown rice consumption on inflammatory marker and cardiovascular risk factors among overweight and obese non-menopausal female adults." M. Kazemzadeh et al. *International Journal of Preventative Medicine.* April 2014, vol. 5, no. 4, pp. 478–488.

Swap white rice for brown: "White rice, brown rice, and risk of type 2 diabetes in US men and women." Q. Sun et al. *Archives of Internal Medicine.* 2010, vol. 170, no. 11, pp. 961–969.

Carotenoids improve attractiveness: "Fruit over sunbed: Carotenoid skin coloration is found more attractive than melanin coloration." C. E. Lefevre et al. *Quarterly Journal of Experimental Psychology.* 2015, vol. 68, no. 2, pp. 284–293.

Carotenoids in whole grains: "Distribution of carotenoids in endosperm, germ, and aleurone fractions of cereal grain kernels." V. U. Ndolo et al. *Food Chemistry.* 2013, vol. 139, pp. 663–671.

Carotenoids and optimism: "Association between optimism and serum antioxidants in the midlife in the United States study." J. K. Boehm et al. *Psychosomatic Medicine.* January 2013, vol. 75, no. 1, pp. 2–10.

Cashews and roasting: "Effect of roasting on phenolic content and antioxidant activities of whole cashew nuts, kernels, and testa." N. Chandrasekara et al. *Journal of Agricultural and Food Chemistry.* 2011, vol. 59, pp. 5006–5014.

Cashews and shelling methods: "Bioactive compounds in cashew nut (*Anacardium occidentale* L.) kernels: effect of different shelling methods." J. Trox et al. *Journal of Agricultural and Food Chemistry.* 2010, vol. 58, pp. 5341–5346.

Catechins, tyrosine, capsaicin, caffeine, and metabolism: "Body fat loss achieved by stimulation of thermogenesis by a combination of bioactive food ingredients: a placebo-controlled, double-blind 8-week intervention in obese subjects." A. Belza et al. *International Journal of Obesity.* 2007, vol. 31, pp. 121–130.

Cayenne, metabolism, and appetite: "The effects of hedonically acceptable red pepper doses on thermogenesis and appetite." M. Ludy et al. *Physiology and Behavior.* March 1, 2011, vol. 102, no. 3–4, pp. 251–258.

Chia seeds, ALA, and EPA: "Supplementation of milled chia seeds increases plasma ALA and EPA in postmenopausal women." F. Jin et al. *Plant Foods for Human Nutrition.* 2012, vol. 67, pp. 105–110.

Chia seeds, ALA, and EPA: "Chia seed supplementation and disease risk factors in overweight women: a metabolomics investigation."

D. C. Nieman et al. *Journal of Alternative and Complementary Medicine.* 2012, vol. 18, no. 7, pp. 700–708.

Chia seeds for athletes: "Omega 3 Chia seed loading as a means of carbohydrate loading." T. G. Illian et al. *Journal of Strength and Conditioning Research.* January 2011, vol. 25, no. 1, pp. 61–65.

Chia seeds background: "What are chia seeds?" Academy of Nutrition and Dietetics, February, 2014, www.eatright.org/resource/food/vitamins-and -supplements/nutrient-rich-foods/what-are-chia-seeds

Chia seeds, thickening properties: "Gelling properties of chia seed and flour." R. Coorey et al. *Journal of Food Science.* 2014, vol. 79, no. 5, pp. E859–866.

Chia seeds, antioxidants, and phytochemicals: "Phytochemical profile and nutraceutical potential of chia seeds (*Salvia hispanica* L.) by ultra high performance liquid chromatography." O. Martínez-Cruz et al. *Journal of Chromatography A.* 2014, pp. 43–48.

Chickpeas and cancer: "Chickpea (*Cicer arietinum*) and other plant-derived protease inhibitor concentrates inhibit breast and prostate cancer cell proliferation in vitro." P. J. Magee et al. *Nutrition and Cancer.* June 2012, vol. 64, no. 5, pp. 741–748.

Cinnamon and blood sugar: "Effects of cinnamon consumption on glycemic status, lipid profile and body composition in type 2 diabetic patients." M. Vafa et al. *International Journal of Preventative Medicine.* August 2012, vol. 3, no. 8, pp. 531–536.

Cinnamon and weight: "Cinnamon: potential role in the prevention of insulin resistance, metabolic syndrome, and type 2 diabetes." B. Qin et al. *Journal of Diabetes Science & Technology.* May 2010, vol. 4, no. 3, pp. 685–693.

Cinnamon's medicinal properties: "Medicinal properties of 'true' cinnamon (*Cinnamomum zeylanicum*): a systematic review." P. Ranasinghe et al. *BMC Complementary and Alternative Medicine.* 2013, vol. 13, no. 275, pp. 1–10.

Citrus foods and stroke: "Can citrus ward off your risk of stroke?" American Academy of Neurology,

February 2014. www.sciencedaily.com/releases /2014/02/140214203851.htm

Cocoa and cardiometabolic health: "Regular consumption of a cocoa product improves the cardiometabolic profile in healthy and moderately hypercholesterolaemic adults." B. Sarria et al. *British Journal of Nutrition.* 2014, vol. 111, pp. 122–134.

Cocoa and cardiovascular risk: "Flavonoid-rich cocoa consumption affects multiple cardiovascular risk factors in a meta-analysis of short-term studies." M. G. Shrime et al. *Journal of Nutrition.* 2011, vol. 141, pp. 1982–1988.

Cocoa flavonoids and arterial stiffness: "Flavonoids and arterial stiffness: Promising perspectives." M. Lilamand et al. *Nutrition, Metabolism & Cardiovascular Diseases.* 2014, vol. 24, no. 7, pp. 698–704.

Cruciferous vegetables and cancer: "Cruciferous vegetables and cancer prevention." National Cancer Institute, June 2012. www.cancer.gov/about-cancer /causes-prevention/risk/diet/cruciferous-vegetables -fact-sheet

Diet and depression: "Diet and depression." A. Ruusunen et al. *Publications of the University of Eastern Finland. Dissertations in Health Sciences.* September 2013, no. 185, pp. 1–118.

Fats and mood: "Dietary Fat Intake and the Risk of Depression: The SUN Project." Almudena Sanchez-Villegas et al. *PLOS ONE.* January 2011, vol. 6, no 1.

Fats and skin: "Healing fats of the skin: the structural and immunologic roles of the Ω-6 and Ω-3 fatty acids." M. M. McCusker and J. M. Grant-Kels. *Clinics in Dermatology.* July–August 2010, vol. 28, no. 4, pp. 440–451.

Fish and the brain: "Men, feed your brain! Go Fish!" Academy of Nutrition and Dietetics, May 2014. www .eatright.org/Public/content.aspx?id=6442463963

Flaxseed or fish and joint health: "Regulation of osteoarthritis by omega-3 (n-3) polyunsaturated fatty acids in a naturally occurring model of disease." L. Knott et al. *Osteoarthritis and Cartilage.* 2011, vol. 19, no. 9, pp. 1150–1157.

Flaxseed and blood pressure: "Potent antihypertensive action of dietary flaxseed in hypertensive patients." D. Rodriguez-Leyva et al. *Hypertension.* October 14, 2013, vol. 62, pp. 1081–1089.

Flaxseed and blood pressure: "Flaxseed consumption reduces blood pressure in patients with hypertension by altering circulating oxylipins via an ⊠-linolenic acid-induced inhibition of soluble epoxide hydrolase." S. P. B. Caligiuri et al. *Hypertension.* April 28, 2014, vol. 64, pp. 53–59.

Flaxseed and breast cancer: "Consumption of flaxseed, a rich source of lignans, is associated with reduced breast cancer risk." E. C. Lowcock et al. *Cancer Causes Control.* 2013, vol. 24, pp. 813–816.

Flaxseed background: "Healthy food trends— flaxseeds." National Institutes of Health. www.medicine plus.gov/ency/patientinstructions/000728.htm

Flaxseed, glucose, and insulin: "Daily flaxseed consumption improves glycemic control in obese men and women with pre-diabetes: a randomized study." A. M. Hutchins et al. *Nutrition Research.* 2013, vol. 33, pp. 367–375.

Flaxseed insulin resistance: "Flaxseed supplementation improved insulin resistance in obese glucose intolerant people: a randomized crossover design." Y. Rhee and A. Brunt. *Nutrition Journal.* 2011, vol. 10, no. 44, pp. 1–7.

Flaxseed metabolic syndrome: "Lifestyle counseling and supplementation with flaxseed or walnuts influence the management of metabolic syndrome." H. Wu et al. *Journal of Nutrition.* 2010, vol. 140, pp. 1937–1942.

Flaxseed, appetite, and blood fat: "Flaxseed dietary fibers suppress postprandial lipemia and appetite sensation in young men." M. Kristensen et al. *Nutrition, Metabolism & Cardiovascular Diseases.* 2013, vol. 23, pp. 136–143.

Flaxseed inflammation and aging: "Elevated levels of pro-inflammatory oxylipins in older subjects are normalized by flaxseed consumption." S. P. B. Caligiuri et al. *Experimental Gerontology.* November 2014, vol. 59, pp. 51–57.

Folate and depression: "Folate and depression—a neglected problem." Simon N. Young et al. *Journal of Psychiatry and Neuroscience.* 2007, vol. 32, no. 2, pp. 80–82.

Fruits and veggies reduce energy intake: "Comparison of three methods to reduce energy density: Effects on daily energy intake." R. A. Williams et al. *Appetite.* 2013, vol. 66, pp. 75–83.

Fruits, veggies, and stroke risk: "Fruits and vegetables consumption and risk of stroke: a meta-analysis of prospective cohort studies." D. Hu et al. *Stroke.* June 2014, vol. 45, no. 6, pp. 1613–1619.

Garlic and heart disease: "Garlic and cardiovascular disease: a critical review." K. Rahman and G.M. Lowe. *Journal of Nutrition.* March 2006, vol. 136, pp. 736S–740S.

Ginger and muscle soreness: "Influence of ginger and cinnamon intake on inflammation and muscle soreness endued by exercise in Iranian female athletes." N.S. Mashhadi et al. *International Journal of Preventive Medicine.* April 2013, vol. 4 (suppl. 1), pp. S11–15.

Ginger and nausea: "Ginger." University of Maryland Medical Center, July 31, 2013. http://umm.edu/health/medical/altmed/herb/ginger

Hair, folate: "Vitamin B$_9$ (Folic acid)." University of Maryland Medical Center, June 21, 2013. http://umm.edu/health/medical/altmed/supplement/vitamin-b9-folic-acid

Hair, iron: "The diagnosis and treatment of iron deficiency and its potential relationship to hair loss." L.B. Trost et al. *Journal of the American Academy of Dermatology.* May 2006, vol. 54, no. 5, pp. 824–44.

Hair, zinc: "Zinc." Office of Dietary Supplements, June 5, 2013. http://ods.od.nih.gov/factsheets/Zinc-HealthProfessional

Hair and nails, protein: "Protein in diet." U.S. National Library of Medicine, April 30, 2013. www.nlm.nih.gov/medlineplus/ency/article/002467.htm

Hiding veggies: "Hiding vegetables to reduce energy density: an effective strategy to increase children's vegetable intake and reduce energy intake." M. K. Spill et al. *American Journal of Clinical Nutrition.* 2011, vol. 94, pp. 735–41.

Honey and wounds: "Honey: its medicinal property and antibacterial activity." Manisha Deb Mandal et al. *Asian Pacific Journal of Tropical Biomedicine.* 2011, vol. 1, no. 2, pp. 154–160.

Powerhouse fruits and veggies: "Defining powerhouse fruits and vegetables: a nutrient density approach." J. Di Noia et al. *Preventing Chronic Disease.* 2014, vol. 11, pp. 1–5.

Functional foods: "Tackling metabolic syndrome by functional foods." M. I. Khan et al. *Reviews in Endocrine and Metabolic Disorders.* 2013, vol. 14, pp. 287–297.

Garlic and colds: "Supplementation with aged garlic extract improves both NK and gd-T cell function and reduces the severity of cold and flu symptoms: A randomized, double-blind, placebo-controlled nutrition intervention." M. P. Nantz et al. *Clinical Nutrition.* 2012, vol. 31, pp. 337–344.

Sprouting garlic has antioxidants: "Garlic sprouting is associated with increased antioxidant activity and concomitant changes in the metabolite profile." A. Zakarova et al. *Journal of Agricultural and Food Chemistry.* February 25, 2014, vol. 62, no. 8, pp. 1875.

Green tea and weight: "The effects of green tea consumption on metabolic and anthropometric indices in patients with type 2 diabetes." A. Mousavi et al. *Journal of Research in Medical Science.* December 2013, vol. 18, no. 12, pp. 1080–1086.

Greens and weight loss: "Body weight loss, reduced urge for palatable food and increased release of GLP-1 through daily supplementation with green-plant membranes for three months in overweight women." Caroline Montelius et al. *Appetite.* 2014, vol. 81, pp. 295–304.

Healthy foods at lower cost: "Healthy Foods Under \$1 Per Serving." American Heart Association, November 2013. www.heart.org/HEARTORG/GettingHealthy/HealthierKids/HowtoMakea HealthyHome/Healthy-Foods-Under-1-Per-Serving_UCM_303809_Article.jsp.#.V5j3kxDMwuc

High-intensity interval training: "Physiological adaptations to low-volume, high-intensity interval training in health and disease." M. J. Gibala et al. *Journal of Physiology.* March 1, 2012, vol. 590, no. 5, pp. 1077–84.

Inflammation and diet: "Inflammation and diet." Academy of Nutrition and Dietetics, September, 2014. www.eatright.org/resource/health/wellness /preventing-illness/inflammation-and-diet

Inulin and weight: "Differential effects of two fermentable carbohydrates on central appetite regulation and body composition." T. Arora et al. *PLOS ONE.* August 2012, vol. 7, no. 8, pp. 1–10.

Legumes and heart health: "Nutritional quality of legumes, and their role in cardiometabolic risk prevention: a review." M. Bouchenak et al. *Journal of Medicinal Food.* 2013, vol. 16, no. 3, pp. 185–198.

Linoleic acid and reducing fat mass: "Efficacy of conjugated linoleic acid for reducing fat mass: a meta-analysis in humans." L. D. Whigham et al. *American Journal of Clinical Nutrition.* 2007, vol. 85, pp. 1203–1211.

Swap mushrooms for beef: "Lack of energy compensation over 4 days when white button mushrooms are substituted for beef." L. J. Cheskin et al. *Appetite.* 2008, vol. 51, pp. 50–57.

Nails, nutrients: "Vitamins and minerals: their role in nail health and disease." N. Scheinfeld et al. *Journal of Drugs in Dermatology.* August 2007, vol. 6, no. 8, pp. 782–787.

Nuts' benefits: "In a Nutshell: The Health Benefits and Culinary Uses of Nut Meats." Academy of Nutrition and Dietetics. www.eatright.org/resource /food/nutrition/healthy-eating/in-a-nutshell

Nuts and diet quality: "Nuts improve diet quality compared to other energy-dense snacks while maintaining body weight." S. L. Tey et al. *Journal of Nutrition and Metabolism.* Aug. 10, 2011, pp. 1–11.

Pecans and heart health: "Pecans acutely increase plasma postprandial antioxidant capacity and catechins and decrease LDL oxidation in humans." C. Hudthagosol et al. *Journal of Nutrition.* 2010, vol. 141, no. 1, pp. 56–62.

Tree nuts and phytochemicals: "Tree nut phytochemicals: composition, antioxidant capacity, bioactivity, impact factors: A systematic review of almonds, Brazils, cashews, hazelnuts, macadamias, pecans, pine nuts, pistachios and walnuts." B. W. Bolling et al. *Nutrition Research Reviews.* 2011, vol. 24, pp. 244–275.

Walnuts and endothelial function: "Effects of walnuts on endothelial function in overweight adults with visceral obesity: a randomized, controlled, crossover trial." D. L. Katz et al. *Journal of the American College of Nutrition.* 2012, vol. 31, no. 6, pp. 415–423.

Walnuts and stress: "Effects of diets high in walnuts and flax oil on hemodynamic responses to stress and vascular endothelial function." S. G. West et al. *Journal of the American College of Nutrition.* December 2010, vol. 29, no. 6, pp. 595–603.

Oatmeal and appetite: "Acute effect of oatmeal on subjective measures of appetite and satiety compared to a ready-to-eat breakfast cereal: a randomized crossover trial." C. J. Rebello et al. *Journal of the American College of Nutrition.* 2013, vol. 32, no. 4, pp. 272–279.

Oats and cholesterol: "Effect of 6 weeks' consumption of b-glucan-rich oat products on cholesterol levels in mildly hypercholesterolaemic overweight adults." K. E. Charlton et al. *British Journal of Nutrition.* 2012, vol. 107, pp. 1037–1047.

Oats and cholesterol: "A randomized crossover study to assess the effect of an oat-rich diet on glycaemic control, plasma lipids and postprandial glycaemia, inflammation and oxidative stress in type 2 diabetes." S. C. McGeoch et al. *Diabetic Medicine.* 2013, vol. 30, pp. 1314–1323.

Oats and inflammation: "Oat-enriched diet reduces inflammatory status assessed by circulating cell-derived microparticle concentrations in type 2 diabetes." X. Zhang et al. *Molecular Nutrition and Food Research.* 2014, vol. 58, pp. 1322–1332.

Oats, blood sugar, insulin: "Effect of oat intake on glycaemic control and insulin sensitivity: a meta-analysis of randomised controlled trials." L. Bao et al. *British Journal of Nutrition.* 2014, vol. 112, pp. 457–466.

Oats, obesity, liver function: "Oat prevents obesity and abdominal fat distribution, and improves liver function in humans." H. Chang et al. *Plant Foods for Human Nutrition.* 2013, vol. 68, pp. 18–23.

Oregano's antibacterial properties and relationship to blood glucose: "Bioactive compounds from culinary herbs inhibit a molecular target for type 2 diabetes management, dipeptidyl peptidase IV." A. M. Bower et al. *Journal of Agricultural and Food Chemistry.* July 2, 014, vol. 62, pp. 6147–6158.

Parsley background: "Parsley." The World's Healthiest Foods. www.whfoods.com/genpage .php?tname=foodspice&dbid=100

Phytochemicals background: "What are phytonutrients?" Fruits and Veggies More Matters, March 2012. www.fruitsandveggiesmorematters.org /what-are-phytochemicals

Pistachios overview: "Pistachio nuts: composition and potential health benefits." M. L. Dreher et al. *Nutrition Reviews.* 2012, vol. 70, no. 4, pp. 234–240.

Pistachio shells reduce calories: "The effect of pistachio shells as a visual cue in reducing caloric consumption." K. Kennedy-Hagan et al. *Appetite.* 2011, vol. 57, pp. 418–420.

Pistachios and calories: "In-shell pistachio nuts reduce caloric intake compared to shelled nuts." C. S. Honselman et al. *Appetite.* 2011, vol. 57, pp. 414–417.

Pistachios, antioxidants, and cholesterol: "Pistachios increase serum antioxidants and lower serum oxidized-LDL in hypercholesterolemic adults." C. D. Kay et al. *Journal of Nutrition.* 2010, vol. 140, no. 6, pp. 1093–1098.

Pistachios, blood pressure, and stress response: "Diets containing pistachios reduce systolic blood pressure and peripheral vascular responses to stress in adults with dyslipidemia." S. G. West et al. *Hypertension.* 2012, vol. 60, pp. 58–63.

Pistachios and cardiometabolic profile: "A moderate-fat diet containing pistachios improves emerging markers of cardiometabolic syndrome in healthy adults with elevated LDL levels." S. D. Holligan et al. *British Journal of Nutrition.* 2014, vol. 112, pp. 744–752.

Pistachios, cardiovascular risk, and diabetes: "Pistachio nut consumption modifies systemic hemodynamics, increases heart rate variability, and reduces ambulatory blood pressure in well-controlled type 2 diabetes: a randomized trial." K. A. Sauder et al. *Journal of the American Heart Association.* June 30, 2014, vol. 3, no. 4, pp. 1–9.

Pistachios and fat absorption: "Measured energy value of pistachios in the human diet." D. J. Baer et al. *British Journal of Nutrition.* 2012, vol. 107, pp. 120–125.

Pistachios, immediate blood sugar and insulin: "Acute effects of pistachio consumption on glucose and insulin, satiety hormones and endothelial function in the metabolic syndrome." C. W. Kendall et al. *European Journal of Clinical Nutrition.* March 2014, vol. 68, no. 3, pp. 370–375.

Pistachios, postprandial blood sugar: "The impact of pistachio intake alone or in combination with high-carbohydrate foods on post-prandial glycemia." C. W. Kendall et al. *European Journal of Clinical Nutrition.* 2011, vol. 65, pp. 696–702.

Pistachios, triglycerides, and weight: "Effects of pistachios on body weight in Chinese subjects with metabolic syndrome." Xin Wang et al. *Nutrition Journal.* 2012, vol. 11, no. 20, pp. 1–19.

Pistachios, antioxidants, and cholesterol: "Pistachios increase serum antioxidants and lower serum oxidized-LDL in hypercholesterolemic adults." C. D. Kay et al. *Journal of Nutrition,* 2010, vol. 140, no. 6, pp. 1093–1098.

Polyphenols, inflammation, diet, and depression: "Inflammatory dietary pattern and risk of depression among women." M. Lucas et al. *Brain, Behavior, and Immunity.* 2014, vol. 36, pp. 46–53.

Polyphenols, skin, and aging: "Skin photoprotection by natural polyphenols: Anti-inflammatory, anti-oxidant and DNA repair mechanisms." Joi A. Nichols et al. *Archives of Dermatology Research.* March 2010, vol. 302, no. 2, pp. 1–19.

Potatoes background: "Potatoes—a natural health food." Academy of Nutrition and Dietetics. www.eatright.org/resource/food/vitamins-and-supplements/nutrient-rich-foods/potatoes-a-natural-health-food

Prebiotics and probiotics background: "Prebiotics and Probiotics: Creating a Healthier You." Academy of Nutrition and Dietetics, October 12, 2015. www.eatright.org/resource/food/vitamins-and-supplements/nutrient-rich-foods/prebiotics-and-probiotics-the-dynamic-duo

Pulses and second-meal effect: "Second-meal effects of pulses on blood glucose and subjective appetite following a standardized meal 2 h later." R. C. Mollard et al. *Applied Physiology, Nutrition and Metabolism.* July 2014, vol. 39, no. 7, pp. 849–51.

Pumpkin seeds and blood sugar: "Second-meal effects of pulses on blood glucose and subjective appetite following a standardized meal 2 h later." G. G. Adams et al. *Critical Reviews in Food Science and Nutrition.* 2014, vol. 54, no. 10, pp. 1322–9.

Pumpkin seed oil and cholesterol: "Improvement in HDL cholesterol in postmenopausal women supplemented with pumpkin seed oil: pilot study." M. Gossell-Williams et al. *Climacteric.* 2011, vol. 14, pp. 558–564.

Quinoa and gluten-free diet: "Quinoa Well Tolerated in Patients with Celiac Disease." American College of Gastroenterology. http://gi.org/media/current-press-releases-and-media-statements/quinoa-well-tolerated-in-patients-with-celiac-disease

Quinoa background: "Quinoa: Nutritional Value." Food and Agricultural Organization, January 2014. www.fao.org/quinoa-2013/what-is-quinoa/nutritional-value/en

Quinoa nutrition facts: "Nutrition facts and functional potential of quinoa (*Chenopodium quinoa* wild), an ancient Andean grain: a review." A. Vega-Galvez et al. *Journal of the Science of Food and Agriculture.* 2010, vol. 90, pp. 2541–2547.

Quinoa, sprouting and antioxidant properties: "Quinoa seeds leach phytoecdysteroids and other compounds with anti-diabetic properties." B. L. Graf et al. *Food Chemistry.* 2014, vol. 163, pp. 178–185.

Swap quinoa for cornflakes: "Metabolic parameters of postmenopausal women after quinoa or corn flakes intake—a prospective and double-blind study." F. G. De Carvalho et al. *International Journal of Food Sciences and Nutrition.* May 2014, vol. 65, no. 3, pp. 380–385.

Raisins for athletes: "Sun-dried raisins are a cost-effective alternative to Sports Jelly Beans in prolonged cycling." H. L. Rietschier et al. *Journal of Strength & Conditioning Research.* November 2011, vol. 25, no. 11, pp. 3150–3156.

Rice and antioxidants: "Rice antioxidants: phenolic acids, flavonoids, anthocyanins, proanthocyanidins, tocopherols, tocotrienols, c-oryzanol, and phytic acid." P. Goufo et al. *Food Science & Nutrition.* 2014, vol. 2, no. 2, pp. 75–104.

Rice background: "A Global Grain: The Health Benefits and Culinary Uses of Rice." Academy of Nutrition and Dietetics, April 29, 2013. www.foodandnutrition.org/May-2013/A-Global-Grain-The-Health-Benefits-and-Culinary-Uses-of-Rice/

Salad and satiety: "Salad and satiety. The effect of timing of salad consumption on meal energy intake." L. S. Roe et al. *Appetite.* 2012, vol. 58, pp. 242–248.

Superfoods background: "What's so super about superfoods?" American Heart Association, March 2014. www.heart.org/HEART.ORG/HeathyLiving/Healthy Eating/Nutrition/whats-so-super-about-superfoods_UCM_457937_Article.jsp#.V4J2sdirLIU

Superfoods background: "Diabetes Superfoods." American Diabetes Association, August 2014. www.diabetes.org/food-and-fitness/food/what-can-i-eat/making-healthy-food-choices/diabetes-superfoods.html

Swap in whole grains and legumes, diabetes: "Replacing with whole grains and legumes reduces lipoprotein-associated phospholipase A2 (Lp-PLA2) activities in plasma and peripheral blood mononuclear cells in patients with prediabetes or newly diagnosed type 2 diabetes." M. Kim et al. *The Journal of Lipid Research*. June 2014, vol. 55, no. 8, pp. 1762–1771.

Sweet potato health benefits: "Sweet Potato (*Ipomoea batatas* [L.] Lam)—A Valuable Medicinal Food: A Review." R. Mohanraj et al. *Journal of Medicinal Food*. 2014, vol. 17, no. 7, pp. 733–741.

Thermic effect of food: "Discrepancy between the Atwater factor predicted and empirically measured energy values of almonds in human diets." J. A. Novotny et al. *American Journal of Clinical Nutrition*. 2012, vol. 96, pp. 296–301.

Tomatoes and breast cancer: "Effects of tomato and soy on serum adipokine concentrations in postmenopausal women at increased breast cancer risk: a cross-over dietary intervention trial." Adana Llanos et al. *Journal of Clinical Endocrinology & Metabolism*. February 2014, vol. 99, no. 2, pp. 625–632.

Tomatoes, lycopene content, raw vs. cooked: "Thermal processing enhances the nutritional value of tomatoes by increasing total antioxidant activity." V. Dewanto et al. *Journal of Agricultural and Food Chemistry*. May 8, 2002, vol. 50, no. 10, pp. 3010–4.

Turmeric background: "Turmeric." World's Healthiest Foods. www.whfoods.com/genpage .php?tname=foodspice&dbid=78

Vinegar and weight/belly fat: "Vinegar intake reduces body weight, body fat mass, and serum triglyceride levels in obese Japanese subjects." T. Kondo et al. *Bioscience, Biotechnology, and Biochemistry*. 2009, vol. 73, no. 8, pp. 1837.

Vinegar and calories: "Vinegar and peanut products as complementary foods to reduce postprandial glycemia." C. S. Johnston et al. *Journal of the American Dietetic Association*. December 2005, vol. 105, no. 12, pp. 1939–1942.

Vinegar and mood: "Functional properties of vinegar." B. H. Nilgun et al. *Journal of Food Science*. May 2014, vol. 79, no. 5, pp. R757–R764.

Vitamin C and aging: "Dietary nutrient intakes and skin-aging appearance among middle-aged American women." M. C. Cosgrove et al. *American Journal of Clinical Nutrition*. 2007, vol. 86, pp. 1225–1231.

Vitamin C and colds: "Vitamin C for preventing and treating the common cold (Review)." H. Hemilä et al. *Cochrane Database of Systematic Reviews*. 2013, no. 1, pp. 1–103.

Vitamin C and heat: "The impact of food processing on the nutritional quality of vitamins and minerals." M. B. Reddy and M. Love. *Advances in Experimental Medicine & Biology*. 1999, vol. 459, pp. 99–106.

Vitamin E background: "Vitamin E." NIH Office of Dietary Supplements, October 2011. http://ods.od.nih .gov/factsheets/VitaminE-Consumer

Vitamin E background: "Vitamin E." World's Healthiest Foods. www.whfoods.com/genpage .php?tname=nutrient&dbid=111

Water and resting energy expenditure: "Influence of water drinking on resting energy expenditure in overweight children." G. Dubnov-Raz et al. *International Journal of Obesity*. 2011, vol. 35, pp. 1295–1300.

Water and weight loss in overweight women: "Drinking water is associated with weight loss in overweight dieting women independent of diet and activity." J. D. Stookey et al. *Obesity*. November 2008, vol. 16, no. 11, pp. 2481–2488.

Water and weight loss while dieting: "Water consumption increases weight loss during a hypocaloric diet intervention in middle-aged and older adults." E. A. Dennis et al. *Obesity*. 2010, vol. 18, pp. 300–307.

Water and weight-review: "Association between water consumption and body weight outcomes: a systematic review." R. Muckelbauer et al. *American Journal of Clinical Nutrition*. 2013, vol. 98, pp. 282–99.

Water and metabolism: "Water-induced thermogenesis." M. Boschmann et al. *Journal of Clinical Endocrinology & Metabolism*. 2003, vol. 88, no. 12, pp. 6015–6019.

Water as replacement for sugary drinks: "Replacing sweetened caloric beverages with drinking water is associated with lower energy intake." J. D. Stookey et al. *Obesity.* December 2007, vol 15, no. 12, pp. 3013–3022.

Water consumed before meals: "Pre-meal water consumption for weight loss." *Australian Family Physician.* June 2013, vol. 42, no. 6, p. 478.

Water, weight, body mass index, and body composition: "Effect of 'water induced thermogenesis' on body weight, body mass index and body composition of overweight subjects." V. A. Vij and A. S. Joshi. *Journal of Clinical and Diagnostic Research.* September 2013, vol. 7, no. 9, pp. 1894–1896.

Swap in whole grains: "Dietary modeling shows that substitution of whole-grain for refined-grain ingredients of foods commonly consumed by US children and teens can increase intake of whole grains." D. R. Keast et al. *Journal of the American Dietetic Association.* 2011, vol. 111, pp. 1322–1328.

Whole grains and diabetes: "Whole grain and refined grain consumption and the risk of type 2 diabetes: a systematic review and dose–response meta-analysis of cohort studies." D. Aune et al. *European Journal of Epidemiology.* 2013, vol. 28, pp. 845–858.

Whole grains and family health: "5 Grains to Keep Your Family Healthy." Academy of Nutrition and Dietetics, April 2013. www.eatright.org/resource/food/vitamins-and-supplements/nutrient-rich-foods/five-grains-to-keep-your-family-healthy

WEEK 2

Advanced glycation end products: "Advanced glycoxidation end products in commonly consumed foods." T. Goldberg et al. *Journal of the American Dietetic Association.* August 2004, vol. 104, no. 8, pp. 1287–1291.

Advanced glycation end products in aging: "Advanced glycation end products: Key players in skin aging?" P. Gkogkolou et al. *Dermato-Endocrinology.* December 2012, vol. 4, no. 3, pp. 259–270.

Alcohol and sleep quality: "Alcohol and sleep I: effects on normal sleep." I. O. Ebrahim et al. *Alcoholism: Clinical and Experimental Research.* 2013, vol. 37, no. 4, pp. 539–549.

Artificial dyes, risks: "Food Dyes: A Rainbow of Risks." Center for Science in the Public Interest, June 2010. http://cspinet.org/new/pdf/food-dyes-rainbow-of-risks.pdf.

Artificial sweeteners and fat production: "Artificial sweeteners stimulate adipogenesis and suppress lipolysis independently of sweet taste receptors." B. R. Simon et al. *Journal of Biological Chemistry.* 2013, vol. 288, pp. 32475–32489.

Artificial sweeteners, background: "Nonnutritive sweeteners, fructose, and other aspects of diet." Zachary T. Bloomgarden et al. *Diabetes Care.* May 2011, vol. 34, pp. 46–51.

Azodicarbonamide, background: "Frequently Asked Questions on Azodicarbonamide (ADA)." US Food and Drug Administration, June 2014. www.fda.gov/Food/IngredientsPackagingLabeling/FoodAdditivesIngredients/ucm387497.htm

Caffeine and weight loss: "Does caffeine help with weight loss?" Mayo Clinic, March 19, 2014. www.mayoclinic.org/healthy-living/weight-loss/expert-answers/caffeine/faq-20058459?p=1

Caffeine, how much: "Nutrition and healthy eating." Mayo Clinic, April 14, 2014. www.mayoclinic.org/caffeine/ART-20045678?p=1

Caramel coloring, background: "Questions & Answers on Caramel Coloring and 4-MEI." US Food and Drug Administration, May 13, 2014. www.fda.gov/food/ingredientspackaginglabeling/foodadditivesingredients/ucm364184.htm

Carcinogens in caramel color: "Developing an effective means to reduce 5-hydroxymethyl-2-furfural from caramel colour." Y. Guan et al. *Food Chemistry.* 2014, vol. 143, pp. 60–65.

Carrageenan and colon cells: "Increased expression of colonic Wnt9A through Sp1-mediated transcriptional effects involving arylsulfatase

B, chondroitin 4-sulfate, and galectin-3." S. Bhattacharyya et al. *Journal of Biological Chemistry*. April 28, 2014, vol. 289, pp. 17564–17575.

Coffee and death risk: "Coffee consumption and total mortality: a meta-analysis of twenty prospective cohort studies." Y. Je et al. *British Journal of Nutrition*. 2014, vol. 111, pp. 1162–1173.

Coffee and diabetes risk: "Changes in coffee intake and subsequent risk of type 2 diabetes: three large cohorts of US men and women." S. N. Bhupathiraju et al. *Diabetologia*. 2014, vol. 57, pp. 1346–1354.

Coffee, benefits: "Four-week coffee consumption affects energy intake, satiety regulation, body fat, and protects DNA integrity." T. Bakuradze et al. *Food Research International*. 2014, vol. 63, pp. 420–427.

Diet and aging: "Does overall diet in midlife predict future aging phenotypes? A cohort study." Tasnime Akbaraly et al. *American Journal of Medicine*. May 5, 2013, vol. 126, no. 5, pp. 411–419.

Diet changes your gut bacteria: "Diet rapidly and reproducibly alters the human gut microbiome." L. A. David et al. *Nature*. January 23, 2014, vol. 23, no. 505, pp. 559–63.

Diet quality and mental disorders: "The association between habitual diet quality and the common mental disorders in community-dwelling adults: the Hordaland Health study." F. N. Jacka et al. *Psychosomatic Medicine*. 2011, vol. 73, pp. 483–490.

Fats and mood: "Dietary fat intake and the risk of depression: the SUN Project." A. Sanchez-Villegas et al. *PLOS ONE*. January 2011, vol. 6, no 1, pp. 1–7.

Food additives, gaps in toxicity testing: "Data gaps in toxicity testing of chemicals allowed in food in the United States." T. G. Neltner et al. *Reproductive Toxicology* 2013, vol. 42, pp. 85–94.

Food additives, lack of oversight, full report: "Fixing the Oversight of Chemicals Added to Our Food." The Pew Charitable Trusts, November 2013. www.pewtrusts.org/en/research-and-analysis /reports/2013/11/07/fixing-the-oversight-of-chemicals -added-to-our-food

Food additives, safety information: "Chemical Cuisine: Learn about Food Additives." Center for Science in the Public Interest, 2014. www.cspinet.org /reports/chemcuisine.htm

Food fears: "Ingredient-based food fears and avoidance: Antecedents and antidotes." B. Wansink et al. *Food Quality and Preference*. December 2014. vol. 38, pp. 40–48.

Food labels and health perceptions: "Food Labels Survey: 2014 Nationally-Representative Phone Survey." Consumer Reports National Research Center. www.greenerchoices.org/pdf /ConsumerReportsFoodLabelingSurveyJune2014.pdf

Food labels and health perceptions: "Truth, lies, and packaging: How food marketing creates a false sense of health." T. Northup et al. *Food Studies: An Interdisciplinary Journal*. 2014, vol. 3, no. 1, pp. 9–18.

Food labels, background: "How to Understand and Use the Nutrition Facts Label." US Food and Drug Administration, November 2004. www.fda.gov/Food /IngredientsPackagingLabeling/LabelingNutrition /ucm274593.htm

Framing of physical activity: "Is it fun or exercise? The framing of physical activity biases subsequent snacking." C. O. C. Werle et al. *Marketing Letters*. May 15, 2014, vol. 26, no. 4, pp. 691–702.

Fructose and metabolic syndrome: "Association of fructose consumption and components of metabolic syndrome in human studies: A systematic review and meta-analysis." R. Kelishadi et al. *Nutrition*. 2014, vol. 30, pp. 503–510.

Genetic engineering, background: "Questions & Answers on Food from Genetically Engineered Plants." U.S. Food and Drug Administration, May 13, 2014. www.fda.gov/Food/FoodScienceResearch /Biotechnology/ucm346030.htm

Grass-fed meat: "A review of fatty acid profiles and antioxidant content in grass-fed and grain-fed beef." Cynthia A Daley et al. *Nutrition Journal*. 2010, vol. 9, no. 10, pp. 1–12.

High-fructose corn syrup, lipids, and body composition: "The effect of normally consumed amounts of sucrose or high fructose corn syrup on lipid profiles, body composition and related parameters in overweight/obese subjects." J. Lowndes et al. *Nutrients.* 2014, vol. 6, pp. 1128–1144.

Junk-food diet and energy levels: "Food quality and motivation: A refined low-fat diet induces obesity and impairs performance on a progressive ratio schedule of instrumental lever pressing in rats." A. P. Blaisdell et al. *Physiology & Behavior,* 2014, vol. 128, pp. 220–225.

Meat and type 2 diabetes: "Red meat consumption and risk of type 2 diabetes: 3 cohorts of US adults and an updated meta-analysis." A. Pan et al. *American Journal of Clinical Nutrition.* 2011, vol. 94, pp. 1088–96.

Meat, heart disease, and mortality: "Association between total, processed, red and white meat consumption and all-cause, CVD and IHD mortality: a meta-analysis of cohort studies." I. Abete et al. *British Journal of Nutrition.* 2014, vol. 112, pp. 762–775.

Organic food and antioxidants: "Higher antioxidant and lower cadmium concentrations and lower incidence of pesticide residues in organically grown crops: a systematic literature review and meta-analyses." M. Baranski et al. *British Journal of Nutrition.* September 14, 2014, vol. 112, no. 5, pp. 794–811.

Organic livestock, background: "Organic livestock requirements." US Department of Agriculture, July 2013. www.ams.usda.gov/publications/content /organic-livestock-requirements

Pesticides and Parkinson's: "Aldehyde dehydrogenase variation enhances effect of pesticides associated with Parkinson disease." A. G. Fitzmaurice et al. *Neurology.* February 4, 2014, vol. 82, pp. 419–426.

Pesticides in produce: "Executive summary." Environmental Working Group, April 2014. www.ewg .org/foodnews/summary.php

Processed foods and aging: "Dietary and genetic evidence for phosphate toxicity accelerating mammalian aging." M. Ohnishi and M. S. Razzaque.

FASEB Journal. September 2010, vol. 24, no. 9, pp. 3562–71.

Refined vs. whole grains: Food Groups. US Department of Agriculture. www.choosemyplate.gov /grains

Short glasses and overindulgence: "Short glasses more likely to lead to over-indulgence." *British Medical Journal,* December 2005. www.eurekalert.org/pub _releases/2005-12/bmj-sgm122105.php

Sugars, background: "Added Sugar in the Diet." The Nutrition Source, Harvard School of Public Health. www.hsph.harvard.edu/nutritionsource /carbohydrates/added-sugar-in-the-diet

Trans fats, background: "Talking About *Trans* Fat: What You Need to Know." US Food and Drug Administration, March 7, 2014. www.fda.gov/Food /IngredientsPackagingLabeling/LabelingNutrition /ucm079609.htm

Trans fats, background: "Trans Fat." Center for Disease Control and Prevention. www.cdc.gov /nutrition/downloads/trans_fat_final.pdf

Western diet and depression: "Association of Western and traditional diets with depression and anxiety in women." F. N. Jacka et al. *American Journal of Psychiatry.* 2010, vol. 167, pp. 1–7.

Western diet, background: "Western diet." Medical Dictionary, 2012. http://medical-dictionary .thefreedictionary.com/Western+Diet

Whole grains and body fat: "Whole and refined-grain intakes are differentially associated with abdominal visceral and subcutaneous adiposity in healthy adults: the Framingham Heart Study." N. M. McKeown et al. *American Journal of Clinical Nutrition.* 2010, vol. 92, pp. 1165–71.

WEEK 3

All you can eat buffets: "The flat rate pricing paradox: Conflicting effects of 'all-you-can-eat' buffet pricing." D. R. Just et al. *Review of Economics and Statistics.* February 2011, vol. 93, no. 1, pp. 193–200.

Food norms, effects on your diet: "Food intake norms increase and decrease snack food intake in a remote confederate study." E. Robinson et al. *Appetite.* 2013, vol. 65, pp. 20–24.

Friends' diets and their effects on yours: "Friends don't let friends eat cookies: Effects of restrictive eating norms on consumption among friends." M. Howland et al. *Appetite.* 2012, vol. 59, pp. 505–509.

Mix up your workouts: "Physical activity variety, energy expenditure, and body mass index." H. A. Raynor et al. *American Journal of Health Behavior.* 2014, vol. 38, no. 4, pp. 624–630.

Sandwiches background: "Discover the History of the Sandwich." PBS Food, January 3, 2013. www.pbs .org/food/the-history-kitchen/history-sandwich

Vice-virtue bundles balance your diet: "Vice-Virtue Bundles." P. J. Liu et al. *Management Science.* 2015, vol. 61, no. 1, pp. 204-228.

WEEK 4

Chill mood and calories: "Fast food restaurant lighting and music can reduce calorie intake and increase satisfaction." B. Wansink, and K. van Ittersum. *Psychological Reports.* August 2012, vol. 111, no. 1, pp. 228–32.

Distract yourself from cravings: "Playing 'Tetris' reduces the strength, frequency and vividness of naturally occurring cravings." J. Skorka-Brown et al. *Appetite.* 2014, vol. 76, pp. 161–165.

Exercise and its effect on food response: "The effects of high-intensity exercise on neural responses to images of food." Daniel R. Crabtree et al. *American Journal of Clinical Nutrition.* 2014, vol. 99, pp. 258–67.

Exercise memories: "Using memories to motivate future behaviour: An experimental exercise intervention." M. J. Biondolillo et al. *Memory.* February 2014, vol. 23, no. 3, pp. 390–402.

Fun or exercise: "Is it fun or exercise? The framing of physical activity biases subsequent snacking." C. O.

C. Werle et al. *Marketing Letters.* 2014, vol. 26, no. 4 pp. 691–702.

Group exercise and hormones: "Biomarkers of vascular function in premenopausal and recent postmenopausal women of similar age: effect of exercise training." Michael Nyberg et al. *American Journal of Physiology: Regulatory Integrative Comparative Physiology.* January 2014, vol. 306, pp. R510–R517.

NEAT: "A NEAT Approach to Weight Loss." National Academy of Sports Medicine, December 19, 2013. http://blog.nasm.org/12-days-of-fitness/exercise -programming/neat-approach-weight-loss

Sleep and obesity: "Both habitual short sleepers and long sleepers are at greater risk of obesity: a population-based 10-year follow-up in women." J. Theorell-Haglöw et al. *Sleep Medicine.* October 2014, vol. 15, no. 10, pp. 1204–1211.

Sleep restriction and added calories: "Effects of experimental sleep restriction on weight gain, caloric intake, and meal timing in healthy adults." A. M. Spaeth et al. *Sleep.* 2013, vol. 36, no. 7, pp. 981–990.

Why we snack: "Reasons for eating 'unhealthy' snacks in overweight and obese males and females." L. Cleobury et al. *Journal of Human Nutrition and Dietetics.* 2013, vol. 27, pp. 333–341.

RECIPES

Baking with flaxseed: "Oxidative stability of flaxseed lipids during baking." Z-Y. Chen et al. *Journal of the American Oil Chemists' Society.* June 1994, vol. 71, no. 6, pp. 629–632.

Celery and blood pressure: "Prospective study of nutritional factors, blood pressure, and hypertension among US women." A. Ascherio et al. *Hypertension.* 1996, vol. 27, pp. 1065–1072.

Fat in salads: "Carotenoid bioavailability is higher from salads ingested with full-fat than with fat-reduced salad dressings as measured with electrochemical detection." M. J. Brown et al. *American Journal of Clinical Nutrition.* 2004, vol. 80, pp. 396–403.

Grass-fed meat: "A review of fatty acid profiles and antioxidant content in grass-fed and grain-fed beef." C. A. Daley et al. *Nutrition Journal.* 2010, vol. 9, no. 10, pp. 1–12.

Green produce and appetite: "Body weight loss, reduced urge for palatable food and increased release of GLP-1 through daily supplementation with green-plant membranes for three months in overweight women." Caroline Montelius et al. *Appetite.* 2014, vol. 8, pp. 295–304.

Honey and wounds: "Honey: its medicinal property and antibacterial activity." M. D. Mandal et al. *Asian Pacific Journal of Tropical Biomedicine.* 2011, vol. 1, no. 2, pp. 154–160.

Monotony and weight loss: "Amount of food group variety consumed in the diet and long-term weight loss maintenance." H. A. Raynor, *Obesity Research.* May 2005, vol. 13, no. 5, pp. 883–90.

Olive oil and antioxidants: "Direct analysis of total antioxidant activity of olive oil and studies on the influence of heating." N. Pellegrini et al. *Journal of Agricultural and Food Chemistry.* 2001, vol. 49, pp. 2532–2538.

Olive oil stability: "Oxidative stability of virgin olive oil enriched with carnosic acid." P. Zunin et al. *Food Research International.* 2010, vol. 43, pp. 1511–1516.

Olive oil heating: "How heating affects extra virgin olive oil quality indexes and chemical composition." Yosra Allouche et al. *Journal of Agricultural and Food Chemistry.* 2007, vol. 55, pp. 9646–9654.

Olive oil frying: "Frying with olive oil." International Olive Council. www.internationaloliveoil.org/estaticos/view/85-frying-with-olive-oil

Sourdough and blood sugar: "Sourdough-leavened bread improves postprandial glucose and insulin plasma levels in subjects with impaired glucose tolerance." M. Maioli et al. *Acta Diabetologica.* June 2008, vol. 45, no. 2, pp. 91–96.

Sweeteners and antioxidants: "Total Antioxidant Content of Alternatives to Refined Sugar." Katherine M. Phillips et al. *Journal of the American Dietetic Association.* 2009, vol. 109, no. 1, pp. 64–71.

Variety stimulates appetite: "Understanding variety: tasting different foods delays satiation." M. M. Hetherington et al. *Physiology & Behavior.* February 28, 2006, vol. 87, no. 2, pp. 263–71.

Vinegar and blood sugar: "Vinegar supplementation lowers glucose and insulin responses and increases satiety after a bread meal in healthy subjects." E. Ostman et al. *European Journal of Clinical Nutrition.* 2005, vol. 59, pp. 983–988.

Vinegar and weight/belly fat: "Vinegar intake reduces body weight, body fat mass, and serum triglyceride levels in obese Japanese subjects." T. Kondo et al. *Bioscience, Biotechnology, and Biochemistry.* 2009, vol. 73, no. 8, pp. 1837.

Vinegar and calories: "Vinegar and peanut products as complementary foods to reduce postprandial glycemia." C. S. Johnston et al. *Journal of the American Dietetic Association.* December 2005, vol. 105, no. 12, vol. 1939–1942.

Yerba mate and fat burning: "Yerba maté (*Illex paraguariensis*) ingestion augments fat oxidation and energy expenditure during exercise at various submaximal intensities." A. Alkhatib et al. *Nutrition & Metabolism.* 2014, vol. 11, no. 42, pp. 1–7.

Wet grains are more filling: "Water incorporated into a food but not served with a food decreases energy intake in lean women." B. J. Rolls et al. *American Journal of Clinical Nutrition.* October 1999, vol. 70, no. 4, pp. 448–55.

Eggs and cholesterol: "Egg consumption and coronary atherosclerotic burden." P. Chagas et al. *Atherosclerosis.* August 2013, vol. 229, no. 2, pp. 381–84.

» INDEX «

Note: Page references in *italics* indicate photographs.

C